An Introduction to Humanities

An Introduction to the Blue Humanities is the first textbook to explore the many ways humans engage with water, utilizing literary, cultural, historical, and theoretical connections and ecologies to introduce students to the history and theory of water-centric thinking. Comprised of multinational texts and materials, each chapter will provide readers with a range of primary and secondary sources, offering a fresh look at the major oceanic regions, saltwater and freshwater geographies, and the physical properties of water that characterize the Blue Humanities. Each chapter engages with carefully chosen primary texts, including frequently taught works such as Herman Melville's *Moby-Dick*, Samuel Taylor Coleridge's "Rime of the Ancient Mariner," Homer's *Odyssey*, and Luis Vaz de Camões's *Lusíads*, to provide the perfect pedagogy for students to develop an understanding of the Blue Humanities chapter by chapter. Readers will gain insight into new trends in intellectual culture and the enduring history of humans thinking with and about water, ranging across the many coastlines of the World Ocean to Pacific clouds, Mediterranean lakes, Caribbean swamps, Arctic glaciers, Southern Ocean rainstorms, Atlantic groundwater, and Indian Ocean rivers. Providing new avenues for future thinking and investigation of the Blue Humanities, this volume will be ideal for both undergraduate and graduate courses engaging with the environmental humanities and oceanic literature.

Steve Mentz is Professor of English at St. John's University in New York City. His academic expertise includes environmental criticism, the blue humanities, Shakespeare studies, early modern European poetry, and critical theory. He has published five single-author books, including most recently *Ocean* (2020), *Break Up the Anthropocene* (2019), and *Shipwreck Modernity* (2015). He has edited or co-edited six other volumes, published many chapters and articles in scholarly journals and collections, and organized exhibitions and symposia on blue humanities topics. His research has been funded by the Rachel Carson Center in Munich, the National Endowment for the Humanities, the Folger Shakespeare Library, the John Carter Brown Library, the National Maritime Museum in London, and other institutions. He received his Ph.D. in English from Yale University in 2000.

An Introduction to the Blue Humanities

Steve Mentz

NEW YORK AND LONDON

Designed cover image: Steve Mentz

First published 2024
by Routledge
605 Third Avenue, New York, NY 10158

and by Routledge
4 Park Square, Milton Park, Abingdon, Oxon, OX14 4RN

Routledge is an imprint of the Taylor & Francis Group, an informa business

ISBN: 978-0-367-76369-5 (hbk)
ISBN: 978-0-367-76366-4 (pbk)
ISBN: 978-1-003-16666-5 (ebk)

DOI: 10.4324/9781003166665

Typeset in Bembo
by Apex CoVantage, LLC

For Alinor, Ian, and Olivia, who buoy me up

Contents

	List of Illustrations	viii
	Acknowledgements	ix
	Personal Preface: Bodies of Water	xi
1	A Poetics of Planetary Water	1
2	Blue Humanities Thinking	17
3	Our Sea of Islands: Voyaging in the Pacific	38
4	The Roaring South	54
5	The Human Sea: Networks in the Indian Ocean	65
6	Surrounded by Land: Mediterranean Examples	80
7	In the Caribbean	93
8	Northern Visions	107
9	The Tornadoed Atlantic	116
10	Conclusion: Touching Moisture	132
	Works Cited	143
	Essential Reading in the Blue Humanities	154
	Index	157

Illustrations

2.1	"Pluralize the Anthropocene!" by Vanessa Daws	22
2.2	Blue Humanities Logo	23
3.1	Geometrical Projections of Two Thirds of the Sphere (Pacific Ocean Central)	38
3.2	"The Society Islands"	41
4.1	The Spilhaus Projection	56

Acknowledgements

First among many collaborators I call out the saltwater ecology of Short Beach, Connecticut, including its sea birds, seaweed, menhaden, bluefish, oysters, and jellyfish. We share a world, and I learn so much from immersing myself in it. I recognize the unceded rights of the Totoket and Menunkatuck bands of the Quinnipiac people and their ancient stewardship of the lands and waters that I inhabit.

I am grateful for the support of my colleagues and administration at St. John's University in Queens, New York. I completed this book as a Landhaus Fellow at the Rachel Carson Center in Munich, and I thank the RCC and its founder, Christof Mauch, for hospitality, generosity, and several very generative questions.

It's impossible to name all the scholars, artists, writers, and water-people who have supported this book and the larger, flowing dream of a blue humanities. Special gratitude goes to Stacy. Alaimo, Josiah Blackmore, Hester Blum, Dan Brayton, Alexandra Campbell, Siobahn Carroll, Jeffrey Jerome Cohen, Margaret Cohen, Vanessa Daws, Bathsheba Demuth, Lowell, Duckert, Marianna Dudley, John Eperjesi, Mary Fuller, Eileen Joy, Philip Hoare, Jonathan Howard, Peter Hulme, Bernhard Klein, Astrida Neimanis, Adam Nicolson, Nancy Nowacek, Serpil Opperman, Craig Santos Perez, Laurence Publicover, Killian Quigley, Brian Russell Roberts, Martha Rojas, James Seth, Dyani Johns Taff, Robert Sean Wilson, Marina Zurkow, and many others. I am especially grateful to institution-builders who are crafting spaces for blue thinking, including Nicholas Allen at the Humanities Institute of the University of Georgia, Ellen Arnold at the Norwegian Institute for Research in the Environmental Humanities, Jonathan Bate at Arizona State University, the Blue Humanities Lab at James Cook University in Queensland, Cristina Brito and the 4-Oceans Project in Lisbon, Floriana Cavello and the editors of *Sirene* in Italy, Joana Gaspar de Freitas and the Dunes Project in Lisbon, Anna Iltnere and her visionary Sea Library in Latvia, Ursula Kluwick and the Beach in the Long Twentieth Century Project in Bern, Isaac Land and his fellow editors at *Coastal Studies and Society*, Helen Rozwadowski at the Maritime Studies Program at the University of

Connecticut, David Worthington and James Smith at the Coastal History Network, and many others.

The pioneering ocean historian John Gillis died in 2021 when I was writing this book. I thank him for his example, his inspiration, and the generosity that he showed to so many of the people whose scholarship appears in these pages.

For hosting me to lecture about this project, I thank the University of Bern, Kyung Hee University in Seoul, the Rachel Carson Center in Munich, the 4-Oceans Project in Lisbon, the Norwegian Research School in Environmental Humanities at Stavanger, the University of Bremen, and Ca' Foscari University in Venice.

Personal Preface: Bodies of Water

Twice each month, near the spring tides, I walk down the street to the low point of Beckett Avenue and watch the ocean bubble up through the sewer grate. Depending on when exactly I get there, and what direction the wind is blowing, the water might be either a damp oval leaching out from the sewer, or the entire street might be covered with around five to ten centimeters of water. The road does not get a lot of car traffic, and it usually remains passable for dog walkers like me, except a few times a year during storms or king tides. A slow exhalation of water passes through an underground channel and up out of the grate onto the street, generating the wet pulse of Short Beach, my little coastal neighborhood in the northeastern United States. The water pools in predictable shapes, fitting itself into slight gradations in the asphalt. It moves subtly in response to wind and the tides that roll shoreward from the open water of Long Island Sound, maybe ten meters away, on the other side of a row of beachfront houses. Sunny day flooding appears only in this one place, a low point across the street from a small public park. Here, at the bottom, the sea invades the land, following the rhythm of the tides, twice each day.

Geographic invasion provides physical evidence, wet and salty, of the presence of sea in this ordinary Connecticut suburb. Other evidence is not far to seek. A few hundred meters inland from the coast, a stub of the New Haven electric trolley line follows a raised railroad bed through the salt marsh. Part of the old "F" trolley route of the Connecticut Company that operated between New Haven and Branford from 1900 through 1947, before the postwar automobile boom displaced it, one last mile of functioning track crosses the salt marsh about a block behind my house.[1] As I walk along the tracks, the tide's inflating lungs follow me, alternately filling and draining the marsh. Living near Long Island Sound means that I see little appreciable surf, but we average a tidal range of two to four meters each cycle.

During the warmer half of the year, I'm a daily high-tide swimmer, and I carry the tidal rhythms in my body. Some days welcome me with afternoon high tides, with plenty of time to swim after a full day's work. But some days I sneak in an early morning dip, or else wait until the water rolls up to swimming depth when I should be cooking dinner for my family. I prefer a midday tide, but I like the cycle. I like tracing tidal changes through each month. All year I watch the water crawl up and then recede, staining the sand, filling the marsh, flooding the paved road.

That saltwater and salt marsh geography frames this book, much of which has been written on the shoreline of Connecticut.[2] Since the blue humanities as an intellectual discourse has grown out of investigations of how humans relate to the ocean, the saltwater film of our planet, it makes sense to begin here, at high tide, walking down the hill to see how much the road has flooded. But my personal saltwater geography does not exhaust the kinds of water with which this book engages. Even the whole World Ocean—shallow and deep, polar and tropical—represents only most, not all, of the water on our planet, and in this book.

Chasing multiple forms of planetary water, this book engages with two bodies of water in each chapter, one large and salty and the other smaller and fresh. Each chapter also takes up one physical property of water as a substance—its polarity, currents, buoyancy, and other things—to explore how this essential compound shapes human and nonhuman life. Each chapter explores several primary water-texts, as well as splashing through a single chapter from Herman Melville's novel *Moby-Dick*, perhaps the English language's greatest hymn to oceanic vastness and the human desires oceanic vistas spur. These five elements—salt water, fresh water, a physical property, primary texts, and a chapter from *Moby-Dick*—comprise the backbone of each of the ensuing chapters. (See Table 1 for all these elements together.) These objects, texts, and properties describe the current state of intellectual, creative, and artistic work in the blue humanities. They also, in their plurality and messy overflows, provide a feeling of how this critical discourse works. These ideas surge and reward immersion. As the American poet Charles Olson rhapsodizes about boats and bodies in his experimental epic *The Maximus Poems*, we must go "in! in! the bow-spirit, bird, the beak/in, the bend is, in, goes in, the form."[3] For Olson-as-Maximus, as for many blue humanities scholars who physically engage the waters they study, to go in means to confront waters and their meanings not just with ideas but with our bodies, sometimes in boats, always through direct contact.

Both the saltwater and freshwater bodies in this preface are my body. Human bodies, like estuaries, mix up the fresh and the salt. The physical property is the tides, in particular my local tides in Long Island Sound. But since tides slosh around the planet's surface in response to lunar gravity on the World Ocean, they are your tides, too, wherever you are. Visible tides are only easy to discern on oceans, or a few large lakes, but all bodies of water respond to the moon's pull. Even the water in my body, and yours, shifts in micro-tidal patterns. In juxtaposing the water that makes up roughly sixty percent of my own body with the forces that move vast basins of saltwater across the surface of the planet, this preface aims to foreground the interpretive challenge of multiple scales. Water surrounds us—in our bodies, our neighborhoods, and our planet. The core intellectual challenge of the

Table 1 Introduction to the Blue Humanities

	Chapter	*Saltwater*	*Freshwater*	*Property*	*Primary Texts*	*Moby-Dick*
0	Preface Bodies of Water	My Body	My Body	Tides	Swimming a Long Way Together	Wheelbarrow
1	Poetics of Planetary Water	World Ocean	Clouds	Phases	An Everywhere of Silver Song of Myself	Brit
2	Blue Humanities Thinking	World Ocean	Storm	Condensation	*The Tempest* Praise Song for Oceania	The Quadrant
3	Our Sea of Islands	Pacific Ocean	Rain	Buoyancy	*from unincorporated territory: [guma']*	The Pacific
4	The Roaring South	Southern Ocean	Wind	Currents	*Rime of the Ancient Mariner*	Will the Whale Diminish?
5	The Connected Sea	Indian Ocean	Rivers	Monsoon	*In An Antique Land* *The Lusiads* *Haroun and the Sea of Stories*	The Grand Armada
6	Surrounded by Land	Mediterranean Sea	Lakes and Springs	Connectivity	*The Odyssey* *Gun Island* *Don Quixote*	Loomings
7	In the Caribbean	Caribbean Sea	Swamps	Sweat	*A General History of the Pyrates* *The Mermaid of Black Conch*	Queequeg in his Coffin
8	Northern Visions	Arctic Sea	Sea Ice	Fish	The Seafarer Dark Traffic	Nantucket
9	The Tornadoed Atlantic	Atlantic Ocean	Humidity	Polarity	*The Interesting Narrative* *The Deep* *The Edge of the Sea*	The Whiteness of the Whale
10	Conclusion Touching Moisture	World Ocean	Immersion	Phases	Swimming Memoirs	Epilogue

blue humanities explores how water functions in and across multiple scales. How does the water that seeps out of a sewer grate at high tide connect to the water that nourishes my muscles and flesh? How might either of these two small bodies of water speak to the vast circulations of the ocean basins? Gear-slipping shifts between inside and outside, salt and fresh, liquid, solid, and vaporous represent interpretive puzzles. Making sense of disorienting movements across scales and spaces captures the pleasure and ambition of the blue humanities.

We who are swimmers, sailors, or simply humans who drink and wash our bodies know the sensation of water on skin. The touch pleases, but it also carries a hint of alienation, because land mammals cannot live in water. The variable opposition between the wet and the dry has long been at the heart of my thinking about blue environments. In *Shipwreck Modernity* (2015), I explored "wet narratives [that] emphasize disorder, disorientation, and rupture" in juxtaposition with "a dry countermovement that attempts to make sense and meaning out of disaster."[4] The contrast between wet swirl and dry structure operates as a fundamental division that animates blue humanities thinking. The conceptual distinction between experience and knowledge and the felt difference between feeling and form flow from the contrast between the wet and the dry. To be wet—to be "in" (in Olson's emphatic word)—generates an experience and distinctive feelings. Drying is the slower process, an imposition of form and accumulation of knowledge. Even though the opposition may feel binary and abrupt—as cold water shocks flesh on a hot day—these two states coexist in tension with each other. The movement of water into and across bodies trickles through many paths, forking often, sometimes unpredictably. The process through which water moves between bodies—which Stacy Alaimo describes through her term "transcorporality," and as I have previously theorized in wetter contexts through the verb "seep"—resists any absolute distinction between wet and dry tendencies.[5] On the driest days our bodies remain full of water, as does our planet even as both droughts and floods disrupt human communities. The felt opposition between wet immersion and dry terrestrial living operates in tension with a broader sense in which water touches everything. It flows through our body's cells, moistens our food and flesh, permeates the earth's crust, and even, scientists have determined, sits frozen on interstellar comets. The burden of the blue humanities follows water's sinuous trails wherever they flow and traces their dampness in our environments and memories.

Writing, thinking, and creative work that flies the flag of the blue humanities responds to water's intimate paradoxes in many modes, from poetry to literary criticism to history, environmental writing, and religious scholarship. This book's second chapter, "Blue Humanities Thinking," sketches out a large but still partial list of the many publications, collaborative books, special issues of journals, and related projects that have appeared in the first two decades of the twenty-first century. Because of my own training, this book leans heavily on literary texts and literary criticism, mostly but not only written in English. Literary culture, as I present it here, aims to be less a narrow specialization than a bridge-discourse to make water-infused ideas accessible for thinkers in many modes. We all read stories, many of us read poems, and the connective tissue of literary culture can, perhaps, form links between disparate modes of analysis and argument. In emphasizing literary studies, I do not mean to decenter the scholarship of historians, ecologists, marine biologists, or many others from whom I have learned and continue to learn so much. Rather, it is my hope that a nontechnical presentation of literary texts, including canonical figures such as William Shakespeare, Emily Dickinson, Walt Whitman, and Herman Melville as well as newer oceanic voices such as Éduoard Glissant, Craig Santos Perez, and Monique Roffey, can provide modes of access for many disciplines.

At the core of this understanding of literature as cultural bridge sits the overdetermined figure of the White Whale in *Moby-Dick*. Whenever I meet someone who works with water in any way—a yachtsman, a marine biologist, a NASA scientist interested in the composition of water on extraterrestrial bodies—*Moby-Dick* almost always sparks affinity. Readers of Melville recognize that the book that contains multitudes—South Sea adventure, cetacean natural history, Calvinist rage, political allegory, Shakespearean pastiche, gay romance, and much more. A recent comprehensive literary-critical study of maritime literature, *A Poetic History of the Oceans: Literature and Maritime Modernity* by Søren Frank, uses Melville as a test case for multiple iterations of Western imaginations of the sea.[6] For me, as for Frank, *Moby-Dick* represents the urtext of the human encounter with the global ocean. Rather than following Frank's lead and orienting my study around a core analysis of Melville, however, I dip briefly into fragments of *Moby-Dick* in each chapter. I hope to spur readers back to Melville, as also to the other primary texts, with newly blue vigor.

At the risk of making this short preface indulgently self-referential, its primary literary text will be a poem that I wrote for a "Swimposium" event that I was unable to attend in Dublin, Ireland, during the summer of 2021. My poem takes its title from a durational art project organized and curated by my friend and blue humanities inspiration, the open-water swimmer and videographer Vanessa Daws. Her project explores the legacy of British long-distance swimming pioneer Mercedes Gleitze, who in 1927 became the first woman to swim the English Channel. The title of Daws's project, and my poem, is "Swimming a Long Way Together":

> To be together, immersed in wetness,
> In-splashing arms in rotation, to catch
> The water, cup and hold, to pull endless
> Flowing the sea backward and me to match
> Leaping forward, through, in, past, and into
> The deep blue. Free! I in the wonder-world

Circumperigrinate to rendezvous
Inside the world-sea, light-bender, dreamworld.
You are here inside too, swimming with me
For a long way. Can't see where we're going.
Arms churn circles and hands cup the salt sea,
Emptiness around, flowing, unknowing.
To school like fish in silver mail so bright
From each day's dawning straight on to the night.[7]

The poem, which I also recorded with a musical background for Daws's project, reimagines the solitary experience of ocean swimming as collective act.[8] It presents three fundamental features of blue humanities thinking that can help introduce this book: physical contact with water, disorientation, and the emergence of new collectivities. The story is hyperlocal and personal, based on the physical feeling of my body in salt water. Principles of contact, disorientation, and collectivity operate across multiple scales. Blue environments disorient and reform collectives on the levels of the community, the nation, and beyond to posthuman networks. They operate on planetary scales, structuring the movements of human and nonhuman populations. We start with the body.

It is not easy to capture in words the feeling of saltwater immersion. This poem holds up the swimmer's effort to "catch/The water, cup and hold" (2–3), as I attempt to follow a long-ago swim coach's advice to grab the water in my cupped palm and pull it backward. Moving through water entails multiple sliding forms exchanging places with each other, "Flowing the sea backward and me to match/Leaping forward" (4–5). As my human body pushes into the water in front of me, the sea swirls in behind to fill up the vacated space. Liquid water always moves; it always responds to things moving inside it. To feel oneself in this element, to move in a practiced way that guides one's body toward a desired goal—this feeling, and the form that enables it, remakes a terrestrial animal. In the poem's concluding couplet, I present a desire to "school like fish" (13). A fish-school represents the collective this book aspires to build, a school of blue knowledge. But experience always wriggles free. The prospect of fish-being, becoming a water-breather whose physical capacities exceed my own, brings me up against the limits of my aquatic embrace. I love immersion, but I can't live in water.

For the brief time that my body goes into a watery environment, my capacity to orient myself in space changes. In the central word of the poem, I feel "free!" (6) from gravity's tug. The space I enter disorients me. "Inside the world-sea, light-bender, dreamworld" (7), physical senses fail. Vision becomes distorted. Sound and smell lose specificity. Touch hypertrophies as my skin vibrates to the surging passage of salt water on all sides. "Can't see where we're going" (9), and since humans lack the echolocation capacities of marine mammals, I swim with little guidance. Keeping a straight course is a technical problem for open-water swimmers, though mostly an annoyance for meditative amateurs like me. I feel water around me water "flowing, unknowing" (12). My experiential world narrows, distorts, and refocuses on buoyancy and motion.

Daws's "Swimming a Long Way Together" project includes multiple art installations, public swims, films, and conversations at different venues in Ireland and the United Kingdom, following the itineraries of Mercedes Gleitze.[9] My poetic contribution, sent across the Atlantic in lieu of my body in August 2021, builds toward a dream of collaboration. I want to shape semiaquatic creatures into knowledge-building collectives. To construct that unity over time, "From each day's dawning straight on to the night" (14), represents a difficult, perhaps impossible, task. Immersion creates communities, but when you're in the water there's a visceral solitude, a shock of being a land mammal out of place in the world. Art, like swimming strokes and intellectual discourses, builds communities through shared experiences. My aim in this book is to provide for readers something resembling the immersive communities that Vanessa Daws and other collaborators have been helping me discover.

Maritime communities construct themselves through reading as well as swimming. One clear example of community-formation appears early in *Moby-Dick*, in the chapter "Wheelbarrow." Ishmael and Queequeg's short voyage from the mainland to Nantucket, from which island they will embark after the White Whale, provides a miniature allegory of how humans engage with the sea. A foolish young greenhorn mocks the exotic South Sea islander, gets himself tossed in the air for his trouble, and in the disorder the maritime operations of the vessel fall to pieces. The captain, defending the landlubber passenger, threatens Queequeg, distracting attention from "the main-sail . . . [and] the weather-sheet," which frees the "tremendous boom" to sweep the deck. The greenhorn who had insulted Queequeg "was swept overboard" instantly, and "all hands were in a panic."[10] In this moment, the human–machine assemblage of a ship under sail falls apart: "Nothing was done, and nothing seemed capable of being done" (63). Into this failure of American seamanship Queequeg steps, first as able sailor and next as powerful swimmer. He deftly secures the boom with a neat bit of rope work that includes "flinging the other end like a lasso." Before the sailors lower a boat to attempt a rescue, Queequeg "stripped to the waist, [and] darted from the side with a long diving arc of a leap" (63). The man goes under, but Queequeg dives to recover him, and swims him back to safety. "From that hour," Ishmael observes, "I clove to Queequeg, like a barnacle" (64). The South Sea Aquaman shows himself the perfect sailor as well as a deep diver, saving the sinking greenhorn. As sailor and swimmer, Queequeg establishes himself as an ideal maritime human.

The reader's adulation for the cannibal harpooner follows the narrator's lustful gaze. "Was there ever such unconsciousness?" (64) rhapsodizes Ishmael after Queequeg emerges from the sea, washes himself with fresh water, and leans along the rail to smoke his pipe. His swimming body presents the narrator and the reader with an erotic covering and uncovering through repeated immersions, as Queequeg appears "throwing his long arms straight out before him, and by turns revealing his brawny shoulders. through the freezing foam" (63). The mystic marriage between Ishmael and Queequeg, initiated earlier when they shared a bed at the Spouter-Inn, represents an intermingling of human longings and oceanic intimacy. While the whale-ship *Pequod* may, in its multiplicity and submission to a tyrant's rage, allegorize the antebellum United States, the bond between schoolmaster and harpooner represents an ideal combination of Queequeg's natural capacities and Ishmael's intellectual curiosity. As Ishmael watches Queequeg smoke after saving both greenhorn and ship, he imagines the water-hero's vision of solidarity. "It's a mutual, joint-stock world, in all meridians," Ishmael ventriloquizes Queequeg, "We cannibals must help these Christians" (64). The contrast between the support Queequeg provides Ishmael and the raging destruction to which Captain Ahab consigns his crew represents oppositional versions of human solidarity in the oceanic encounter. Some mariners seek domination and find destruction. Others practice immersion and manage to save at least one swimmer.

After this brief preface, *An Introduction to the Blue Humanities* continues with two agenda-setting chapters: "A Poetics of Planetary Water" and "Blue Humanities Thinking." The first explores the diverse physical shapes and phases of water on our planet, in dialogue with nineteenth-century American sea poetry by Emily Dickinson and Walt Whitman. The next chapter provides a broad overview of the surge of critical publications, events, and collaborations in this growing discourse over the first two decades of the twenty-first century, while also articulating a contrast between Shakespeare's play *The Tempest* (1611) and new sea poetry by Craig Santos Perez. The seven chapters that follow each engage with a body of salt water, from Pacific to Atlantic, as well as different freshwater reservoirs from lakes to swamps. The blue geography that structures these chapters unfurls many varieties of planetary waters, as my project aims to provide points of entry into the critical, creative, and activist impulses that characterize blue humanities thinking today. A conclusion on the meditative poetics of swimming in the Anthropocene rounds out the book with the hope of imagining possible futures for human intimacy with water. As seas rise, glaciers melt, and warmer air absorbs more moisture, the blue humanities will have much to say and do in our changing ecological conditions.

Notes

1 For the local history as maintained by the Shoreline Trolley Museum in East Haven, CT, see https://shorelinetrolley.org/about/local-history/. Accessed 5 October 2022.

2 During the final two months of writing, I was a Landhaus Fellow at the Rachel Carson Center in Munich, Germany. I am deeply grateful for the hospitality and intellectual intensity of the Center.

3 Charles Olson, *The Maximus Poems* (Berkeley: University of California Press, 1983), 8.

4 Steve Mentz, *Shipwreck Modernity: Ecologies of Globalization, 1550–1719* (Minneapolis: University of Minnesota Press, 2015), 11.
5 Stacy Alaimo, *Bodily Natures: Science, Environment, and the Material Self* (Bloomington: Indiana University Press, 2010); Steve Mentz, "Seep," *Veer Ecology: An Ecotheory Companion* (Minneapolis: University of Minnesota Press, 2017).
6 Søren Frank, *A Poetic History of the Oceans: Literature and Maritime Modernity* (Leiden: Brill Publishing, 2022). The Melville material comprises chapter 1.5, "The Four World Pictures of *Moby-Dick*," 146–71.
7 First published in *Belfield Literary Review* 2 (Spring 2022), 198. The poem also appears in Steve Mentz, *Swim Poems* (Massapequa: Ghostbird Press, 2022), 28.
8 The recording can be found on Soundcloud: https://soundcloud.com/user-182078240/swimming-a-long-way-together-poem-steve-mentz. Accessed 30 November 2022.
9 For more on this ongoing project, see www.swimmingalongwaytogether.com/. Accessed 5 October 2022.
10 Herman Melville, *Moby-Dick*, Hershel Parker and Harrison Hayford, eds. (New York: W. W. Norton & Company, 2002), 63.

1 A Poetics of Planetary Water

Scholarship in the blue humanities and related discourses during the early decades of the twenty-first century has been dazzled by oceanic vastness.[1] As Helen Rozwadowski eloquently frames the subject in *Vast Expanses* (2018), her one-volume history of the ocean, the "world ocean" comprises "the dominant feature of planet Earth."[2] The massive circulating systems that connect all the saltwater basins on the surface of our planet have captured the attention of scholars and thinkers in multiple fields. As ocean-focused scholarly discourses have been developing, attention has radiated out from oceans to include rivers, lakes, glaciers, and many other forms of water.[3] The rapid growth of blue scholarship across literary studies, environmental history, anthropology, art, and related discourses has produced a riot of intellectual plurality in the early twenty-first century. As the seas rise, oceanic scholarship spills its bounds. These intellectual currents can be conceptualized under the rubric of a "poetics of planetary water." The flexible and speculative nature of this concept enables it to speak across multiple disciplines, geographies, and human histories. A focus on planetary water responds to the global concerns of today's ecocatastrophic times. The aims of watery criticism, to adapt a phrase, include both describing the complex workings of water and imagining ways to change our relationships to it. While many neologisms have been proposed, from hydro-criticism to critical ocean studies to ocean history, the sub-disciplinary modes of cultural and literary studies in the early 2020s mostly gather themselves together under the banner of the "blue humanities."[4]

The project of describing blue humanities scholarship in the first decades of the twenty-first century embraces a wide range of academic writing, artistic work, and activism on many continents. In presenting the outlines of this discourse, I return to some foundational poetic texts for my local watery environments, speaking as an American who lives on the northeastern coast of the United States. The two poetic fragments at the center of this chapter, by Emily Dickinson and Walt Whitman, represent intimate encounters between human bodies and planetary water. They also, not coincidentally, frame my own personal oceanic geography. Whitman's poem describes swimming off an Atlantic beach on Long Island or perhaps

DOI: 10.4324/9781003166665-1

New Jersey. Dickinson draws on the Massachusetts coastline, just a bit up the ragged edge of the continent to the northeast. My personal daily ocean is in Connecticut, roughly midway between these two poets and poems. I emphasize these specific oceanic margins because of my commitment to linking human-sized encounters to planetary forces. Bringing a taste of my local Atlantic into a global scholarly conversation will keep these thoughts tangible, even though the poetics operates across planet-sized, human-sized, and other scales. Dickinson's and Whitman's poems operate as exemplary texts in dialogue with scholarship from a variety of water-thinkers. To display the multimodal nature of blue humanities work, I turn near the end of this chapter to a recent book by an English nature writer to help consider relationships among different locations, modes of thinking, and human encounters with water. The blue humanities, as I pursue it, combines literary, historical, and critical modes.

In moving beyond oceans, blue humanities scholarship follows an impulse that has long been present in oceanic writing. Spillover appears in our urtext, *Moby-Dick*. One of the most widely quoted phrases from the novel holds that "meditation and water are wedded for ever."[5] This phrase, however, does not exclusively describe the salt sea that is the novel's primary setting. It instead emerges from Ishmael's contemplation of desert wells, the Hudson estuary, and the god-infused springs of Greek myth. The ocean itself generally appears as a figure of excess and flood. For example, in "Brit," Ishmael describes the ocean as rebellious: "Panting and snorting like a mad battle steed that has lost its rider, the masterless ocean overruns the globe" (224). This sentence, one of many in which the narrator rhapsodizes oceanic excess, emphasizes how the great waters "overrun" all boundaries. The ongoing shift in blue humanities scholarship from a largely saltwater and liquid focus to more varied analyses of planetary water extends this expansive impulse beyond the ocean itself. To surge over boundaries and encircle the globe require us to embrace not only each bay and basin but also smaller bodies of fresh water, as well as solid ice and water vapor. A poetics of planetary water does not so much turn its back on the sea as follow ocean-logic to its logical conclusions.

The term "poetics" captures the dynamism of blue humanities thinking because in English it resembles both a singular and plural noun. As I employ it, poetics functions as a singular concept: a poetics of planetary water aims to clarify the relationships between humans and water in all its forms and phases. In a similar vein, I treat the blue humanities as a singular collective: the blue humanities combines water with human ideas. *The Oxford English Dictionary* observes that the English word "poetics" has taken both singular and plural verbs in historical usage. The central meaning for my purposes defines poetics as a "theory of form" (1b). This definition usually takes a singular verb, though hints of plurality cling to the concept. My use of the term "poetics" echoes Aristotle's descriptive approach in his *Poetics* (330 BCE), in which the philosopher describes what poetry is by observing the examples he has to hand. The key term for Aristotle, and also for me, is *mimesis*, or "modes of imitation."[6] Aristotle builds his structures out of his reading of Homer and Greek drama, while blue humanities scholarship splashes around with a wetter range of exemplary texts. Aristotle's claim that poetics combines pleasure and pain seems noteworthy for a focus on watery parts of the world that allure and threaten human bodies. Aristotle emphasizes the pleasure of representing something that can be painful: "though the objects themselves may be painful to see, we delight to view the most realistic representations of them" (227). The pleasure that emerges from the threat of pain represents an important element in blue aesthetics. A blue poetics always engages with the awkward fit between humans and water; we depend upon it and love it, but it cannot be our home. The human–water relationship occupies the realm Aristotle names "poetics" in that it is distinct from the human world that he theorizes as politics, or the science of the *polis*. "There is not the same kind of correctness in poetry," the philosopher writes, "as in politics" (260). The pleasure–pain of poetic order instead asks humans to touch and engage more-than-human-beings and systems. My aim is to construct a poetics of planetary water that employs the flexibility and dynamism of the term "poetics."

Three Phases of Planetary Water

Cultural analysis of the multiphasic nature of the human encounter with water can begin with a famous phrase from Evangelista Torricelli. The sixteenth-century Italian humanist and scientist, inventor of the barometer, once remarked that humans live "at the bottom of a vast sea of air."[7] Torricelli accurately described the surface of our planet as covered by two bodies: a heavy and liquid one above which humans usually stand, and a lighter gaseous one to the bottom of which we generally sink. Alongside these two oceans, we should also add the global presence of ice, sometimes called the cryosphere. In our current interglacial period, the ice-ocean has been fragmented into large ice caps near the poles, including those on Antarctica and Greenland, and high-altitude glaciers. Blue humanities scholarship tends to oscillate between rigorous materiality and attention to detail and more expansive or poetic ideas.[8] For literary writers and scholars, the ocean seems especially attractive because of its metaphorical vastness. The great waters represent a principle of narrative fecundity that Salman Rushdie has described as the "sea of stories."[9] The ocean, in Rushdie's formulation, constructs an allegory for literary history and literary culture on a global, connected scale.

But that ocean is not all the water that humans encounter. Above the ocean, clouds circulate as ephemeral fragments of water vapor and water droplets. The sea of air contains massive amounts of water—roughly 142 million-billion liters—but that vapor hangs mostly unseen, occasionally forming into the visible patterns of clouds. While much could be said about the poetics of humidity, clouds present the most visible images of water vapor in the atmosphere.[10] I take my cue from a famous exchange in Shakespeare's *Hamlet.* The prince, in mockery and in jest, attempts to interpret clouds. "Do you see yonder cloud," he says to the counselor Polonius, "that's almost in shape of a camel?" (3.2.367–68).[11] His interlocutor, good subject to the royal throne, concurs: "By th' mass and 'tis like a camel indeed" (3.2.369). The counselor goes on to agree, as Hamlet's mind changes, that the cloud is "backed like a weasel" (3.2.371) and "very like a whale" (3.2.373). The joke that camels are unlike weasels are unlike whales obscures the more complex interpretive issue. The hybridization that Polonius accomplishes as cloud-reader, in which he starts with an initial identification, camel, then bends it into two new forms, weasel and whale, essentially follows a hybridizing theory of interpreting forms of water. Clouds appear as many different things to prince and advisor. Hamlet and Polonius may only be pretending to read cloud shapes—the scene takes place indoors and at night, though perhaps the playwright is imagining outdoor views from the open-air Globe Theater—but the dialogue implies a theory of how vaporous forms assume multiple meanings. The prince's efforts to appear smarter than the old man he will murder in their next scene together do not fully cut through the interpretive problems that clouds pose. Hamlet's building aggression toward Polonius does, however, obscure the imaginative flexibility of the older man. Clouds are camels, weasels, whales, and other shapes. The challenge is devising a language to understand their forms.

Often with reference to this passage in *Hamlet,* clouds are sometimes taken to represent a prototypical problem for hermeneutics. John Durham Peters, in his book *The Marvelous Clouds* (2015), notes that "clouds are often thought of as the thing par excellence without inherent meaning."[12] Peters further suggests that clouds represent "a crucial step in the prehistory of recording media" (259), and he notes that they "resist ontology" (260). Lorraine Daston, in a 2016 analysis of nineteenth-century scientific and artistic efforts to categorize cloud shapes, suggests that the project demonstrates the limits of categorization itself. "All classification," she observes, "depends on some degree of abstraction from the blooming, buzzing world of particulars."[13] Clouds, she continues, challenge all projects of classifying nature. Bringing clouds, as Daston describes the process, from "Ovidian fluidity to Linnaean fixity" (48) represents a key task of the cloud atlas-makers she explores. She posits a structural opposition between the Enlightenment scientist and the classical poet. Ovid, unlike Linnaeus, invites a poetic interpretive frame. Combining Daston's exploration of scientific practices with Peters's media analysis suggests that the connection in *Hamlet* between Polonius as naïve cloud-gazer and Polonius as goofy theorist of media forms is not accidental. Neither static nor visible in the same aspect over time, clouds coalesce into forms briefly, fragmentarily, impermanently. Mobile water-in-air structures present all form and no substance, no clear lines of descent or connection but a tantalizing possibility of partial repetition over time. The critical water-thinker's task distinguishes itself from the cataloging projects of nineteenth-century cloud morphologies. The project today asks us to assimilate fleeting clouds to robust if still dynamic forms.

The third, and for many humans the rarest, form of planetary water comprises the ice-ocean or cryosphere. Ice is the least mobile phase of planetary water, but as explorers and writers from John Davis to John Muir to Barry Lopez have emphasized, glacial ice feels alive.[14] The paradoxical qualities of living ice have motivated blue humanities scholarship on the polar regions. Hester Blum has recently noted, in scholarship informed by her personal voyages to ice-filled latitudes, "Ice in the Arctic and Antarctic appears both silent and still and yet is spectacularly on the move, and not just in epochs of climate crisis: in its vibrance ice carves valleys, levels mountains, and deposits moraines over hundreds of miles."[15] In an ecocritical analysis of early modern Arctic narratives, Lowell Duckert asserts that the "ice age is never over."[16] Christopher Heuer's art historical study *Into the White: The Renaissance Arctic and the End of the Image* (2019) describes the recovery of a frozen cache of engravings from the doomed expedition of Willem Barents to Novaya Zemlya in 1596–97 as representing the "frozen words" of premodern explorers.[17] These and other writers about planetary ice, from adventure writers such as Bill Streever to Indigenous activists such as Sheila Watt-Cloutier, demonstrate that the ice-ocean is as dynamic and humanly present as the liquid and vaporous oceans, even if ice is not very accessible for the human populations that live in temperate and tropical regions.[18]

Even as this chapter's two poetic texts lure me back toward human-scaled beach scenes, the blue humanities project keeps all these disparate world-seas in mind. The goal is an interpretive method that embraces all three phases of planetary water. Poetry and poetics seem powerful tools because poems originate in and are directed to individual humans while also imagining vaster scales. The pressure of human-sized encounters generates mobile reminders that water permeates our planetary existence across multiple contexts. Roughly seventy percent of the planet's surface is covered by liquid and solid water, human bodies are composed of approximately sixty percent liquid water, and the vast gaseous atmosphere contains around four percent water vapor. Human bodies and cultures form themselves in encounters with water in all three phases: liquid, solid, and gas. Water is, in fact, the only substance commonly present in all three phases though, by applying heat and pressure, all compounds can be liquefied or boiled.

Multiple forms of planetary water can be integrated into what James Smith and I recently called an inclusive blue humanities.[19] While my co-author and I used the term to indicate openness to multiple human cultures, I am also committed to exploring how multiple forms of water shape human bodies and human histories. Different narratives become legible through depictions of liquid salt water and fresh water, gaseous vapor, and solid ice.[20] The globe-embracing ocean of stories contains and constrains the circulation of literary narratives, texts, cultures, and traditions. Above the great waters, invisible but circulating, the semitranslucent sea of air overflows with ephemeral fragments, forms without substance, lacking clear lines of descent but hanging heavy in the air like fog. To reconcile these forms of circulation into a flexible and interwoven theory of planetary water as subject and shaper of human culture remains an unfinished task of twenty-first century ecocritical literary studies.

The Example of John Gillis: "The Blue Humanities" (2013)

In introducing the recent history of blue humanities scholarship, I begin with the works of the late ocean historian John Gillis, who died at the end of 2021 in California. The final decades of Gillis's career saw him publish two influential books in maritime environmental history: *Islands of the Mind: How the Human Imagination Created the Atlantic World* (2004) and *The Human Shore: Seacoasts in History* (2012). For this book, however, I start with a short open-access essay he wrote for the online magazine of the National Endowment of the Humanities in 2013 entitled "The Blue Humanities."[21] The oceanic turn in historical and literary scholarship was already very much underway by that time, in part through Gillis's own efforts, and I had been testing the terms "blue humanities" or "blue cultural studies" in publications since around 2009.[22] In a generous summation, Gillis's short article contextualizes the "cultural turn to the sea" as part of a trend he calls the "historicization of the oceans." Drawing on disciplines from archeology, anthropology, maritime history, biology, and environmental history, as well as on poetry, painting, narrative fiction, and other arts, Gillis frames human cultural history around a series of discoveries of new oceans, including the fifteenth-century discovery by European mariners of transoceanic trade routes and the subsequent fictional discoveries of writers such as Melville, Richard Henry Dana, Daniel Defoe, and others. Beyond a focus on Romantic and modern ideas about the sea, which he reads as being intertwined with the progressive alienation of industrial societies from any "working knowledge of the sea," Gillis treats the great waters as a resource for the imagination. Engaging with literary critic Margaret Cohen's ideas about the "sublimation of the sea," Gillis puts forward a paradoxical dual motion.[23] As the sea recedes from the everyday working life of nonprofessional sailors, it grows more and more central to the cultural imagination. "We have come to know the sea," he concludes, "as much through the humanities as through science." Artistic, poetic, and humanistic knowledge, he insists, define the sea's centrality to modern Western culture.

I first read this article in 2013, two years after meeting Gillis at a conference and later visiting him on the remote island on the Maine coast where he often spent the summer months. I remember feeling particularly pleased that he cited me as the coiner of the phrase "blue humanities," because reading my name in his article reflected my ideas back to me in the way that a reader's response can convince a writer that our thinking is not happening in isolation. The animating idea of Gillis's article, that in returning to the ocean "we are returning to our beginnings," seems both demonstrably true and a partial deflection of the challenges of the environmental present. Since the early 2010s I have been phrasing the project a bit differently. The reason to study the water, as I would phrase the point now, is that we are going to be seeing more of it, closer, in the near future. Rising sea levels and high-intensity rainstorms are making our environment wetter. Higher temperatures produce heavier rains since warm air holds more moisture. I have witnessed disorientingly tropical rainstorms in my nontropical neighborhood in Connecticut. In high elevation areas, glacial melt and retreat are fracturing long-established waterscapes. Global climate change defines the central challenge of the current generation, and scholarship about water in all its forms will be necessary to make sense of our disrupted ecosystems.

The changes in planetary water emerging from climate instability are not best represented by polar bears or the threatened Thwaites Glacier in Antarctica. Water-changes appear intimately and tangibly. We feel them on our skin. A closing detail in Gillis's "Blue Humanities" essay takes up the heroic case of Rachel Carson, perhaps the greatest American writer about the sea during the twentieth century. Carson, who like Gillis spent much of her professional life on the Atlantic seaboard of the United States, focused her scientific and poetic attention on tide pools and beaches, as well as writing powerfully about the ecosystems of the deep oceans. Gillis notes, however, that she "never really learned to swim." For an everyday swimmer like me whose understanding of water is inseparable from immersing my body in oceans, pools, rivers, and lakes, I find that shocking. How would it feel to be Carson, gifted with a poet's eye and a biologist's training, while also being excluded from water's embrace? What insights are available from the beach? To explore that question, I turn now to Emily Dickinson.

"An Everywhere of Silver"

There may be no more finely observed portrait of the beach than Emily Dickinson's tiny lyric poem "An Everywhere of Silver." Written in 1865, the final year of the American Civil War, this poem miniaturizes the conflict of sea and land into an aesthetic of barely contained rupture. In Dickinson's framing, we stand on sand facing an alien sea:

> An Everywhere of Silver,
> With Ropes of Sand
> To keep it from effacing
> The Track called Land.[24]

The poem structures itself through three echoing lines, each of which has two strong stresses and two capitalized nouns. The first line features Everywhere of Silver, the second Ropes of Sand, the fourth the Track called

Land. These three repetitive lines encircle the weakly stressed and uncapitalized third line, with its central verb "effacing." The action of effacing, which the poem both presents and disavows, communicates the vulnerability of sand and land to watery incursion. The Silver does not efface the Land in this poem, but we all know what high tides do to marks upon the strand. Dickinson may well be thinking of Edmund Spenser's famous Elizabethan sonnet "One day I wrote her name upon the strand," but the association of the beach with impermanence was and remains familiar.[25] As so often in Dickinson's poetry, the tiny space of this poem captures objects in motion, the silver ocean spreading itself "Everywhere," the Sand twisted into Ropes, the Land humanized into Tracks. Our bodies do not get wet, as they do in some of her other sea poems. The waterline conjures an alien space, a lure, and a temptation. Its surges will not efface the dry worlds on which humans walk, and yet we cannot help being drawn, perhaps by ropes of sand, toward the water. The sea-silver the poet presents feels like a cloud when you walk through it on an alpine hike—soft, wet, intangible, insistently present. Like Hamlet's camel-weasel-whale clouds, Dickinson's poem assumes new forms as we observe it. The lyric exercises our capacity to think about our environment in multiple forms, a valuable technique for the blue humanities and other environmental critical modes.

Reading Dickinson's poetry in the context of ecological crisis has led the literary ecocritic Anne-Lise Francois, in her essay "Ungiving Time: Reading Lyric by the Light of the Anthropocene," to assert that the tensile instability of lyric makes these poems especially well-suited to environmental shifts in scale. "In the suddenness with which they can shift gears without it feeling like a shock," she writes, "poems can help make palpable the contradictions of the simultaneously slow and fast times of the Anthropocene."[26] Francois demonstrates that Dickinson's intricate formal tensions and releases, the animating music of her lines, move her poetry in ecological directions. I extend Francois's reading in a watery context by suggesting that the "Everywhere" of the nonhuman sea bears a distinctive environmental meaning for the poet. Salt water overwrites beaches and human bodies. Watery "Silver" leaves us no dry place for our feet. But the formal pressure within the poetry, which Francois defines as "those delicate practices of transmission inseparable from the work of release and abandonment" (256), creates the poem itself as a beach of partial legibility, a blankness onto which human meaning can, for a time, make marks. Poems thus enable two slightly opposed human responses to rising seas and watery overflows: we accommodate ourselves to inevitable effacements, and we align ourselves to the Ropes and Tracks that, for now, keep us on human courses. In a sense, Dickinson's beach is a cloud—one that has not yet rained down on us.

Standing at the water's edge every year in late spring, I murmur Dickinson's sea poems to myself. Each year, I recite "An Everywhere of Silver" or the more famous "Exultation is the going" to myself before my first swim of the season. I know no more inspiring environmental art than Dickinson's poems. Her lines bring my body back into the cold water from which I have been excluded over a long winter. With my toes on wet sand, I think of Rachel Carson, who knew so much and wrote so insightfully but did not swim. I also think of my departed friend John Gillis. And into that silver Everywhere I plunge my body, shudder with cold, and meditate on how to endure in inhospitable environments. To support both physical experiences and thinking, poetry helps.

Theoretical Legacies: Islands and Shores

The scholarly work of John Gillis that most influences the blue humanities appeared primarily in the books *Islands of the Mind* and *The Human Shore.* These wide-ranging global histories have been especially inspiring because of the efforts Gillis makes to focus on the imagination. He notes early in *Islands of the Mind* that the condition he explores, "isolomania" or obsession with islands, represents "in its many different guises a central feature of Western culture."[27] He draws ideas about islands and oceans from many sources, but it seems revealing that the first two quotations in the book are from the English novelist Lawrence Durrell and the American geographer Yi-Fu Tuan. The project, as Gillis presents it, combines creativity with geography. The more comprehensive *Human Shore* begins with the demographics of the global human population's "unprecedented surge to the sea," but it also turns to poetry on the next page, in this case a local Maine poet from near Gillis's summer home on Great Gott Island.[28] These two books initiate an ocean-centric historiography that includes personal experiences, poetry, and fiction, as well as assorted methodologies in the social sciences, arts, and humanities.

In *Islands of the Mind*, the bridges that connect islands into archipelagos include literature. The island-centered world-making of transatlantic movements has become in subsequent scholarship a principle of global connection with special relevance for our age of environmental disruption. In Jonathan Pugh and David Chandler's book *Anthropocene Islands* (2021), perhaps the most direct extension of Gillis's early work, islands have become both "a figure for thought" and "key sites of 'relational entanglements' in the Anthropocene."[29] Employing sophisticated eco-materialist theoretical vocabulary, including such terms as "correlation" and "storiation," Pugh and Chandler present islands as key geographical concepts for an anxious age. "The island," they write, "has regularly been employed as a key figure which explicitly disrupts the grasp of modernist, linear and reductionist 'mainland' thinking" (5). Drawing especially on the postcolonial Caribbean writings of Éduoard Glissant and Kamau Brathwaite, Pugh and Chandler frame the island as figure and reality. Like Gillis, they engage with historical realities through the lens of poetry.

Both their work and Gillis's island-thinking connect, in an underwater context, to a recent book by the marine archeologist Sara Rich, who animates the presumed-dead spaces of wrecks in *Shipwreck Hauntography* (2021). Rich's ecotheoretical project enlivens the wreck and views it as assemblage and "gathering."[30] To bring together the once-living and now-living objects that one encounters in undersea shipwrecks entails creating what Pugh and Chandler would call "entanglement," but which Rich terms "the autonomy that comes with brokenness" (231). She suggests that "the broken thing, the wrecked ship, refuses the *telos* imposed from beyond, and in *gathering* forces, it opens up to new becomings" (231, emphasis in original). These scholars employ eco-materialist and high theoretical terms that the more traditional historian Gillis mostly eschewed. But his model of global water-poetics infuses this new work.

The "alternative account of global history" (4) that Gillis presents in *The Human Shore* is vaster in geographic and chronological scale than *Islands of the Mind*. In identifying the coast as "humankind's first Eden" (38), Gillis gestures toward a deep cultural and biophysical affinity between humans and watery borders. Considering the expansion of beachfront real estate in the twentieth and twenty-first centuries, he emphasizes that the beach is "the least natural place on earth" (172), despite its cultural affinity with the "pristine." His insights about the connection between human bodies and water have been extended recently by ecotheoretical feminist scholarship. Melody Jue, who includes scuba diving in the kelp beds of southern California in her research practice, emphasizes in her book *Wild Blue Media* (2020) that she aims for "conceptual displacement as a method of defamiliarization to make our terrestrial origins visible."[31] What Jue calls a "science fictional method of thinking with the ocean" (6) seeks to interrogate the great waters as both "medium of change" and "storage medium for the preservation of sunken objects" (112–13). "Seawater," Jue emphasizes, "changes how we think about the porosity of embodiment" (19). Jue extends scholarship about human connections to water and coastal ecotones by engaging directly with undersea experience.

Jue's analysis draws on the feminist eco-materialist scholar Astrida Neimanis, who emphasizes in the title of her monograph that humans are all *Bodies of Water* (2017). This ecofeminist work takes seriously the waters within and without human forms. Neimanis has recently provided a glimpse into the future of literary water-studies in dialogue with Black studies in a brilliant rereading of Adrienne Rich's celebrated poem of queer liberation "Diving into the Wreck." Neimanis's analysis entangles Rich's queer feminist poetics with Christina Sharpe's analysis of the "weather of anti-blackness," so that she can read the mythic structures of descent in ways that challenge racially innocent conceptions of white feminism and queerness.[32] As Neimanis notes in *Bodies of Water*, water "can only serve as a connector *because* it expresses or facilitates difference."[33] Expanding her notions of connection and distinction, she writes, "*Intimacy is not mastery*" (112, emphasis in original). Neimanis's scholarship humanizes Gillis's global oceanic history while it also informs Jue's and Rich's underwater theorizing. These works of embodied water-scholarship represent a theoretical leading edge of blue humanities scholarship in the 2020s.

I distinctly remember reading *The Human Shore* for the first time. It was Monday, 29 October 2012, the night that Hurricane Sandy came onshore near New York City. Though the storm ended up doing most of its damage to the south and west of my home in Connecticut, the evening before I gathered the family together in the living room—me and my wife and our two not-yet teenage children. While the kids tried to sleep, I was reading by a headlamp and anticipating a week without electricity. Hurricanes like Sandy were one of the features of the American weather system that most terrified and baffled early European travelers.[34] The hurricane season in the western Atlantic, which has become increasingly destructive in the Anthropocene, represents one of the most visceral reminders of human dependence on the seas of water and air that circulate around our planet's surface. Sometimes I think back to that moment on the living room floor—trying to hide my fear from my family while my imagination was afire with global forces—as an allegory of my intellectual and physical engagement with planetary waters. They are awesome and always a bit frightening.

Song of Myself

The second poem that I will interpret to span personal and planetary waters is an ecstatic and immersive fragment from Walt Whitman's "Song of Myself." I have written about it before, and as a child of the Jersey Shore, I never fail to be moved by its urgent and inviting physicality.[35] When reading Whitman's sea poetry, as Jeffrey Yang notes in his introduction to *The Sea is a Continual Miracle: Sea Poems and Other Writings by Walt Whitman* (2017), "it's easy to feel that [the sea's] primordial waters permeated his whole unconsciousness, its briny air smelt everywhere in his work, breaking the surface of all content."[36] In these lines, the poet pulls us under the surf with him:

> You sea! I resign myself to you also. . . . I guess what you mean,
> I behold from the beach your crooked inviting fingers,
> I believe you refuse to go back without feeling of me;
> We must have a turn together. . . . I undress. . . . hurry me out of
> sight of the land,
> Cushion me soft, dash me with amorous wet . . . . I can repay you.
> *(10)*[37]

The surf surges into view with the physical energy of these lines, the invitation, refusal, turning, undressing, hurrying out of sight. If Dickinson drops precise droplets, Whitman floods like a wave. The poem assaults the ear with relentless attention to tactile sensation, the cushioning feel of wetness and amorousness. The bravado of the line "I can repay you" represents the poet's egotism at its most titanic, most outward-facing, and most uncompromising. What would it mean to repay the sea? Sometimes I think of the white surf surrounding Whitman as if it were an iceberg, alien and threatening. But his mobile cryosphere refuses to stay isolated at high altitudes or latitudes. Whitman insists on a sea he can repay. His waters always touch flesh.

In the context of blue humanities scholarship, the naked male poet in the Atlantic surf represents as an image of global forces, even of the Anthropocene itself. Waves that break on the east-facing coast of New Jersey and New York roll in from the north Atlantic. The ocean beach on the Jersey Shore, where Whitman swam and where I have been swimming since I was a boy, faces the ocean around 40 degrees north, the latitude of Madrid, Sardinia, and northern Greece. When Whitman plunges into that water—when I dive into those waves—we each receive a measure of planetary force on our skin. The waves may cushion or dash, in the poet's words, but in order not to be tumbled about by its force, I usually tuck my head and dive under. Locally, in that space and time, I can join briefly with waves, if I do not resist them.

As anyone who reads the environmental news or who has lived through a storm like Sandy knows, human forces motivate oceanic transgressions in the Anthropocene. The agent here is the figure I like to call Old Man Anthropos. This giant, his vast and aging body full of carbon and smoke, has become, as geologists have recognized, a planet-sized force.[38] Whitman's pale body, and my own, frolicking in the waves, carry on our skin the guilt and violence of ecological catastrophe. I would like to believe, and sometimes I do believe, that inside the chaos of the surf we can derive succor and pleasure from the buoyancy that poetry creates. But it is hard not to recall the other creatures who depend upon the ocean, the fish and crabs, and microscopic plankton, that will pay a harsher price.

Heraclitus at the Shore

The micro-focus of lyric poetry shows how human bodies encounter water. Reading Dickinson and Whitman enables blue humanities scholarship to engage with planetary waters. But since the scales of that encounter always shift, we also need to think about systems. One further image of the Anthropocene beach that combines a global view with local experiences comes from the contemporary English writer Adam Nicolson.[39] In a book with the wonderful title *The Sea is Not Made of Water* (2021), Nicolson describes building by hand concrete tide pools near a coastal property in Scotland. Observing life in these artificial spaces, he learns what kinds of biotic worlds thrive on the margins of sea and land. His engagements with poetry, history, and marine biology reach a pitch of intensity in the book's central chapter, "Heraclitus at the Shore."[40] Meditating on his father-in-law, a classical scholar, Nicolson connects the Greek philosopher Heraclitus's theories of change with the evidence he finds in his tide pools. The Heraclitean vision, Nicolson avers, is "not static or closed but dynamic and open" (148). "There is no sense of calm in Heraclitus" (149), Nicolson continues, but only a world in which "strife is justice" (150). The central functions of disequilibrium and partial stability—strife and justice—connect Nicolson's reading of Heraclitus to the fundamental insights of ecological and oceanic biology. "Nothing is stable," he writes in joint paraphrase of Heraclitus and the coastal biologist Bob Paine, "and yet everything coheres" (159). In fact, it is only through instability and disequilibrium that systems arrive at any coherence, however temporary. In these tense vibrating systems, tide pools and Greek philosophy both resemble poems.

To understand a shoreline, a ship under sail, a poem, or a human community requires us to recognize that "its strife is its order" (158). This position represents a shift away from "green" ecological ideas that center stasis and sustainability. This insight becomes especially visible from a water-centric point of view. The argument that all ecologies are "dynamic" and all stable mixtures potentially unstable has been emerging in the ecological sciences since the work of Daniel Botkin in the 1990s.[41] As Nicolson describes this change, "It is a paradigm of nature opposite to the idea that living things hang happily and stably together in a set of mutually accommodated niches" (158). In place of stability, the tide pools and the world become "yet another theatre in which Heraclitean strife-and-justice held sway" (162). A vision of ecological dynamism has been central to the way I see literature responding to ecological catastrophe since I first used Botkin's ideas to read *King Lear* in 2010.[42] In extending this vision of strife and justice to all the planet's waters, the blue humanities crafts critical languages for dynamic partial orders that respond to strife while also seeking justice for humans and nonhumans alike.

Conclusions: Encounters, Transitions, Methods

In concluding these thoughts about the planetary and multiphasic turn in blue humanities scholarship, I turn to a trio of human-focused terms: encounters, transitions, and methods. Exploring these terms through a lens both poetic and Heraclitean, the logical future of this scholarly discourse requires a flexible and posthuman approach to our watery planet. The assimilation of dynamic ecologies and the accommodation of watery environments turn out to resemble each other and to resemble the complex forms and turns characteristic of poetry. As Anne-Lise Francois has demonstrated, poetry represents one of the best tools we have for communicating across different scales simultaneously. A holding-together of multiple registers of thinking and interpretation within a single poetic image represents how poets forge meaning. When Emily Dickinson describes a beach, it is both place and alien symbol. When we dash our bodies in the surf with Walt Whitman, we feel the world on our flesh, while knowing that collective human actions are marring and marking that world.

Encounters

Touch brings objects together, with pain or pleasure or both. When poets write about encounters, they animate an environment that in some modern scientific or even historical discourses can feel lifeless. The models of Astrida Neimanis, Melody Jue, Sara Rich, and others make water animate and viscerally present. The global vision of John Gillis describes the long-standing physical and imaginative integration of humans and oceans to locate these encounters in pan-historical contexts. Responses to encounters with planetary water challenge us to engage the world as it is, not as we would like it to be.

Transitions

But as soon as we encounter water, it changes. Dickinson's calm silver becomes Whitman's amorous churn becomes Nicolson's strife-filled tide pools. The sea's liquid evaporates into vapor in the heat and freezes into ice in the cold. Transition seems a weak word to describe processes that are more universal than occasional. Phases change, always. The project of blue humanities thinking across oceans, seas, islands, and beaches asks us to recognize and celebrate transitions across scales and encounters. In cold water, on ice, when hiking through clouds or fog, our bodies crave water and are water. To feel that and to know it may enable us to endure uncertain times ahead.

Methods

The thoughts and interpretations this book hazards amount to something less direct than a set of methods for blue humanities scholarship. The most productive methods, it seems to me, will require scholars and writers to seek out plural poetics rather than a singular theory. In a broad sense, blue humanities scholars should follow the grooves carved by Aristotle's descriptive theory of poetic genres and Heraclitus's creative understanding of tension and strife. Variation for these classical thinkers becomes the essential fact of human life; change is both a phenomenon to be explained and an engine to drive further inquiry. Poems and other products of creative thinking thus become exemplary representations of how humans respond to dynamic environments while being themselves representations of that dynamism. The intimacy between humans and water, an element that surrounds our planet and permeates our bodies, provides a rich reservoir for ideas about change, resilience, and the possibilities for new ways of thinking and living.

Notes

1 A slightly different form of this chapter has appeared as "A Poetics of Planetary Water: The Blue Humanities after John Gillis," *Coastal Studies & Society* (2023). E-published in October 2023. https://journals.sagepub.com/doi/abs/10.1177/26349817221133199. Accessed 20 November 2023.

2 Helen Rozwadowski, *Vast Expanses: A History of the Oceans* (London: Reaktion, 2018), 7.
3 On varied types of water in literary history, see Margaret Cohen, "Chronotypes of the Sea," *The Novel, Vol. 2*, Franco Moretti, ed. (Princeton: Princeton University Press, 2007), 647–66. On ice in the global water-system, see Hester Blum, *The News at the Ends of the Earth: The Print Culture of Polar Exploration* (Durham: Duke University Press, 2019). On multiple forms of water in ecocritical studies, see Steve Mentz, "Ice/Water/Vapor," *The Cambridge Companion to Environmental Humanities*, Jeffrey Jerome Cohen and Stephanie Foote, eds. (Cambridge: Cambridge University Press, 2021), 185–98.
4 Origin stories for academic terms are often suspect, but I first used the terms "blue humanities" and "blue cultural studies" in print around 2009. The related term "coastal history" was coined by Isaac Land in 2007; along with his collaborators Land has been advancing this discourse in the new journal *Coastal Studies and Society*.
5 Herman Melville, *Moby-Dick*, Hershel Parker and Harrison Hayford, eds. (New York: Norton Critical Edition, 2002), 19.
6 Aristotle, *The Rhetoric and The Poetics of Aristotle*, Friedrich Solmsen, ed. and trans. (New York: Modern Library, 1954), 223.
7 John B. West, "Torricelli and the Ocean of Air: The First Measurements of Barometric Pressure," 2013. https://journals.physiology.org/doi/full/10.1152/physiol.00053.2012?rfr_dat=cr_pub++0pubmed&url_ver=Z39.88-2003&rfr_id=ori%3Arid%3Acrossref.org. Accessed 12 May 2022.
8 Metaphor remains important to blue humanities thinking even though a signature rallying cry scholarship has long insisted, in Hester Blum's words, that "the sea is not a metaphor." Hester Blum, "The Prospect of Oceanic Studies," *PMLA* 125:3 (2010), 670–77.
9 Salman Rushdie, *Haroun and the Sea of Stories* (New York: Granta, 1991). I return to this novel in chapter 5.
10 On humidity in William Faulkner, Eudora Welty, and elsewhere, see Mentz, "Ice/Water/Vapor," 187–88.
11 William Shakespeare, *Hamlet*, Ann Thompson and Neil Taylor, eds. (London: Arden Shakespeare, 2006), 323. Further citations in the text by act, scene, and line numbers.
12 John Durham Peters, *The Marvelous Clouds: Toward a Philosophy of Elemental Media* (Chicago: University of Chicago Press, 2016), 254.
13 Lorraine Daston, "Cloud Physiognomy: Describing the Indescribable," *Representations* 135 (Summer 2016), 45–71, 48.
14 See, for example, Albert Hastings Markham, ed., *The Voyages and Works of John Davis the Navigator* (London: Routledge, 2016); William Cronon, ed., *John Muir: Nature Writings* (New York: Library of America, 1997); Barry Lopez, *Arctic Dreams: Imagination and Desire in an Arctic Landscape* (New York: Vintage, 2001).
15 Blum, *The News at the Ends of the Earth*, 9.
16 Lowell Duckert, *For All Waters: Finding Ourselves in Early Modern Wetscapes* (Minneapolis: University of Minnesota Press, 2017), 146.
17 Christopher Huer, *Into the White: The Renaissance Arctic and the End of the Image* (New York: Zone Books, 2019), 164.
18 Bill Streever, *Cold: Adventures in the World's Frozen Places* (New York: Little, Brown, 2009); Sheila Watt-Cloutier, *The Right to Be Cold: One Woman's Fight to Protect the Arctic and Save the Planet from Climate Change* (Minneapolis: University of Minnesota Press, 2018).
19 See Steve Mentz and James Smith, "Learning an Inclusive Blue Humanities: Oceania and Academia through the Lens of Cinema," *Humanities* 9 (2020), 67. www.mdpi.com/2076-0787/9/3/67. Accessed 12 May 2022.
20 See Mentz, "Ice Water/Vapor," 185–98.

21 John Gillis, "The Blue Humanities," *Humanities: The Journal of the National Endowment for the Humanities*. Unpaginated web publication. www.neh.gov/humanities/2013/mayjune/feature/the-blue-humanities. Accessed 12 May 2022.
22 See Steve Mentz, "Toward a Blue Cultural Studies: The Sea, Maritime Culture, and Early Modern English Literature," *Literature Compass* 6/5 (2009), 997–1013, and *At the Bottom of Shakespeare's Ocean* (London: Bloomsbury, 2009).
23 Margaret Cohen, *The Novel and the Sea* (Princeton: Princeton University Press, 2012), 106–8.
24 Emily Dickinson, *The Poems of Emily Dickinson*, Ralph W. Franklin, ed. (Cambridge: Belknap Press/Harvard University Press, 1999), 398.
25 Edmund Spenser, "One day I wrote her name . . .," *Amoretti 75, The New Oxford Book of Sixteenth-Century Verse*, Emrys Jones, ed. (Oxford: Oxford University Press, 1991), 282.
26 Anne-Lise Francois, "Ungiving Time: Reading Lyric by the Light of the Anthropocene," *Anthropocene Reading: Literary History in Geologic Times*, Tobias Menely and Jesse Oak Taylor, eds. (University Park: Penn State University Press, 2017), 239–58, 251.
27 John Gillis, *Islands of the Mind: How the Human Imagination Created the Atlantic World* (London: Palgrave Macmillan, 2004), 1.
28 John Gillis, *The Human Shore: Seacoasts in History* (Chicago: University of Chicago Press, 2012), 1.
29 Jonathan Pugh and David Chandler, *Anthropocene Islands, Entangled Worlds* (London: Westminster University Press, 2021), x–xi.
30 Sara Rich, *Shipwreck Hauntography: Underwater Ruins and the Uncanny* (Amsterdam: Amsterdam University Press, 2021), 228.
31 Melody Jue, *Wild Blue Media: Thinking Through Seawater* (Durham: Duke University Press, 2020), 6.
32 Astrida Neimanis, "The Weather Underwater: Blackness, White Feminism, and the Breathless Sea," *Australian Feminist Studies* 34:102 (2019), 490–508, 498.
33 Astrida Neimanis, *Bodies of Water: Posthuman Feminist Phenomenology* (London: Bloomsbury, 2017), 67.
34 See Steve Mentz, "Hurricanes, Tempests, and the Meteorological Globe," *The Palgrave Handbook of Early Modern Literature and Science*, Howard Marchitello and Evelyn Tribble, eds. (London: Palgrave Macmillan, 2017), 257–76.
35 Steve Mentz, "After Sustainability," *PMLA* 127:3 (2012), 586–92, 588–89.
36 Jeffrey Yang, "Introduction: Apologia for the Sea," *The Sea Is a Continual Miracle: Sea Poems and Other Writings by Walt Whitman* (Hanover: University Press of New England, 2017), xxxii.
37 Walt Whitman, "Song of Myself," *The Sea Is a Continual Miracle*, 10.
38 Steve Mentz, *Break Up the Anthropocene* (Minneapolis: University of Minnesota Press, 2019).
39 On Nicolson, see my public humanities essay, "The Restlessness of the Tides," *Sirene* 15 (2022), 78–85.
40 Adam Nicolson, *The Sea Is Not Made of Water: Life between the Tides* (London: William Collins, 2021), 144–62. Further citations by page numbers in the text. The American edition, published by Farrar, Straus & Giroux in 2022, employs the simpler title, *Life between the Tides*.
41 Daniel Botkin, *Discordant Harmonies: A New Ecology for the Twenty-First Century* (Oxford: Oxford University Press, 1990).
42 Steve Mentz, "Strange Weather in *King Lear*," *Shakespeare* 6:2 (2010), 139–62.

2 Blue Humanities Thinking

The blue humanities comprises a current of scholarly and artistic discourses that foreground human relationships with water in all its forms. While over the past several decades, many writers and thinkers have emphasized oceans, blue humanities thinking also explores fresh water and even water vapor from lakes and glaciers to groundwater and humidity.[1] During the first two decades of the twenty-first century, an early wave of blue humanities writing and thinking has emerged from Anglophone literary contexts, with emphases on Atlantic, Mediterranean, and Caribbean locations.[2] Writers in the 2020s are widening the focus to engage global, non-Western, and Indigenous materials. This chapter takes the measure of the past two decades of work in this fast-flowing discourse and suggests some ways that newer turns toward Indigenous and Pacific ideas seem to be modifying the blue humanities in the early 2020s. To an extent, this overview requires me to return to my own early work in this mode, especially the article "Toward a Blue Cultural Studies" and the book *At the Bottom of Shakespeare's Ocean*, both of which appeared in 2009.[3] Those two publications represented my first ventures into blue-critical waters. There are things I still like about those writings, things I see now that I did not yet recognize then, and questions that I am still trying to figure out how best to answer. This chapter attempts to do justice to the surge of blue humanities scholarship in multiple modes since the mid-2000s and also to provide some sense of future developments now emerging.

The biggest change I will chart between the 2009 version of the blue humanities and the early 2020s version is the increasingly visible effort to move beyond the Atlantic centrism of my own, and Anglophone literary criticism's, history. While I remain shaped by my own education and training as a Shakespearean, my aim in this chapter is to unpack ways in which my background in Renaissance English literature has been confining and should be pried open. The blue humanities in what I like to call its "offshore trajectory" should move beyond the Atlantic and beyond Shakespeare, though without leaving either of them, or English-language literature, entirely behind. This chapter considers the benefits of moving toward the Pacific as default ocean basin. The shift would not entail ignoring the

DOI: 10.4324/9781003166665-2

Atlantic, Mediterranean, Caribbean, or other waters salt and fresh, but it would shift the normative baseline from the Anglophone North Atlantic to the global Pacific. To suggest the contours of that shift, I will chart my own efforts to supplement Shakespeare studies with analysis of the Indigenous Chamorro poet Craig Santos Perez.[4] The shift from Atlantic to Pacific expands geographical range and reconsiders oceanic patterns of connection and communication. Shifting from the uber-canonical Renaissance figure Shakespeare to the new voice of Perez inverts the focus of much Anglophone scholarship. While the Pacific dwarfs the Atlantic in size, Perez's public visibility remains tiny compared to Shakespeare's. This chapter considers the benefits and costs of either an Atlantic or Pacific focus and the different representations of the human–ocean relationship in Shakespeare and Perez. I argue the future of the blue humanities requires a truly global, multilingual, and inclusively creative methodology inspired by and ranging alongside the cultural practices of Oceania.

The offshore vision of the blue humanities emerges, in this telling, across the time and space between Perez's Oceania and Shakespeare's Thamesside Globe Theatre. Reading these two authors together will enable close textual analysis to tease out some essential features of the blue turn in humanities scholarship and creative practices. Dividing this chapter's analysis between the most canonical author of the English Renaissance and a distinctive new twenty-first century poetic voice, however, inevitably glosses over a wide range of practices and voices. To some extent, Shakespeare in this reading can be imagined as a symbol for traditional ideas about the literary canon, encompassing established works from the Mediterranean epics of Homer and Virgil to the nineteenth-century surge of oceanic narratives in authors such as Melville and more terrestrial figures such as Jane Austen. Other versions of oceanic literary history place more emphasis on the nineteenth-century transatlantic novel or on contemporary world literature.[5] An ocean-centric retelling of human history seems to me a valuable thing, but this chapter focuses somewhat narrowly on two literary authors to show by juxtaposition how blue humanities narratives and poetic tropes have been and continue to be operating in English-language literary culture.[6]

My focus on these two literary examples contrasts with the global surge in blue humanities criticism, writing, and thinking over the past two decades. Not all authors working in this mode use the term "blue humanities," although many do, and not all of their works speak directly to each other. But the blue humanities represents a thriving community of voices and visions, rapidly expanding year by year. A private, shared Zotero bibliography grouped by the rubric "Coastal Studies" currently includes more than 495 entries contributed by forty-four international scholars who are registered users.[7] A more compact and curated bibliography of the blue humanities created by Alison Maas and hosted by Searchable Sea Literature and the Williams-Mystic Program contains 108 entries.[8] (Maas has more recently transformed this static bibliography into a collaborative Zotero database.[9]) Both bibliographies continue to be updated actively, and neither is fully comprehensive. New blue humanities publications continue to appear in single-author books, collaborative collections, articles, and exhibitions. Without aspiring to be exhaustive, which is not feasible during this dynamic stage of the discourse, this chapter aims to provide a sense of the range, variety, and perspectives of blue humanities work at the start of the third decade of the twenty-first century.

The critical practice of the blue humanities has come into focus during the first two decades of the twenty-first century, although the practice draws on ideas of water-inflected reading and writing that are as old as Homer's *Odyssey* and the creation stories of Oceania. Many of the critics whose works have come to exemplify this trend first published ocean-focused criticism in the 2000s. Influential early studies include John Peck's *Maritime Fiction* (2001), Philip Steinberg's *Social Construction of the Ocean* (2001), Bernhard Klein's edited collection *Fictions of the Sea* (2002) and his co-edited collection *Sea Changes* (2003), Elizabeth DeLoughrey's *Routes and Roots: Navigating Caribbean and Pacific Island Literatures* (2007), Hester Blum's *View from the Masthead: Maritime Imagination and Antebellum American Sea Narratives* (2008), my own *At the Bottom of Shakespeare's Ocean* (2009), and Margaret Cohen's *Novel and the Sea* (2012).[10] These scholarly forays built on earlier trends in late twentieth-century scholarship, including historiographical trends such as Atlantic history, the Black Atlantic, and postcolonial Caribbean studies.[11] In bringing together these discourses in an approach that focuses directly on the watery substrate, the blue humanities self-consciously distinguishes itself from familiar terrestrial (or "green") models of the relationship with the nonhuman environment. While much of value has emerged and continues to emerge from green ecostudies, the blue turn aims to redress what Dan Brayton and, more recently, Sidney Dobrin term our "ocean deficit."[12] Blue discourses also reject traditional conceptions of the human, especially in the more theoretical versions of blue thinking advanced by critics such as Steinberg, DeLoughrey, and Stacy Alaimo.[13] Even scholars who begin by engaging with familiar works of Western literary culture, such as Peck, Blum, Brayton, Klein, Mentz, and Cohen, untether their literary analysis from terrestrial narratives that center traditional categories such as nation, race, and language. By around 2010, the blue humanities had found its name, though cognate forms such as "blue cultural studies" and "hydro-criticism" continue to appear.[14] The next decade would see a rapid expansion of the discourse.

The 2010s witnessed the maturation of the blue humanities as scholarly discourse. This emergence appears most clearly through cataloging the nine different clusters or special issues of English language scholarly journals dedicated to this critical method published between 2010 and 2020. These compilations together contain more than ninety separate essays exploring human interactions with oceans in different forms and phases, analyzed from various perspectives and modes. The decade's blue scholarship began with an important cluster of essays in the flagship journal of American literary studies, *PMLA*, which published an "Oceanic Studies" collection edited by Patricia Yaeger in 2010.[15] A few years later in 2013, Americanist Hester Blum, who had contributed to Yaeger's collection, edited a special issue of *Atlantic Studies* under the rubric of "Oceanic Studies."[16] Several years later in 2017, Isabel Hofmeyr and Kerry Bystrom co-edited a special issue of *Comparative Literature* on the topic of "Oceanic Routes."[17] During the same year, but operating in a very different historical period and critical context, two scholars of medieval literature, Matthew Boyd Goldie and Sebastian Sobecki, co-edited a special issue of the journal *Postmedieval* under the title "Our Sea of Islands: New Approaches to British Insularity in the Late Middle Ages."[18] In 2019, Laura Winkiel's special issue of *English Language Notes* introduced a new way to describe this critical trend with the term "Hydro-Criticism."[19] During the same year, an expansive transdisciplinary Special Forum in the *Journal of Transnational American Studies* employed the compound title "Archipelagos/Oceans/American Visuality."[20] Another large special issue on "Blue Humanities" appeared in the journal *symploke* in 2019.[21] The three most recently published collections, including Di Leo's, appear to have provisionally settled on the term "blue humanities" for this discourse. Theoretical feminist scholar Stacy Alaimo guest-edited an issue of *Configurations* in 2019 under the title "Science Studies and the Blue Humanities."[22] In the following year, Alexandra Campbell and Michael Paye co-edited an issue of the open-access journal *Humanities* under the title "World Literature and the Blue Humanities."[23] Together these issues comprise around ninety articles by at least eighty distinct critical voices over the course of a decade. This body of work defines an emerging new discourse.

These nine journal issues have shaped the blue humanities alongside a series of monographs published in the 2010s, including new studies by Blum (*The News at the Ends of the Earth*, 2019), Mentz (*Shipwreck Modernity*, 2015, and *Ocean*, 2020), and DeLoughrey (*Allegories of the Anthropocene*, 2019).[24] As with the multiple journal issues, however, the rapid growth of this subfield appears most clearly in collective works, especially a series of edited volumes that brought together different voices and methodologies. Steve Mentz and Martha Elena Rojas combined British and American scholarship from multiple periods of literary study in their 2017 co-edited volume *The Sea and Nineteenth-Century Anglophone Literary Culture*.[25] Nicholas Allen, Nick Groom, and Jos Smith co-edited *Coastal Works: Cultures of the Atlantic Edge* (2017), which treats the multiple islands of Great Britain and Ireland as containing diverse literary and cultural possibilities.[26] Cecilia Chen, Janine MacLeod, and Astrida Neimanis's *Thinking with Water* (2013) announced a theoretical turn in blue criticism that Neimanis's monograph *Bodies of Water* (2017) would do much to extend.[27] Stefanie Hessler and the Thyssen-Bornemisza Art Collective's

Tidalectics: Imagining an Oceanic Worldview through Art and Science (2018) brings together creative and scientific responses to ocean thinking inspired by Caribbean poet Kamau Brathwaite.[28] Another substantial multidisciplinary volume that bridges the divide between historical and literary analysis, *The Routledge Companion to Marine and Maritime Worlds, 1400–1800*, co-edited by Claire Jowitt, Craig Lambert, and Steve Mentz, appeared in 2020.[29] Margaret Cohen followed up her study of the oceanic novel in 2020 with a co-edited volume with Killian Quigley, *The Aesthetics of the Undersea*.[30] Edging just into the next decade with a publication date of April 2021, Cohen's magisterial six-volume *Cultural History of the Sea* (Bloomsbury 2021) represents the most comprehensive portrait available of the state of the discourse at the start of the 2020s. The six individual volumes are edited by Marie-Claire Beaulieu (Antiquity), Elizabeth A. Lambourn (Medieval), Steve Mentz (Early Modern), Jonathan Lamb (Age of Enlightenment), Margaret Cohen (Age of Empire), and Franziska Torma (Global Age).[31] At the cusp of a new decade, the blue humanities seems both well-established and surging forward.

Preexisting academic and personal networks make citation-counting a somewhat unreliable measure, and this gathering of articles, monographs, and book collections does not exhaust the production of blue humanities scholarship in the 2010s. The names that appear multiple times among this sample of well roughly two hundred books, articles, and chapters, however, may be taken as a rough gathering of some early movers in this discourse. These include Stacy Alaimo, Hester Blum, Dan Brayton, Margaret Cohen, Adriana Craciun, Elizabeth DeLoughrey, Isabel Hofmeyr, Claire Jowitt, Bernard Klein, Astrida Neimanis, Steve Mentz, Meg Samuelson, Teresa Shewry, Sebastian Sobecki, and Philip Steinberg. The full range of these essays and collections, while not quite representing a comprehensive account of blue humanities scholarship published in the 2010s, provides a view into a thriving scholarly current that seems likely to continue to expand in the 2020s.

Making sense of the recent history of the blue humanities also entails coming to terms with the challenges and affordances of engaging an element defined by mobility and evanescence. The poet John Keats asked a friend to carve onto his gravestone "Here Lies One Whose Name Was Writ in Water." The famous inscription emphasizes water's incapacity to endure. To write on, in, or perhaps even about water may doom a discourse to dangerous proximity with the limits of language itself, as the poet implies. In contrast with other forms of environmental studies and with more traditional discourses in the humanities, the blue humanities foregrounds ephemerality and experimental writing practices. Blue humanities scholars and artists shape our words and images in dialogue with water's physical and cultural instabilities. The surge in watery writing in the past decade suggests that the challenge of water writing is proving attractive to the current generation of environmental scholars.

Images of the Blue Humanities

In addition to this substantial bibliography of recent scholarship, the first half of this chapter will explore a pair of images that capture some of the aims and challenges of this work. These images may appear somewhat idiosyncratic or personal, which they are, but I hope that they represent important trends in blue humanities thinking, in particular about an emerging turn toward the Pacific as well as long-standing efforts to engage with global climate change and ocean pollution. The first image is a small acrylic painting of an imaginary seascape that the artist Vanessa Daws painted in 2019. The second is a digital logo that I commissioned in early 2021.

The painting was drawn by the Dublin-based blue humanities artist, swimmer, and videographer Vanessa Daws in 2019. The image was made to accompany a workshop and public lecture on the blue humanities that I gave at the University of Lausanne in Switzerland.[33] The title of the painting, "Pluralize the Anthropocene!," and its riot of slightly unsettling colors together create the sensation of crisis and uncertainty, with perhaps a touch

Figure 2.1 "Pluralize the Anthropocene!" by Vanessa Daws[32]

of seasickness. Daws paints a boat crammed full of faceless souls, perched precariously on a wave that is itself full of stormy ocean trash. Atop the mast a single figure peers down toward murky water, and behind him the tail of a monstrous beast seems about to strike. The sea monster is modeled on a creature that decorates a celebrated seventeenth-century European atlas; Daws found the image in the flyleaf of a first edition copy of Rachel Carson's *Sea Around Us*.[34] The painting represents the twenty-first century Anthropocene Ocean as we have broken it and filled it with garbage. This space has become hostile to humans and hard to endure, but it still pulses with an eerie attraction. This ocean is not only blue—many other colors are present—and it may be better understood as the prismatic (in Jeffrey Jerome Cohen's sense) or multihued subject of the blue humanities.[35] The painting presents alien oceans in which terrestrial mammals like humans cannot easily live. With the crowd of sailors, we fear the ocean's waves. With the solitary figure on the masthead, we cannot see as far ahead as we would like.

Figure 2.2 Blue Humanities Logo

Source: Digital file by T.J. Piccirillo, 2021[36]

The second image is a logo that T.J. Piccirillo, an American graphic designer, created for me during early 2021. The image deliberately presents a more hopeful vista than Daws's painting. The logo echoes the global view of the Earth made famous by the "blue marble" photograph taken by the crew of the Apollo 17 spacecraft in 1972. In reframing the image, I asked the designer to place the Pacific Ocean at the center. Australia and New Zealand are visible in the lower left of the globe, and the northern coasts of North America and Asia frame the upper half. If the image quality is good enough, the viewer can pick out Korea, Japan, and several other large Pacific land features including Borneo and New Guinea. The empty blue heart of the image, however, is the vast Pacific itself, here depicted without famous islands such as Hawaii or Tahiti. The image highlights a planetary ocean that pushes human settlements to the edges of our sight. The inhuman great waters occupy the frame. In important ways, the dehumanized content of this image is false—the central waterways of the Pacific have been sites of human travel and settlement for millennia, as poets and scholars of Oceania have shown—but since we almost always see maps that put land in the middle, I wanted this image to center the ocean. The blue humanities aims to keep this dominant feature at the focus of our attention.

These two images, like this chapter, participate in efforts to define the blue humanities. Over the years, many scholars have been using a variety of short definitions. The blue humanities represents a form of literary and cultural criticism that puts water at the center. It poses a blue counterchallenge to the obsessively green visions of ecocriticism.[37] It puts water where the land used to be. It is animated by the effort to craft new vocabularies and critical methods that enable a richer connection between humans and water in all its forms. I should emphasize, by the way, that while I often get credit for "inventing" the term blue humanities, I assert no claim of ownership. Like any robust scholarly endeavor, this discourse is plural and collective; many people contribute to and practice blue humanities thinking, and many of them do not connect it with me or my work. That seems perfectly fine and right—we are on the open sea where no one owns anything!

The analysis that follows of Shakespeare and Perez will engage with some histories and some definitions. However, I want to emphasize that the two positions made visible in these images—the ship-as-catastrophe and the ocean as nonterrestrial vastness—represent central poles between which blue humanities thought oscillates. Like many blue humanities writers and thinkers, I find something enticing about that wild blue, even if I remain self-conscious about my own lingering Romanticism. Some of those alluring qualities are the same things that make the human experience of the ocean painful. The sea down the street from me, where I swim every day between May and November, is the same sea of troubles on which the transatlantic slave trade floated and into which the bones and bodies of suffering humans were consigned. The blue waters represent both difference and capacity, or perhaps it is clearer to say that they represent difference *as* capacity. To engage with the blue means to step at least provisionally outside of familiar land-bound concerns. Sometimes that is a welcome change, and at other times, it can feel catastrophic.

The Tempest (1611) and "Praise Song for Oceania" (2020)

The blue humanities is not always or only a literary practice, though for me it often starts with sea poetry. The remainder of this chapter juxtaposes two literary texts to help show the contours of blue humanities thinking and analysis, both recently and, insofar as I can predict, in the future. I start with perhaps the most canonical vision of the ocean in English literary culture: Shakespeare's late play *The Tempest*, first performed in London around 1611 and first published in 1623.[38] I have been writing obsessively about this play since at least the mid-2000s. It remains for me a core text in the history of human–ocean interactions. Recognizing that not all blue humanities scholars share my fascination with early modern literary history, I juxtapose *The Tempest* with Craig Santos Perez's recent poem "Praise Song for Oceania," published in 2020 in his book *Habitat Threshold*.[39] These two texts represent, in their similarities and their differences, some essential qualities of the blue humanities as a discourse. *The Tempest* represents literary history, particularly in Anglophone context. Every one of the six chapters in my 2009 book *At the Bottom of Shakespeare's Ocean* has a *Tempest*-section, and I continue to wrestle with the play's capacious view of watery enmeshment, as well as its representations of colonial domination, racism, political conspiracy, and patriarchy.[40] Perez's poetry has been a more recent discovery. Part of the reason to juxtapose these writers is their contrasting places in the discourse of literary criticism, though I am not interested in fights about canonicity or transcendent value. Perez's "Praise Song," which names in its verse "your blue humanities" (71) among the oceanic qualities it singles out for celebration, represents a more current vision. The poem draws together multiple voices, spaces, practices, and tributes to represent the living legacy of Oceania, its inhabitants both human and nonhuman, and its joys and terrors. Shakespeare's play also presents oceanic horror and beauty, and it also dramatizes nonhuman forces as well as social injustices. Despite the play's long history of contextualization regarding English colonial expansion, as well as its direct connections with seventeenth-century voyages to Bermuda and Virginia, I would not term *The Tempest* anything like a praise song for English or European mariners.[41] Like most of Shakespeare's works, the play seems more critical and ambivalent than celebratory. My hope in reading Shakespeare and Perez in watery entanglement with each other will be to mix up a new flavor of blue humanities, one that adequately responds to Atlantic and Pacific strains, to old and new poetics, and to shared human feelings and experiences.

Offshore Capacity

I am tempted to claim that "blue humanities" is my favorite short phrase in Perez's poem, but the repeated word I keep diving into is "capacity." The first seven stanzas of the twenty-nine-stanza poem begin by repeatedly emphasizing oceanic capacity as the measure of praise. "Praise your capacity for birth" (66), Perez opens his first stanza, in a perhaps unconscious echo of Rachel Carson's first-page invocation of the sea as "that great mother of life" in *The Sea Around Us* (1951).[42] Birth and capacity together drive the poem's fecundity, its rhythmic sense of the sea's generative surges and flows. The primary rhetorical mode of Perez's song-poem is accumulation, and the opening stanzas pile qualities atop qualities, so that the ocean's features end up jumbled together like the detritus on the wrack line of a beach that marks high tide. The sea presents a capacity for "renewal," and further capacities "to endure," "to survive," "to dilute," "to bury," and ultimately "to remember" (66–67). These stanzas oscillate between physical qualities of the ocean, which dilutes everything that flows into it, and which is the fluid matrix from which planetary life emerged, and metaphorical capacities such as survival and endurance. These physical and metaphysical movements back and forth suggest that the poem traces exchanges among multiple meanings. The poem's title, too, especially the word "Oceania," performs another slight dislocation of simple meaning: much of the poem appears to describe qualities of the physical ocean, but the word "Oceania" also refers to humans and human cultures, in particular the ocean-intimate peoples and cultures from whose experiences and histories Perez, an Indigenous Chamorro poet from the island of Guam (Guahan), speaks. To Perez, ocean-Oceania and its constellation of islands and sea routes represent an ancestral home, a "library of drowned stories" and "vast archive of desire" (67). This oceanic archive is one that I can read somewhat and perhaps interpret, but for me—a white male American professor living on the Atlantic coast almost thirteen thousand kilometers from Guam—some aspects of it remain distant.

Or do they? Reading about Perez's Pacific also returns me to my personal and physical engagement with local waters, bracingly cold every spring as I begin my cycle of high-tide immersions. In a global blue humanities sense, my (Atlantic) waters are the same global fluid body as Perez's (Pacific) ocean, whether in his native Guam or his current Hawaiian home. As soon as my cold feet leave the gritty bottom, I am "offshore," which means I am in the same World Ocean as Perez's daughter, who dangles her toes in the tropical surf on the cover of *Habitat Threshold*. The offshore trajectory of the blue humanities means that you arrive in this placeless place as soon as you step off land. To offshore oneself—to move from land to sea—defines this practice in terms of location, method, and direction. To always be moving offshore, into water, away from land—that is the vector that this form of inquiry seeks. In my native Atlantic, where the water is bitter cold half the year, I may be differently aware of the alienation of my terrestrial body from the generative waters. Shakespeare, also a North Atlantic figure who may or may not have ever learned to swim, figures the ocean as transformative but also deadly. Each of these two poets, when considering human encounters with the ocean, reads the beauty without forgetting the pain. Ariel's song in *The Tempest*, which the critic Ian Baucom has called the "theme song of postmodernity,"[43] shows both the capacity that Perez presents and an offshore alienation that lingers:

> Full fathom five thy father lies,
> Of his bones are coral made,
> Those are pearls that were his eyes,
> Nothing of his that doth fade
> But doth suffer a sea change
> Into something rich and strange
> *(1.2.397–402)*

Ariel's "sea change" combines beauty with underwater death, even though it turns out that the king neither sank nor drowned. At the core of this famous passage is salt water's power to transform. Both Perez and Shakespeare write about capacity, and both also engage with transformative movements offshore. Like many other sea-poets, from Ovid to Byron to Alice Oswald, they register the salt touch of the sea as lure and danger. The central project of blue humanities criticism seeks to respond to both challenges. To do that, we need to head out.

Beyond the Atlantic

For me personally, and I think also for many others in this discourse, the trajectory of the blue humanities in the early 2020s requires moving beyond the Atlantic. An American and Anglophone scholar, I have lived, studied, and thought near the Atlantic Ocean for most of my life, growing up in New Jersey, going to graduate school and living now in Connecticut, and teaching in New York City since 2000. The Atlantic has a particular history, especially for American literary scholars. It is the ocean across which European colonizers and slave traders traveled from the late fifteenth century forward, and the legacies of that traffic remain deeply present in the North American and European literary cultures in which I was trained. My home sits about 100 meters from an inlet of Long Island Sound, a relatively calm bay just north and east of New York City. When I swim my local waters, I am immersing myself in the World Ocean, but necessarily from a local position. The offshore vision of my current work aims to bring me farther out and deeper in. Partly this happens through scholarship about global geophysical structures, like the Coriolis force and the ocean gyres, both of which have shaped patterns of colonization, the slave trade, and modern global exchange. The events that I call "wet globalization," meaning a globalization structured through maritime labor and technologies, speak to and beyond my Atlantic surroundings.[44]

My scholarship comes into the Atlantic from a different direction as well. The writings of William Shakespeare, the core subject of my academic training, teaching, and research, emerge from the Atlantic port of London and draw on classical and Renaissance Mediterranean settings. Shakespeare is an Atlantic writer by birth, though by choice and cultural influences he may be more a Mediterranean one. To a significant extent the blue humanities, as I have experienced it, grew out of a scholarly history of environmental engagement that emerged in the mid-twentieth century through the work of French historian Fernand Braudel, whose multivolume work *The Mediterranean and the Mediterranean World in the Age of Philip II* was originally published in France in 1949.[45] Braudel's combination of hyperlocalism, archival density, and attention to varied environmental conditions proved invaluable, including through the international success of the *Annales* School of research he helped found. More-recent Med-centric scholarship, such as Peregrine Horden and Nicholas Purcell's *Corrupting Sea: A Study of Mediterranean History* published in 2000, acknowledges Braudel as the point of departure for what they call a "new thalassology" in Mediterranean studies.[46] *The Tempest* is one of Shakespeare's many Mediterranean-centered plays; others include *Othello, The Merchant of Venice, Twelfth Night, The Comedy of Errors, Timon of Athens*, and *Pericles*—all of which I explore in *At the Bottom of Shakespeare's Ocean*.[47] My aim in launching the blue humanities from my home base in Shakespeare studies was to connect the plays and their author to larger global and transoceanic currents. I started where the plays put me: in the classical seas of Rome, Greece, and the Ottoman Empire.

Shakespeare makes few references to the New World in his plays. Unlike some of his contemporaries, he mentions neither Peru nor Virginia, and his one use of the word "America" is a metaphorical reference to a globe.[48] *The Tempest*, however, has long been considered an Atlantic play, because the spirit Ariel makes an offhand reference to being sent "to fetch dew/From the still-vexed Bermudas" (1.2.228–29), referring to an Atlantic island that would soon host a British colony, and because the shipwreck that opens the play draws upon eyewitness accounts of the wreck of the Virginia Company ship *Sea-Venture* off Bermuda in 1609, roughly two years before *The Tempest* was first staged. Since the middle of the twentieth century, scholars such as the British Shakespearean Frank Kermode and the American literary critic Leo Marx have treated *The Tempest* as, in Marx's phrase, Shakespeare's "American fable."[49] Generations of writers from the Americas, including Spanish-language and Francophone writers from the Caribbean, have written back against Shakespeare's representation of European mastery and native enslavement, in such influential works as Aimé Césaire's Francophone inversion of Shakespeare, *Un Tempête* (1969), and Derek Walcott's post-Homeric epic *Omeros* (1990).[50] Shakespeare scholars have engaged critically with these analyses in the decades since Kermode, Marx, and others advanced American-centric readings of *The Tempest*, but the sense that this play speaks to the emerging transatlantic world being remade by sea travel, colonization, and enforced servitude remains strong. Late twentieth-century developments in Caribbean literary studies have contributed to the play's New World contexts.

The personal archive from which I began my first voyages into the blue humanities, then, centered itself around Atlantic experiences and Mediterranean literary heritage. Thinking over a dozen years later about the oceanic spaces and narratives that beckon beyond those models leads me to Perez's sense of the ocean as living archive—varied, dynamic, and always offering more than it is possible to read at any one time. Two stanzas of the "Praise Song" suggest the dialectical method through which oceans consume and preserve historical knowledge. "Praise your capacity to bury," Perez writes, emphasizing "shipwrecks and ruined cities" (67). In sinking human designs and desires, the Ocean captures a radicalizing urge that counters colonial and mercantile fantasies of mastery. The second archival act the sea accomplishes, Perez continues, is "to remember." Ocean memory creates a "vast archive of desire" (67) through techniques such as "your tidalectics/your migrant routes/and submarine roots" (68). Perez gestures here toward "tidalectics," the poetic theory of Barbadian writer Kamau Brathwaite, and to American scholar Elizabeth DeLoughrey's influential first book *Routes and Roots* (2007), which juxtaposes Caribbean and Pacific literatures.[51] In gesturing to Caribbean poetry and twenty-first century comparative literary studies, Perez suggests that his poetic Oceania overspills its boundaries.

Trajectories of the Blue Humanities

My hope for the blue humanities, when I started publishing this kind of work in 2009, was to help generate something like the offshore trajectory that Perez's poetry makes explicit in 2020. I did not know Perez's work at the time—his first book of poems appeared in 2008, but I did not discover him until almost a decade later. In the 2010s, I worked out a series of shorthand terms that defined the things I was hoping to move toward. Phrases such as "wet globalization," "blue ecocriticism," and "shipwreck modernity" represent efforts to make the blue humanities into a series of claims about the historical and still-living shapes of the human relationship with watery spaces.[52] Wet globalization has been for me a central idea about the early modern period, which I have come to understand as fundamentally structured by the interface between maritime technologies, especially the sailing ship, and the environmental forces of the ocean basins. The riskier side of these encounters underwrote my 2015 book *Shipwreck Modernity*, and a less disaster-centric version of this claim about globalization appears as the introduction to *A Cultural History of the Sea in the Early Modern Age*.[53] "Salt aesthetics," a phrase that I left out of some early descriptions of my blue humanities practice, speaks to the experimental and creative elements that characterize much of this work. The phrase "shipwreck modernity," which became a book title, indicates my ambitions to connect maritime experience to large questions about periodization and history. What is "modernity" anyway? I suggest that, from an oceanic point of view, it is not possible to imagine historical change, or transoceanic travel, without the looming threats of shipwreck and catastrophe.

These modes remain meaningful today, and I will speak more directly about "blue ecocriticism" shortly, since that term has recently been used to criticize my work in interesting ways. As I think about blue humanities scholarship in 2023, however, my former structures resemble doors that appear only partway ajar. Early globalizing scholarship on Anglophone colonies should open wider to embrace the Pacific and Indian Ocean basins. Ecocriticism and environmental studies are themselves in the middle of a massive transformation, in which some of the most exciting areas include the eco-materialist theories of such figures as Jeffrey Cohen, Serenella Iovino and Serpil Opperman, Alaimo, and Neimanis, as well as many theory-rich articles published in such venues as the journal *Environmental Humanities*, among others. Utopian water-structures are also being conjured by novelists such as Kim Stanley Robinson, eco-philosophers such as Timothy Morton, and artists such as Marina Zurkow.[54] Scholarly interest in oceanic technologies, which has drawn on older schools of maritime and naval historiography, is coming into contact with newer theories of distributed cognition and cyborg identities, including the critical theories of Edwin Hutchins, Andy Clark, Donna Haraway, and others.[55] The turn beyond the Atlantic and the northern hemisphere opens up massive new archives of historical, literary, and cultural materials. In this broader context, the notion that Western ideas of the sea were themselves a symptom only of the nineteenth-century Romantic movement, as the poet W.H. Auden influentially argued in *The Enchaféd Flood* in 1950, and against which I have been arguing for more than a dozen years, seems less constricting now that the horizon beckons far beyond Atlantic and Mediterranean shores.[56]

The challenge in the 2020s seems not merely to chart a new course but to develop the ability to orient in fast-flowing waters. Once again Perez's "Praise Song" uncovers an appropriate oceanic metaphor for finding oneself in dynamic spaces. On the last page of the printed poem, he enjoins us to "praise your capacity for echolocation" (72). Along with many scholars of premodern navigation, I have long explored sailors' techniques, from maps and charts to celestial observations and compass readings, as models for orientation.[57] Perez's leap to the sonar used by cetaceans, and mimicked by modern technology, suggests a different degree of physicality in reading the sea environment. The stanza continues to celebrate the languages of Oceania and the acts of translation that preserve them: "praise our names for you that translate/into creation songs and song maps/tasi: kai: tai: moana nui: vasa:/tahi: lik: wai tui: wonsolwara" (72). These words from multiple languages of Oceania refer to oceans and the humans who live near them. Perez suggests in his English poem that we who live in the Anglosphere may wish to expand our vocabularies.

That project of vocabulary expansion seems quite urgent for my own work and that of other blue humanities scholars who began with canonical literary authors. In 2009, at the end of *At the Bottom of Shakespeare's Ocean*, I wrote a challenge for future criticism that was also a challenge to myself:

> Reading Shakespeare for the sea thus launches the vast and slightly quixotic project of a blue cultural studies, a way of looking at terrestrial literary culture from an offshore perspective, as if we could align ourselves with the watery element.[58]

Looking back at this sentence today, I wonder at my assumption that the object I would be looking at would remain confined to "terrestrial literary culture." I am not the only one who wonders. In his 2021 book *Blue Ecocriticism and the Oceanic Imperative*, Sidney Dobrin takes me to task for my lingering attachment to canonical writers like Shakespeare. Dobin writes:

> While I concur with Mentz's diagnostic, it is his loyalty to canonical literary texts that necessarily must be cast off. . . . [Blue humanities criticism] cannot be limited to maritime canon or even Anglophone literatures more generally.[59]

While maintaining some residual loyalty to the earlier-me who wrote the lines Dobrin criticizes, I think he is basically right. The blue humanities is not, and should not be, limited to canonical writers, or Anglophone literature, or even to literary culture. I very much agree with Dobrin's diagnosis that ecocriticism and humanities scholarship in general suffer from what he calls a "critical ocean deficit."[60] Not everyone can do everything all the time, but the project of expanding the discourse—beyond the Atlantic, beyond the traditional canon, beyond English, and beyond literature as such—seems exactly what the blue humanities should be undertaking in the 2020s. In juxtaposing Perez's "Praise Song" with Shakespeare's *Tempest* in this chapter, I aim to show that my own perspective is no longer as narrow as it may have appeared in 2009. New work on *The Tempest* has productively engaged with the Black Atlantic, the histories and legacies of the slave trade, and Afro-Indigenous alliances.[61] Creative–critical work on the legacies of the Black Atlantic by writers such as Dionne Brand, Saidiya Hartman, Christina Sharpe, and Alexis Pauline Gumbs provides new ways to reconfigure Atlantic histories, ecologies, and poetics.[62] One constant in the evolution of the blue humanities has been the desire to intermingle creative and critical processes and modes of writing. That is one way, I hope, to address Dobrin's accurate and helpful critique while not confining ourselves inside a just-slightly-larger box.

Blue Humanities as Collaboration and Connection

In concluding this chapter, I want to isolate one further stanza of Perez's "Praise Song," the only stanza that takes up a full printed page by itself. It is a short three-line stanza that represents the ocean as ocean, alone and independent:

> praise your halcyon nests
> praise your pacific stillness
> praise your breathless calm
> *(70)*

Each line in this stanza shifts our perspective out of a merely human register. The "nests" of the first line, paired with the weather term "halcyon," gesture toward nonhuman denizens beneath the waves. In the second line, by using the word "pacific" to mean peaceful, rather than as the (European) name given to the largest ocean basin on the planet, Perez performs the stilling and quieting that his line describes. Again, the poem moves past human ideas and European names into watery spaces. Even the "breathless calm" of the stanza's final line gives rise to a literal reading. Is the poet thinking about sea creatures who do not breathe—maybe jellyfish?—as it also shifts our imagination past mere human experiences? This ocean is alien and beloved, known and unknowable, peaceful if not, at this point, named "Pacific." I admire a lot about Perez's poetry, and the "Praise Song" in particular, but this still moment of oceanic representation, in which the sea gets praised only for being the sea, seems central to the poem's blue humanities insight. There may be a few comparable moments in English-language sea writing that capture the paradoxical double sensation of connection and alienation between humans and the ocean—Emily Dickinson's "An Everywhere of Silver," Melville's vision of Pip gazing into impossible depths in *Moby-Dick*, Ariel's song in *The Tempest*, perhaps the anonymous Old English elegy "The Seafarer"—but I think Perez gets at something distinctive here. The great waters that comprise the fluid substrate of Oceania connect to human ways of knowing and float beyond them. The project of the sea-poet, Perez shows, includes knowing when to watch, when to listen, and when to touch.

These lines help imagine possible futures of blue humanities criticism. The most important things to discover may not be scholarly sources or archives or theories. Instead, the key question remains: how can we write in collaboration and co-conspiracy with planetary water? How can we write in alliance and entanglement with the water that flows and freezes over our blue planet, including the water inside our bodies and the invisible water vapor in the air? Water is life, as Perez repeats in another poem, "Chanting the Waters" (27–30). Making these waters substantial partners in creative and critical work has supported some untraditional academic practices, including swim poetry, collaborations with visual artists and musicians, and convincing a bunch of professors to body surf in the Pacific or plunge into frigid Lake Michigan before conference panels. The blue humanities lends itself to immersive performances. Writers such as Perez can open new whale-roads for scholars and artists. Recognizing and valuing the cultural legacies of Oceania can revitalize the thinking and writing of Anglo-European scholarship.

Smashing the Quadrant, or Why the Blue Humanities Needs Oceania

When European sailors encountered the wayfinders of Oceania in the sixteenth century, two contrasting modes of oceanic orientation came into contact for the first time. Western navigators used charts and the tools of celestial navigation to locate ships in relationship to the fixed stars in the sky. Wayfinders, by contrast, used local knowledges of prevailing winds, ocean currents, and the distinctive formations that clouds assume over islands to guide their trackless navigation. The next chapter, on the Pacific, will explore wayfinding and its humanizing of oceanic space. This chapter closes with a crisis of celestial navigation in "The Quadrant" chapter of *Moby-Dick* that demonstrates the limits of premodern Western maritime technology.

When the *Pequod* arrives on the Pacific waters beloved of both Ishmael and the White Whale, Ahab smashes the quadrant to rupture his connection to the sun and the fixed structures it represents. As the captain takes his final noon observation, solar order still controls the great waters. Ishmael describes an "unblinkingly vivid Japanese sun [that] seems the blazing focus of the glassy ocean's immeasurable burning-glass" (378). Into this fire Ahab gazes, protected by the quadrant's "colored glasses, through which to take sight of that solar fire" (378). Like a divine GPS satellite, the sun represents inhuman surveillance, through which the captain attempts to glimpse his prey. "Where is Moby Dick?" he asks the sun, "This instant thou must be eyeing him" (378). In smashing the quadrant, Ahab breaks with solar order, visual divinity, and Apollonian reason. Recalling his boast to Starbuck that "I'd strike the sun if it insulted me" (140), Ahab rejects the quadrant as part of his progressive rejection of all human and divine systems of order.

The ocean-underworld into which Ahab casts himself and his ship does not lack meaning, but its guiding forces are maritime, not solar. Cursing the instrument and rejecting the logic of its earth–sky system, Ahab growls, "no longer will I guide my earthly way by thee" (378). In place of celestial navigation, he clings to knowledge not from sky above but sea below: "the level ship's compass, and the level dead-reckoning, by log and line; *these* shall conduct me, and show me my place on the sea" (378, emphasis in original). A compass provides direction through the pull of the planet's magnetic poles, so it seems possible to imagine this instrument operating beneath the ocean. As the quest continues, however, the compasses become unreliable after they invert themselves in a massive magnetic storm ("The Needle," chapter 124). The practice of "dead-reckoning," however, which estimates the ship's position by plotting previous locations, bearing, and speed on a map, locates the *Pequod* inside an entirely maritime system. All orienting principles—place, speed, location—vary with oceanic movements. Human pilots like Ahab can only approximately find "my place on the sea." In this moment of rejection and release, Ahab casts himself and his ship into a blue and inhuman logic. Starbuck, still partially resisting his captain, names Ahab at this point "Old man of oceans" (379). To steer only by watery means will guide Ahab to the White Whale, but never again to land. His hand on the tiller pilots the *Pequod* in antisolar and antihuman directions; he smashes connections to both sky and land. His doomed quest does not capture all of Melville's blue humanities vision—Ishmael's survival and Queequeg's sacrifice each in some ways counterbalances Ahab's suicidal velocity—but Ahab's efforts to orient only by sea capture the fatal mismatch between terrestrial humans and oceanic space. The current turn toward the Pacific and Oceania positions itself against this doomed impulse and its Western origins.

Notes

1 See Bernhard Klein, ed., *Fictions of the Sea: Critical Perspectives on the Ocean in British Literature and Culture* (London: Routledge, 2002); Hester Blum, *The View from the Masthead: Maritime Imagination and Antebellum American Sea Narratives* (Chapel Hill: University of North Carolina Press, 2008); Bernard Bailyn, *Atlantic History: Concept and Contours* (Cambridge: Harvard University Press, 2005); Steve Mentz, "Ice/Water/Vapor," *The Cambridge Companion to the Environmental Humanities*, Jeffrey Jerome Cohen and Stephanie Foote, eds. (Cambridge: Cambridge University Press, 2021), 185–98.
2 Dan Brayton, *Shakespeare's Ocean: An Ecocritical Exploration* (Charlottesville: University of Virginia Press, 2012); Nicholas Purcell and Peregrine Horden, *The Corrupting Sea: A Study of Mediterranean History* (London: Wiley-Blackwell, 2000); Édouard Glissant, *Poetics of Relation*, Betsy Wing, trans. (Ann Arbor: University of Michigan Press, 1997).
3 Steve Mentz, *At the Bottom of Shakespeare's Ocean* (London: Bloomsbury, 2009); Steve Mentz, "Toward a Blue Cultural Studies: The Sea, Maritime Culture, and Early Modern English Literature," *Literature Compass* 6:5 (2009), 997–1013.
4 Craig Santos Perez, "Praise Song for Oceania," *Habitat Threshold* (Oakland: Omnidawn Publishing, 2020).
5 Margaret Cohen, *The Novel and the Sea* (Princeton: Princeton University Press, 2010); John Peck, *Maritime Fiction: Sailors and the Sea in British and American Novels, 1719–1917* (London: Palgrave Macmillan, 2001); Alexandra Campbell and Michael Paye, eds., "World Literature and the Blue Humanities," *Humanities* 9:3 (2020).
6 Steve Mentz, *Ocean* (London: Bloomsbury, 2020).
7 Giacomo Parrinello, ed., "Coastal Studies," Private Shared Zotero Bibliography. www.zotero.org/groups/2503094/coastal_studies. Accessed 19 November 2022.
8 Alison Maas, ed., "A Bibliography to the Study of Sea Literature." https://sites.williams.edu/searchablesealit/a-bibliography-to-the-study-of-sea-literature/. Accessed 9 September 2020.

9 Alison Mass, ed., "Blue Humanities/Searchable Sea Literature." www.zotero.org/groups/4421701/blue_humanities_searchable_sea_literature/library. Accessed 13 October 2022.

10 Peck, *Maritime Fiction*; Philip E. Steinberg, *The Social Construction of the Ocean* (Cambridge: Cambridge University Press, 2001); Klein, *Fictions of the Sea*; Bernhard Klein and Gesa Mackenthun, eds., *Sea Changes: Historicizing the Ocean* (London: Routledge, 2003), Elizabeth DeLoughrey, *Roots and Roots: Navigating Caribbean and Pacific Island Literatures* (Ann Arbor: University of Michigan Press, 2007); Hester Blum, *The View from the Masthead*; Steve Mentz, *At the Bottom of Shakespeare's Ocean*; M. Cohen, *The Novel and the Sea.*

11 Bailyn, *Atlantic History*, Jack P. Greene and Philip D. Morgan, eds., *Atlantic History* (Oxford: Oxford University Press, 2008); Paul Gilroy, *The Black Atlantic: Modernity and Double Consciousness* (Cambridge: Harvard University Press, 1993); Glissant, *Poetics of Relation*; Sylvia Wynter, *Sylvia Wynter: On Being Human as Praxis*, Katherine McKittrik, ed. (Durham: Duke University Press, 2014).

12 Brayton, *Shakespeare's Ocean*, 15–42; Sidney Dobrin, *Blue Ecocriticism and the Oceanic Imperative* (London: Bloomsbury, 2021), 8–9.

13 Philip E. Steinberg and Kimberly Peters, "Wet Ontologies, Fluid Spaces: Giving Depth to Volume through Oceanic Thinking," *Environment and Planning D: Society and Space* 33:2 (2015), 247–64; Elizabeth DeLoughrey, *Allegories of the Anthropocene* (Durham: Duke University Press, 2019); and Stacy Alaimo, *Exposed: Environmental Politics and Pleasures in Posthuman Times* (Minneapolis: University of Minnesota Press, 2016).

14 Mentz, "Toward a Blue Cultural Studies"; Laura Winkiel, ed., "Hydro-Criticism," *ELN* 57:1 (2019).

15 Patricia Yaeger, ed., "Oceanic Studies," *PMLA* 125:3 (2010).

16 Hester Blum, ed., "Oceanic Studies," *Atlantic Studies* 10 (2013).

17 Kerry Bystrom and Isabel Hofmeyer, eds., "Oceanic Routes," Special Issue of *Comparative Literature* 69:1 (2017).

18 Matthew Boyd Goldie and Sebastian Sobecki, eds., "Our Sea of Islands: New Approaches to British Insularity in the Late Middle Ages," *Postmedieval* 7 (2016).

19 Winkiel, "Hydro-Criticism."

20 Hester Blum, M. Eyring, I. Liang, and B.R. Roberts, eds.,"Archipelagos/Oceans/American Visuality," *Journal of Transnational American Studies* 10:1 (2019).

21 Jeffrey R. Di Leo, ed., "Blue Humanities," *symploke* 27:1 (2019).

22 Stacy Alaimo, ed., "Science Studies and the Blue Humanities," *Configurations* 27:4 (2019).

23 Campbell and Paye, "World Literature and the Blue Humanities."

24 Hester Blum, *The News at the Ends of the Earth: The Print Culture of Polar Exploration* (Durham: Duke University Press, 2019); Steve Mentz, *Shipwreck Modernity: Ecologies of Globalization, 1550–1719* (Minneapolis: University of Minnesota Press, 2015); Mentz, *Ocean*; DeLoughrey, *Allegories of the Anthropocene.*

25 Steve Mentz and Martha Elena Rojas, eds., *The Sea and Nineteenth-Century Anglophone Literary Culture* (London: Routledge, 2017).

26 Nicholas Allen, Nick Groom, and Jos Smith, eds., *Coastal Works: Cultures of the Atlantic Edge* (Oxford: Oxford University Press, 2017).

27 Cecilia Chen, Janine MacLeod, and Astrida Neimanis, eds., *Thinking with Water* (Montreal: McGill-Queens University Press, 2013).

28 Stefanie Hessler, and Thyssen-Bornemisza Art Contemporary, eds., *Tidalectics: Imagining an Oceanic Worldview through Art and Science* (Cambridge: MIT Press, 2018).

29 Claire Jowitt, Claire, Craig Lambert, and Steve Mentz, eds., *The Routledge Companion to Marine and Maritime Worlds, 1400–1800* (London: Routledge, 2020).

30 Margaret Cohen and Killian Quigley, eds., *The Aesthetics of the Undersea* (London: Routledge, 2020).
31 Margaret Cohen, ed., *A Cultural History of the Sea,* 6 vols. (London: Bloomsbury, 2021).
32 Vanessa Daws, "Pluralize the Anthropocene!" Watercolor painting, 2018. Image reproduced by permission of artist.
33 Steve Mentz, "Blue Humanities," *Posthuman Glossary*, Rosi Braidotti and Maria Hlavajova, eds. (London: Bloomsbury, 2018), 129–32.
34 For a fuller account of the painting and its seventeenth-century source, see Steve Mentz, *Break Up the Anthropocene* (Minneapolis: University of Minnesota Press, 2019), ix–xii.
35 Jeffrey Jerome Cohen, ed., *Prismatic Ecology: Ecotheory beyond Green* (Minneapolis: University of Minnesota Press, 2013), xv–xxxv.
36 T.J. Piccirillo, Blue Humanities Logo. 2021. Image file used by permission of artist.
37 Mentz, *At the Bottom*; Brayton, *Shakespeare's Ocean*; Dobrin, *Blue Ecocriticism*.
38 William Shakespeare, *The Tempest*, Virginia Mason Vaughan and Alden T. Vaughan, eds. (London: Bloomsbury, 2011).
39 Perez, "Praise Song for Oceania."
40 Mentz, *At the Bottom*.
41 On *The Tempest* and Bermuda, see Mentz, *Shipwreck Modernity*, 51–74.
42 Rachel Carson, *The Sea around Us* (Oxford: Oxford University Press, 1951), 3.
43 Ian Baucom, "Hydrographies," *Geographical Review* 89:2 (1999), 301–13.
44 Steve Mentz, "Plural Anthropocenes in Lausanne," Blog post, 2018. https://stevementz.com/plural-anthropocenes-in-lausanne/. Accessed 9 September 2021.
45 Fernand Braudel, *The Mediterranean and the Mediterranean World in the Age of Philip II*, 2 vols, Sian Reynolds, trans. (New York: Harper and Row, 1972). Orig. French 1949.
46 Horden and Purcell, *The Corrupting Sea*.
47 Mentz, *At the Bottom*.
48 Gavin Hollis, *The Absence of America: The London Stage 1576–1642* (Oxford: Oxford University Press, 2015).
49 Frank Kermode, Introduction to William Shakespeare, *The Tempest* (London: Methuen, 1954); Leo Marx, *The Machine in the Garden: Technology and the Pastoral Ideal in America* (Oxford: Oxford University Press, 1964).
50 Aimé Césaire, *A Tempest*, Richard Miller, trans. (New York: Theatre Communications Group, 2002). Orig. Pub. 1969 in French; Derek Walcott, *Omeros* (New York: Farrar, Straus, & Giroux, 1990).
51 DeLoughrey, *Roots and Routes*.
52 Mentz, *Shipwreck Modernity*.
53 Steve Mentz, "Wet Globalization: The Early Modern Ocean as World-System," *A Cultural History of the Sea in the Early Modern Age*, Steve Mentz, ed., Vol. 3, *A Cultural History of the Sea*, Margaret Cohen, ed. (London: Bloomsbury, 2021), 1–23.
54 Jeffrey Jerome Cohen, *Stone: An Inhuman Ecology* (Minneapolis: University of Minnesota Press, 2015); Serenella Iovino and Serpil Opperman, eds., *Environmental Humanities: Voices from the Anthropocene* (London: Rowman & Littlefield, 2016); Stacy Alaimo, *Exposed*; Astrida Neimanis, *Bodies of Water: Posthuman Feminist Phenomenology* (London: Bloomsbury, 2017); Kim Stanley Robinson, *New York 2140* (New York: Orbit, 2017); Timothy Morton, *Hyperobjects: Philosophy and Ecology after the End of the World* (Minneapolis: University of Minnesota Press, 2013); Marina Zurkow, *More & More (The Invisible Oceans)* (Brooklyn: Punctum, 2016).
55 Edwin Hutchins, *Cognition in the Wild* (Cambridge: MIT Press, 1995); Andy Clark, *Being There: Putting Brain Body, and World Together Again* (Cambridge: MIT Press,

1996); Donna Haraway, *Staying with the Trouble: Making Kin in the Chthulucene* (Durham: Duke University Press, 2016).

56 W.H. Auden, *The Enchafed Flood, or The Romantic Iconography of the Sea* (London: Faber and Faber, 1950); Mentz, "Toward a Blue Cultural Studies."

57 Hester Blum, *The News at the Ends of the Earth: The Print Culture of Polar Exploration* (Durham: Duke University Press, 2019); Brayton, *Shakespeare's Ocean*; Klein, *Fictions of the Sea*.

58 Mentz, *At the Bottom*, 99.

59 Dobrin, *Blue Ecocriticism*, 39.

60 Dobrin, *Blue Ecocriticism*, 40.

61 Tiffany Lethabo King, *The Black Shoals: Offshore Formations of Black and Native Studies* (Durham: Duke University Press, 2019).

62 Dionne Brand, *A Map to the Door of No Return: Notes to Belonging* (Toronto: Vintage Canada, 2001); Saidiya Hartman, *Lose Your Mother: A Journey along the Atlantic Slave Route* (New York: Farrar, Straus, and Giroux, 2007); Christina Sharpe, *In the Wake: On Blackness and Being* (Durham: Duke University Press, 2016); and Alexis Pauline Gumbs, *Undrowned: Black Feminist Lessons from Marine Mammals* (Chico: AK Press, 2020).

3 Our Sea of Islands

Voyaging in the Pacific

To a first approximation, the Pacific Ocean comprises the surface of our planet. Shifting from the somewhat simplistic Blue Humanities logo from the previous chapter, I introduce the Pacific's vastness through a nineteenth-century imperialist map produced by the War Office in London in 1862–63. The map, entitled "Geometrical projection of two thirds of the sphere (Pacific Ocean Central)," presents a Pacific-centered view of the planet.

Like the Blue Humanities logo but with greater geographical precision, this image centers the Pacific and displaces Europe and most of the North Atlantic. The major islands of Oceania are visible in this detailed image,

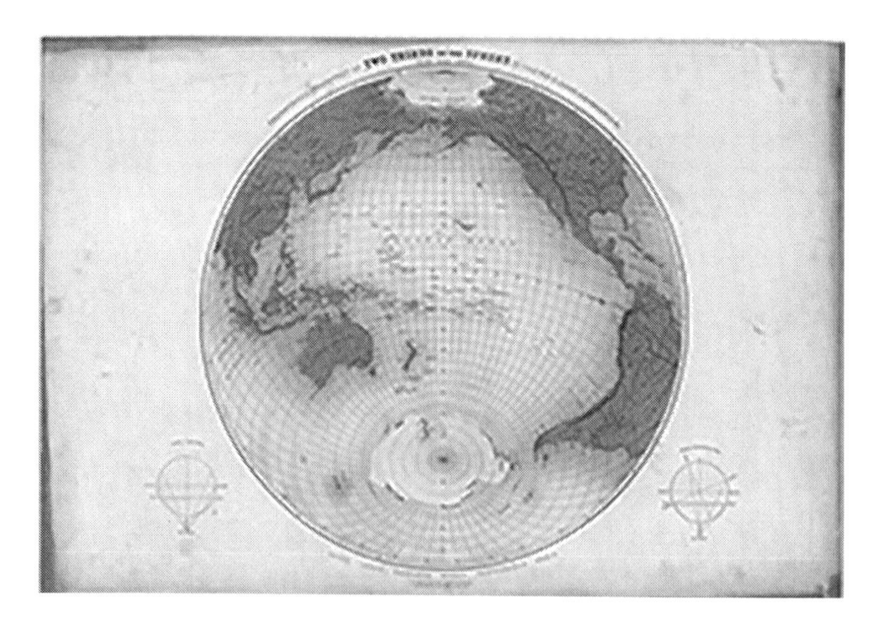

Figure 3.1 Geometrical Projections of Two Thirds of the Sphere (Pacific Ocean Central)

Source: National Library of Scotland, 1862–63[1]

DOI: 10.4324/9781003166665-3

but the bulk of the Pacific still appears empty, the deep sea a hollow white, distinct from blue coastal shallows and brown land. In the view of the nineteenth-century British Empire, which was consolidating its holdings in the regions explored by navigators such as Captain James Cook, the Pacific core was vacant. Empire was a terrestrial concern.

European sailors long imagined these waters as forbiddingly empty. The first trans-Pacific voyage, by Ferdinand Magellan and his crew in 1520, sighted land only once between entering the Pacific on 28 November 1520 and reaching Guam on 6 March 1521. German philosopher Peter Sloterdijk argues that the fleet's ninety-odd days at sea, "with consistently favourable winds—on a north-westerly course through an immeasurable, unknown sea," represents the shocking arrival of the transoceanic modernity that would transform the world. These sailors proved by experience, Sloterdijk claims, "that the *oceans* are the carriers of global affairs, and thus the natural media of unrestricted capital flow."[2] For Sloterdijk, this moment, the hinge at the center of the first European circumnavigation, created the modern globe. "Only the sea," he asserts, "offered a foundation for universal thoughts" (43). Sloterdijk treats Magellan's voyage in the South Pacific as the core moment when the World Ocean was discovered as a unity, a single global whole. What an earlier era of Western historiography framed as the "discovery of the oceans" appears to Sloterdijk as a moment of supreme recognition, in which the global ocean makes possible global capitalist and colonial expansion.[3]

A kernel of historical truth animates Sloterdijk's overly celebratory and Eurocentric vision, but it seems more accurate to see European globalization in the sixteenth century as what the Marxist eco-historian Jason W. Moore calls the birth of "world-ecology." In Moore's model, the defining features of global maritime modernity are less economic expansion than exploitation, colonialism, and transoceanic slavery.[4] From an oceanic perspective, while Moore's attention to the plight of impoverished and exploited humans and nonhumans seems essential, both Sloterdijk's celebration and Moore's condemnation view global maritime modernity as a European project imposed upon the Americas and other parts of the colonized world. While many scholars, including me, remain bounded by European languages and Anglophone educations, a quick glance at the Pacific-centered map should remind us about the location of the world's true center.

Placing the Pacific at the core, and at the start of this book's survey of oceanic geographies, requires attention to the human networks and communities that have populated its blue heart for millennia. The peoples and cultures of Oceania live, and have lived for hundreds of centuries, within the central watery confluences of our globe. One of the insights that blue humanities scholarship has been developing in recent years has been to center the cultures of Oceania. This aspect of ocean-thinking has not always been visible for those of us trained in European scholarly modes, but the influence of Tongan sociologist Epeli Hau'ofa, whose essay

"Our Sea of Islands" was first published in 1993, has been significant. As American literary scholar Robert Sean Wilson observes, Hau'ofa's voice connects his Oceanic heritage with the globalizing American presence, from Tonga to the University of Hawai'i to the global Anglophone world.[5] In the revisionist history that Hau'ofa helped bring forward, two key presences offset older visions of Pacific emptiness: people and islands. " 'Oceania,' " Hau'ofa writes, "denotes a sea of islands with their inhabitants."[6] The crucial technology that enables peoples and their descendants to maintain cultural unity across vast oceanic spaces is navigation.[7] As Hau'ofa describes it, navigation transforms space into a network of known places: "The sea was open to anyone who could navigate a way through it" (34). This process, which would prove harrowing and deadly to Magellan's men and generations of European sailors, represents the enabling technological core of Oceanic culture.[8]

Christina Thompson's *Sea People: The Puzzle of Polynesia* (2019) emphasizes cultural continuities across the breadth of the Pacific, noting that "at its widest, the Pacific is nearly 180 degrees across—more than twelve thousand miles, or almost half the circumference of the earth."[9] The historical secret of cultural connections between all the points within the so-called Polynesian triangle—Hawai'i in the north, Rapa Nui (Easter Island) to the east, and Aotearoa (New Zealand) to the southwest—is the ancient practice of wayfinding or oceanic navigation. Unlike the European mariners who they encountered after the sixteenth century, the sailors of Oceania did not use compasses, astrolabes, or fixed maps. Ahab's destructive rage against the quadrant would have been incomprehensible to them. Wayfinding, as the practice has become known in the West after the historical research of David Lewis and others, requires a complex set of practices of orientation on the ocean to sail toward not-yet visible islands.[10] Alice Te Punga Somerville's study *Once Were Pacific: Māori Connections to Oceania* (2012) demonstrates how the "intersections of Indigeneity and migration" show the vast connections of this culture across oceanic space.[11] Like many writers who engage the Euro-Oceanic encounter, Te Punga Somerville considers the exemplary case of Tupaia, the priest-navigator from Ra'iatea who sailed with Captain Cook and whose extraordinary map of Polynesia now sits in the British Library. The case of Tupaia, among the first Polynesians to sail on a European ship whose experience has been preserved, albeit filtered through the journals of Cook and Sir Joseph Banks, represents a fascinating example of transoceanic crossover. Tupaia's map or chart of the islands of central Oceania, as recently reexamined by Lars Ecstein and Anja Schwarz, represents a "collaborative, cross-cultural process."[12] The contrast between the blue void of the War Office's view of the Pacific and the human continuities of Tupaia's map represents the sharp disjunction between Oceanic connection and the rationalist views of European science.

Blue humanities scholars have been using ideas about oceanic connection from figures such as Hau'ofa and Tupaia to reimagine oceanic spaces.

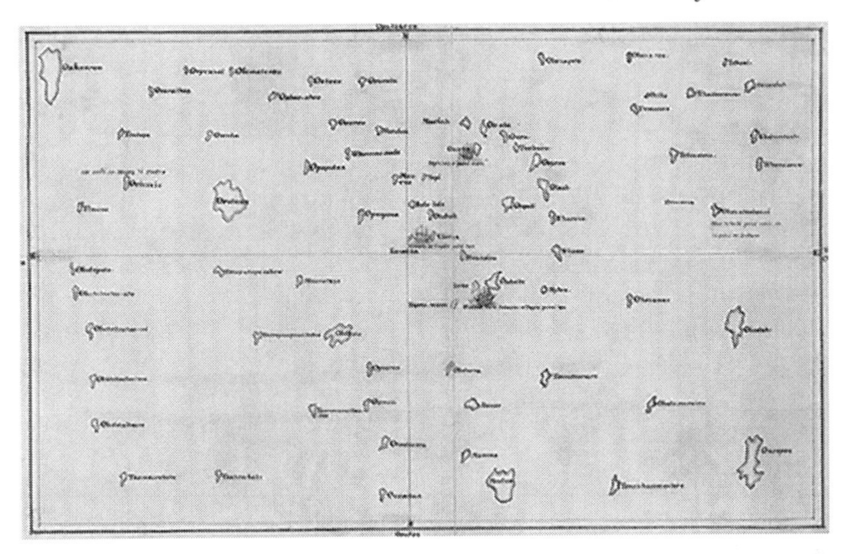

Image 3.2 "The Society Islands"
Source: Copy of Tupaia's Map by Captain James Cook[13]

Elizabeth DeLoughrey, in her book *Roots and Routes* (2007), emphasizes the critical power of Oceania as a window onto watery spaces:

> Pacific models of ocean navigation differ from western paradigms because they do not flatten and stabilize space through the bird's eye view of natural charts. Instead, Pacific navigators have developed a complex system of charting a vessel's movement through space where the voyaging canoe is perceived as stable while the island and cosmos move toward the traveler.[14]

As David Lewis describes the navigational practice of *etak*, its "conception of moving islands is an essentially dynamic one that is not easy to fit into the framework of abstraction that to us is so familiar—the static two-dimensional chart" (184). The "dynamism" that Lewis and DeLoughrey find in Oceanic navigational practices emerges from physical and philosophical intimacy with the sea. As Teresa Shrewry has observed, in the context of late twentieth-century oceanic literatures, "Literary writers and theorists from the Pacific usually situate the ocean as a framework of daily life . . . rather than take it as a primary singular setting."[15] Ocean-intimacy serves an exemplary function for blue humanities thinkers, and it seems likely that a significant amount of the growth in the discourse over the coming years will engage with the cultural products of Oceania and other Indigenous water-cultures. A resonant example appears in Noelani Arista's book about Hawai'i, *The Kingdom and the Republic* (2019). Before investigating cultural relations between sovereign Hawai'i and the United States in the nineteenth century, Arista foregrounds an oral chant that describes the origins of the archipelago and its human history. The land that punctuates the sea, she writes, is not "a random set of islands, nor [are the historical leaders] a random set of chiefs; rather, it is an intertwined genealogy, a history relating the emergence of islands to lineages of chiefs. In this discourse, we see the inextricable interconnection of island home and generations of Hawaiian people."[16] Arista's genealogy shows a relationship between human culture and oceanic spaces that emerges from "bone, birth, movement, and deep knowledge of home place: of islands, seas, and stars" (17). The bone-intimate connection between the Hawaiian people and their terraqueous environment epitomizes Pacific culture.

Craig Santos Perez, *from unincorporated territory [guma']*

Another route into oceanic identities arises through poetry, especially global postcolonial poetry that engages with Pacific Islander identities. In addition to the works of Robert Sullivan, Keri Hulme, and other Māori writers, many of whose works are explored in Te Punga Somerville's *Once Were Pacific*. The multivolume project of the Chamorro poet Craig Santos Perez, in his ongoing collection *from unincorporated territory* (2008–present), opens a window onto Pacific identity as seen from his native Guam. In the collection *[guma']* (2014), Perez traces the fate of the Micronesian kingfisher across four separate lyrics.[17] These poems, scattered within the slim volume, describe the kingfisher's global trajectory. The last surviving birds have been removed from Guam to zoos in the United States, where the threatened population has been preserved since the early 1980s. The last sighting of a Micronesian kingfisher in the wild occurred in 1989, though some have since been returned to zoos in Guam. Perez takes the bird's fate as an allegory for the native cultures of the Pacific. These birds may also represent a possible trajectory for blue studies.

The first of the four lyric fragments depicts "the zookeepers" who "captured [*i sihek*] and transferred/the last/twenty-nine micronesian kingfishers/to zoos for captive breeding" (24). The loss of these birds threatens Indigenous identity, but the italicized voice of the colonizer insists that "*if it weren't for us/your birds [i sihek]/would be gone/forever*" (24). The poem introduces a refrain about history, "what does not change" (24). By establishing the kingfisher/*i sihek* as symbol of loss and identity, the poet inscribes the colonial relationship alongside efforts to preserve an endangered species. To preserve a native population from extinction, in this model, also means to control them in their exile. From the point of view of Perez, members of whose family have emigrated to California and who himself currently teaches in the United States at the University of Hawai'i, the bird represents self and other, the fragile possibilities of island life and the struggle to maintain identity in the face of larger conglomerates.

The second kingfisher poem focuses on the conditions of the birds in captivity in the United States. A rare chick, "weighing five grams" (31), is born in the National Zoo in Washington, DC. Against a possibly triumphant story of extinction averted appear grim structures of imprisonment: "the minimum enclosure/size for breeding pairs: ten feet by eight feet/with a height of ten feet containment" (31). The survival of the species frames itself inside these cubes, made "either [of] solid material wire mesh or glass" (31). Inside these cages, the bird "is born and fed and grows and dies" (31) without any connection to its Pacific home. Identity survives oceanic dislocation, but in cruel circumstances.

Violence arises in the third poem, in which the imprisoned kingfisher attacks its own reflection. "Kingfishers have attacked/their images reflected/ in glass cage fronts" (62), Perez writes. The return to Guam of a pair bred in captivity in 2008 appears to counterbalance the grim tale of the self-attacking imprisoned bird. But the refrain of alienation recurs, as it does in all four poems of the sequence: "what does not change/is the will/to see" (63). Birds in cages cannot see the ocean, and instead they attack their own images in the glass. Seeing registers self-alienation in conditions of captivity. The allegory of Oceania under geographic and biological stress refuses any optimistic solution.

The final lyric section makes explicit the way the kingfisher represents the exiled Chamorro population spread across California and elsewhere in the Pacific. "When land is/caged [we]/. . . / are caged within/[our] disappearance" (71), Perez writes. The story of the exiled birds becomes a saga of colonial control, in which "invasion is/a continuous chair of/immeasurably destructive/events in time—" (71). The last iteration of the refrain gets printed in the italics that had previously indicated the voice of the colonizer: "*what does not change/is the will to colonize*" (72). But although the birds remain in captivity, the sequence does not end with colonial imposition. Instead, Perez releases the birds and their Indigenous names in a flight of lyric opening:

> As weapons
> mount— *[i sihek]*
> risk
> being Chamoru *[i sihek]*
> rise
> above fences *i sihek*
> *(72)*

The freeing of the *i sihek* from its square brackets on its third repetition might represent a form of textual freedom, but the left-hand column of the poem traces a struggle to escape "above fences." The situation of the birds remains tenuous, and the power of the colonizer considerable, but the poem provides a small glimpse at a possible route out.

Perez's poetry, which DeLoughrey has singled out for its "challenges to western binary thinking [and to] the uniformity of traditional genre," provides a voice through which Oceania can speak back to Western ears.[18] His kingfishers pluralize and estrange the cultural odysseys of contemporary Oceania. The experimental flair and local roots of the poetry can help correct overly geometric views of the Pacific in Western criticism. The situation of the endangered birds and ocean-circulating poems may instructively be thought of as representations of the lived experience of globalization, in which Perez himself resembles his beloved kingfishers. The Western imperial ocean remains a fantasy, and the ocean of exile painfully real—but both visions speak to the modern experience of oceanic cultures, connections, and identities.

Rain and Oceanic Space: Wet Ontologies

Consider a human sitting in a boat in the Pacific during a rainstorm. The water-filled body becomes subject to a complex mixture of waters and spaces. The boat's position at the cusp of two fluid bodies—the heavy, wet one below it and the gaseous, humid one above—gets further complicated by liquid water falling from the sky. The experience of rain at sea brings together two forms of water, salt and fresh. This juxtaposition combines multiple experiences of water. To take a literary example, when the narrator of Yann Martel's *Life of Pi* (2001) encounters a sudden thunderstorm while adrift in the Pacific, he sees rain and lightning as visionary and even redemptive:

> I was breathless and wordless. I lay back on the tarpaulin, arms and legs spread wide. The rain chilled me to the bone. But I was smiling. I remember that close encounter with electrocution and third-degree burns as one of the few times during my ordeal when I felt genuine happiness.[19]

The shock of the encounter, which Martel emphasizes through the Christ-like posture of his hero, provides insight. Water touches Pi's body not just through its salty immensity, but also through the sudden and violent arrival of the storm. Wetness appears in multiple forms.

The complex experiential and philosophical implications of these encounters with wetness become legible in the influential work, separately and together, of the geographers Philip Steinberg and Kimberly Peters. Steinberg's book *The Social Construction of the Ocean* (2001) presents a synthetic overview of how human cultures have imagined and understood oceanic space across history.[20] The major subsequent contributions of Steinberg and Peters to blue humanities thought have come in four collaborative articles in which they explore "wet ontology."[21] These articles clarify and particularize the human relationship with water. These two scholars, both located in departments of geography, begin with the "paradoxical" (2014: 247) nature of the ocean in geographical terms. The project of "wet ontology" turns from human conceptions of the global to "the ocean itself . . . its three-dimensional and turbulent materiality" (2014: 247). Steinberg and Peters's analysis of complex materiality and the place of material water inside and outside human bodies and our planet's surfaces challenges theoretical understandings of space. Their initial emphasis, following the suggestion of geographer Stuart Elden, recalls that "water is simultaneously encountered as a depth and as a surface, as a set of fixed locations but also as an ungraspable space that is continually being reproduced by mobile molecules" (2014: 252). They articulate the force of water in "wet ontology" by keeping its dual function in mind, noting that water is mobile and contained, dynamic and limited. Drawing on the experiential epistemologies of surfers and kayakers in the work of Jon Anderson, they propose models such as "churning," "drifting," and "rebordering" for the human–water encounter (2014: 257–60).[22] Bringing the ocean into geographical thinking enables Peters and Steinberg to provide new structures for dynamic understanding.

In 2019, these two collaborators extend "wet ontology" in what they describe as a "more-than-wet" direction. This article engages with theories of the ocean as "assemblage and convergence" while also radicalizing their initial focus on "thinking *through* and *from* the ocean's liquid materiality" (2019: 294, emphasis in original). Exploring three new oceanic vistas—the ocean "within" bodies, "beyond" its liquid boundaries, and "imagined" in fictions—they suggest that wet ontological thinking can find oceanic disruptions in unfamiliar locations. Steinberg and Peters look inside bodies, beyond borders, and into imagined spaces for water's decisive presence. Drawing on literary works, including *Life of Pi*, Samuel Taylor Coleridge's "Rime of the Ancient Mariner," and William Wordsworth's "Sea Shell," the geographers create an expanded theoretical model by considering imaginary representations of human encounters with oceans. Recognizing the "limit of analytic prose in describing such a destabilizing ontology" (2019: 304–5), the authors nonetheless generate a multiply-entangled ocean. To return to the image of a human body in a boat in the rain on the Pacific, a wet/more-than-wet ontological approach would describe connections among the waters below and above, inside and outside, as well as considering vectors of transmission from one wetness to another. These ontological and experiential complexities define how humans pass through and along watery bodies of many kinds and phases. To be wet and more-than-wet, in the theoretical modes that Steinberg and Peters have constructed, means to cultivate an awareness of the constant proximity of bodies and different kinds of moisture.

Ishmael's "dear Pacific"

Beyond the sophisticated formulations of Steinberg and Peters, the Pacific looms in the Western imagination as a figure of desire. Deep longings show themselves in the erotic colonial fantasies of Paul Gauguin and in South

Sea adventure stories including the early novels of Herman Melville. But no clearer literary testament to the Western conception of the Pacific as lure and sublimity appears than the moment in which Ishmael describes the whaleship's arrival on the ocean that he calls "my dear Pacific" (367). By this time, in chapter 111 (out of 135), the reader knows that Pacific waters are the special haunts of the White Whale. But Ishmael's hymn to these waters celebrates harmony instead of violence:

> Thus this mysterious, divine Pacific zones the world's whole bulk about; makes all coasts one bay to it; seems the tide-beating heart of earth. Lifted by those eternal swells, you needs must own the seductive god, bowing your head to Pan.
>
> (367)

Melville's through line uncovers blue humanities ideas throughout the novel. Ishmael's dear Pacific connects human longing to planetary waters. To the sole survivor of the *Pequod's* doomed chase, the ocean represents the "divine," the "seductive god," and "Pan." This passage echoes many moments in Western and other traditions that associate the sea with religious insight, from Psalm 107 ("They that go down to the sea in ships") to the stories of Sinbad, Odysseus, Jonah, and many others. As Kimberly Patton observes in *The Sea Can Wash Away All Evil* (2006), the ocean represents a sacralizing space in many religious traditions, an antidote for the sins of land.[23] To Ishmael's desiring eyes, the Pacific reveals divinity and access to "the world's whole bulk." This great ocean is the "tide-beating heart of earth"—which is to say, the earth's core has been overrun by water. In making "all coasts one bay to it," the Pacific conjures the image of universal flood that Melville explores elsewhere ("Noah's flood is not yet subsided; two-thirds of the fair world it yet covers," 225). As Charles Olson analyzes Melville in *Call Me Ishmael* (1947), "With the Pacific opens the NEW HISTORY. . . . The Pacific is the end of the UNKNOWN which Homer's and Dante's Ulysses opened men's eyes to."[24] That sublime vision of vastness, described by Melville in 1850 and launched into American culture after the postwar Melville revival by Olson among others, places the Pacific as World Ocean in central view. There are other waters for the blue humanities, but none loom vaster than these.

Tim Winton's Surfing Sublime: Buoyancy as Lure[25]

One important Western response to global oceans has been the discourse of the sublime. Especially since the Romantic period in the nineteenth century, writers and thinkers who engage with oceanic space have often had recourse to classical and modern theories of sublime power. In the mid-twentieth century, the poet W.H. Auden claimed that the invention of the Romantic sublime was tantamount to the cultural invention of the sea.[26]

To uncover within Anglophone Pacific literature a critique and reformulation of these traditional ideas of sublimity, masculinity, and power, I close this chapter with an analysis of Australian writer Tim Winton's surf novel *Breath* (2008). Winton, one of Australia's most celebrated authors, writes with a close focus on the surfer's encounter with the waves of a remote Australian location.

For the blue humanities, the oceanic sublime represents an ecological problem. Mammalian breathing poses an entangled solution. Surfing, in which a human body stands upright on a rotating barrel of unbreathable whitewater, provides a way to imagine the connection between these two things.

The sublime has represented an elevated category of literary language since the Greek writer Longinus's *On the Sublime* (~first century CE). From this moment, the sublime style captures grandeur and an excess that challenges human thinking. Many of the essential Romantic and Post-Romantic tropes of the sublime that later appear in philosophical accounts from Edmund Burke and Immanuel Kant to Jean-François Lyotard and Jacques Derrida show themselves embryonically in Longinus's brief description.[27] The key force of sublime style, Longinus emphasizes, is irrationality: "A lofty passage does not convince the reason of the reader, but takes him out of himself. That which is admirable ever confounds our judgment" (1.4).[28] The conceptual violence of the sublime strains our imaginations, and Longinus's intuition that sublimity always sits on the far side of human comprehension becomes a central feature of this idea throughout literary history. Although we know very little about Longinus—neither his name nor the century in which he lived is certain—he pinpoints the pleasurable pain and rupture of coherence that would become the signature of the sublime in Western poetics. The problem with the sublime perspective is that it craves rupture, centers the human imagination, and refuses space for nonhuman collaborators. The opposite of the sublime's imaginative conquest of the world may be the simple act of breathing, the taking of alien air into one's lungs and body, and the environmental enmeshment that each breath marks.

The philosopher Graham Harman has recently traced the sublime lineage of Burke and Kant to Lyotard, Emmanuel Levinas, Derrida, and other twentieth-century thinkers, in order to reject the concept as fundamentally anthropocentric. Harman instead advocates for a posthuman philosophy that does not require the shaping structures of humanity. He argues for an ecological art that engages with the world beyond the merely human perspective, "art that explores unforeseen interactions between the different *parts* of the external world."[29] What Harman terms "unsublime ecology" might reasonably be described as an inhuman ecological perspective. The philosopher reminds us that the sublime has always been—starting with Longinus and, in a line from Kant and Burke to Lyotard and Derrida—a ju-jitsu trick in which the imagination of a (white male) subject reintegrates what it cannot comprehend. The list of poems whose language most commonly appears as exemplary of the sublime—Milton's *Paradise Lost*, Shelley's

"Mont Blanc," Shakespeare's *King Lear*, Wordsworth's *Prelude*—suggest that the mode appeals to poetic egoists of a particularly masculine type.[30]

The heroic sublime of these poets and theorists falters on the physical fact of breathing. Each day of their lives, more than 20,000 times per day, every one of these men, even stern blind Milton dictating his prophetic poem to dutiful daughters after his revolution had failed, drew nonhuman air into and out of his lungs, exchanging oxygen and carbon dioxide and processing water vapor. Each man's thinking continued, while their minds ignored the ways that the human body's dependence on alien matter to suspire might impinge upon the heroic sense of self. Even prophets and geniuses, even Wordsworth and Derrida, depend on unconscious forces. Even the greatest of poets breathes.

Winton's novel illustrates this point. *Breath* comprises a minor-key epic of surfing against breathing.[31] All of novel's core figures devote themselves to intentional oxygen deprivation: the teenage narrator–hero Pikelet, his rebellious buddy Loonie, Sando the Australian surf-seer they both follow, and Sando's American, one-time freestyle skier wife Eva. The unsubtle symbolism of Eva's name underlines her disruptive function in the otherwise-male story; her injured knee keeps her off the snow but does not prevent her from chasing sublimity through self-suffocating games that involve sex, a plastic bag, and eventually Pikelet. To court mortality by cutting off one's access to air, Winton suggests, replicates by physical force the sublime rupture that poets and theorists seek in impossible cogitation, or that surfers find in a wicked break. The language the novel uses for extreme surfing—the practice involves "appointments with the undiscovered" (71) and hits you "like you've felt the hand of God" (78)—echoes the familiar literary topos of sublime disorientation and reintegration. These men and boys, and one injured woman, crave nearness to the forces that nearly shatter their bodies and their selves. By connecting an experience that resembles the sublime to an intentional suppression of breathing, Winton makes this rarefied literary concept visceral.

A more fluid language of aesthetic beauty also punctuates Winton's gorgeous and apparently sincere hymns to surfing as practice. On the last page of the novel, the shattered Pikelet takes consolation in the infrequent days when his adult daughters watch him surf. He enjoys having them observe him as "a man who dances . . . [and] does something completely pointless and beautiful" (218). The notion of surfing as a (mostly) masculine aesthetic practice, something "pointless and elegant, as though nobody saw or cared" (25), threads through the novel. It might be tempting to follow Winton's word choice and call this kind of surfing "the beautiful," thinking about the contrast between the sublime and the beautiful that has exercised critics since Edmund Burke.[32] But beauty is not really what Winton's novel is after. His dominant vision treats extreme surfing, and less often extended breath-hold free diving, as chasing the sublime. These practices entwine themselves in a masculine world of competition and violence whose goal is to get all the way to "the weird, reptilian thing that happened to you" (113). Sando the guru, previously described as having the "stink of chalk on him" (78), lays out the surf sublime as if he were a literary theorist:

> It's like you come pouring back into yourself. . . . Like you've explored and all the pieces of you are reassembling themselves. You're new. Shimmering, Alive.
>
> (113)

Or, as Loonie, the more daring of the two teens, who eventually ends up dead in a drug deal gone bad in Baja, California, puts it upon seeing the great white shark who guards the first of several secret surf breaks—

> That eye . . . was like a fuckin hole in the universe.
>
> (76)

To surf-seek in these places of extremity, for Winton, means looking for tears in the fabric of reality, driving your mouth and nose into whitewater or, in a pinch, into a plastic bag, driving mortal bodies to their limits and then—hoping, most of the time, for reassembly. For a while, it works.

No Ecological Heroes! No Ecological Sublime!

On a theoretical level, there can be no heroes and no sublimity in an ecological system. The sublime and its necessary heroic egotism, which requires excess, danger, and assertive individuation, lack meaning from an ecosystem perspective. What does the wave think of the surfer, the mountain of the climber, the storm of the naked despairing king? Nothing—the wave, the mountain, and the storm do not care about human emotions. As Pikelet observes, the surf sublime represents "a rebellion against the monotony of drawing breath" (43), which is to say a complete rejection of human entanglement within and dependence on nonhuman environments. When the boys are kids, before they meet Sando and Eva, they think free diving is just "cheap weirdness in the days before we knew about drugs" (44). To dive down and "hold our breaths so long that our heads were full of stars" (16) places these boys with Wordsworth on Snowdon, Lear in the storm, Shelly on Mount Blanc. There is a retrospective pleasure in foolhardiness and danger—if you survive.

Sando and Eva, the guru and his damaged wife, appear in the novel as precursors of the extreme-sports faux-heroism that now spans the global worlds of surfing, skiing, climbing, free diving, and similar sports. A cutting observation late in the novel suggests that Sando, having outlived his wife Eva and disciple Loonie, goes on to rule a commercial empire, selling "snowboards, alpine apparel—all dripping radical chic" (207). Figures like Sando can never be ecological heroes because there is no such thing: an ecological point of view requires that we live without heroes. That may be why the Western world's hero-centric culture is having such a hard time with the Anthropocene. A posthuman blue humanities offers an alternative, but no clear heroes.

What could make an ecological hero? Can human self-assertion ever be compatible with ecological interconnectedness? The sublime tells a story in which the heroic ego can be reabsorbed into a divine or aesthetic whole. That vision of wholeness looks either like super-charged egotism or some radically ascetic version of religious practice. Neither vision offers much to the nonhuman environment that surrounds us and fills our lungs.

The problem with heroism is a problem of all human-centered thinking. Sando surfs like a god, but he's a bad teacher who leads Loonie to his death, abandons his wounded wife, and ignores Eva and Pikelet until they conduct a masochistic affair while the guru is away. All human heroes, by virtue of being human, exacerbate through self-assertion the problem of anthropocentrism. Even surfers who fixate on waves and sharks remain human when their skin dries. To the extent that we as humans crave examples of ecological heroism, figures such as Rachel Carson or Al Gore or Greta Thunberg, we resist the full force of the ecological thought that decenters the merely human. Perhaps we should instead worship the air we breathe.

To some extent, the flexible practice of literature, including Winton's ambivalently macho surf novel, may help address the problem of heroes. Winton and his narrator Pikelet know that Sando's a monster, though neither can help loving his drive. The novel attempts, perhaps successfully, to unravel the surf mythology, or at least to illuminate the conflict between the cultural prestige of male heroism and the counterpressure of ecosystemic thinking. The massive surge of ecocritical responses to literature and culture since the 1990s, of which the blue humanities is a part, suggests that the human–nature relationship may be in the process of being reimagined. Perhaps the sublime, one of the most prestigious literary modes that addresses the nexus of humanity, power, and nonhuman nature, may be ripe for reinvention. If so, I suspect that Winton's surf aesthetic may have a contribution to make as tragic counterexample and reminder that breathing may be monotonous but it keeps us human.

Suffocation Aesthetics

It may come as no surprise that I remain uncertain that Winton's novel can on its own accomplish the urgent task of reimagining or replacing the Romantic sublime for the Anthropocene. But he has assembled some important elements of the project and shown how a blue humanities approach might address this issue. The most generative of Winton's moves is assuming an oceanic perspective. To imagine a post-sustainability ecology, we need to exchange green fields for blue seas. We need swimmers and sailors to replace our oversupply of warriors and conquerors.[33] Surfers may help, too, though some of them may be too macho. The ocean, because it is not and has never been a home for humans, contains in its history many non-anthropocentric stories. Oceanic heroes, who exert themselves in intimate and dangerous contact with the fluid element, may provide models for surviving the present era of environmental crisis and disruption. As the seas rise, heed the swimmers.[34] And the surfers.

The second point about counter-heroism in Winton's *Breath* emerges from the novel's not-quite-completed critique of heroic masculinity. The surfers, especially Sando and Loonie, are too violent and selfish to be heroes. Winton admittedly shows little feminist generosity toward wounded Eva, whose Biblical name anticipates her role as sexual temptress for Pikelet, and who ends up dying by accidental self-strangulation in a hotel room in Portland after the events of the novel have long passed. But Winton clearly rejects Sando and Loonie's distinctly Australian machismo, even if Winton, as leading man of Australian fiction, himself may sometimes slide uncomfortably close to that role himself.[35]

A final counter-heroic element in *Breath* comes via the frame story. The adult Pikelet looks back at the wreck of his life, including a failed marriage and several unsuccessful attempts at suicide. He has ended up a paramedic who lives for the danger and urgency of emergency calls. In the opening scene of the novel, he finds a dead teenager who appears to have committed suicide but who Pikelet knows, via his own experience and keen eye, has been playing with the sublime rush of near-death by suffocation. The unnamed boy has, the narrator pronounces near the novel's end, "strangled himself for fun" (216), just like Eva in her hotel room. That death-by-error shadows the sublime contests at the center of the novel: the competitive breath holding, surfing with sharks, and deadly offshore storm breaks. When Pikelet reflects on his life, he finds the pattern of the return from chaos to selfhood that typifies the sublime encounter. But enduring privation no longer brings Pikelet to the heights of ecstasy or glory. "I cohered" (215), he announces, as if bare coherence were the most he could manage after his breath-rupturing life. Coherence is an essential quality of the narrative, and the novelist Winton needs it for his plot. Pikelet arrives at a non-ecstatic form of coherence. These days he exhausts his breath by blowing a didgeridoo instead of surfing or diving. He is a diminished figure, but he represents a safe descent from the heights of the sublime.

Since the sublime is not an ethos for ecology, this novel might more modestly suggest that partial coherence replace sublime unity. There's a place in ecological thinking for coherence, or at least I hope so. A blue humanities reading of *Breath* might end not with the didgeridoo but with adult Pikelet surfing a modest beach break, accommodating himself to nonhuman rhythms. This model may not arrive at the full cultural integration of humans and oceans that is the living legacy of Oceania. But as Pacific Island cultures are progressively threatened by climate change, accommodation with water may be a worthwhile goal to cultivate.

Notes

1 National Library of Scotland, "Geometrical Projection of Two Thirds of the Sphere (Pacific Ocean Central)," 1862–63. https://maps.nls.uk/view/140179373. Accessed 27 October 2022.
2 Peter Sloterdijk, *In the World Interior of Capitalism: For a Philosophical Theory of Globalization*, Wieland Hoban, trans. (Boston: MIT Press, 2013), 40–46.
3 For an older, and Eurocentric, description of this globalizing era, see J.H. Parry, *The Discovery of the Sea* (New York: Dial Press, 1974).
4 Jason W. Moore, *Capitalism in the Web of Life: Ecology and the Accumulation of Capital* (London: Verso, 2015).
5 Robert Sean Wilson, *Be Always Converting, Be Always Converted: An American Poetics* (Cambridge: Harvard University Press, 2009), 119–42.
6 Epeli Hau'ofa, *We Are the Ocean: Selected Works* (Honolulu: University of Hawai'I Press, 2008), 32.
7 For a short history of South Polynesia, see Madi Williams, *Polynesia, 900–1600* (York: ARC Humanities Press, 2021).
8 On the suffering of European circumnavigators, especially in the Pacific, see Joyce Chaplin, *Round About the Earth: Circumnavigation from Magellan to Orbit* (New York: Simon and Schuster, 2012).
9 Christina Thompson, *Sea People: The Puzzle of Polynesia* (New York: Harper, 2019).
10 See David Lewis, *We, the Navigators: The Ancient Art of Landfinding in the Pacific*, Sir Derek Oulton, ed., 2nd ed. (Honolulu: University of Hawai'i Press, 1994).
11 Alice Te Punga Somerville, *Once Were Pacific: Māori Connections to Oceania* (Minneapolis: University of Minnesota Press, 2012).
12 Lars Ecstein and Anja Schwarz, "The Making of Tupaia's Map," *The Journal of Pacific History* 54 (2019), 1–95. Also on Tupaia's map, see Steve Mentz and James Louis Smith, "Learning an Inclusive Blue Humanities: Oceania and Academia through the Lens of Cinema," *Humanities* 9:3 (2020). www.mdpi.com/2076-0787/9/3/67/htm#B5-humanities-09-00067. Accessed 19 July 2022.
13 The British Library catalog lists the map as "The Society Islands," and describes it as made by Captain James Cook, as a copy of Tupaia's original. Shelfmark Add. MS 21593 C. www.bl.uk/collection-items/the-society-islands. Accessed 27 October 2022.
14 Elizabeth DeLoughrey, *Roots and Routes: Navigating Caribbean and Pacific Literatures* (Honolulu: University of Hawai'I Press, 2007), 3.
15 Teresa Shewry, *Hope at Sea: Possibles Ecologies in Oceanic Literature* (Minneapolis: University of Minnesota Press, 2015), 18.
16 Noelani Arista, *The Kingdom and the Republic: Sovereign Hawai'i and the Early United States* (Philadelphia: University of Pennsylvania Press, 2019), 17.
17 Craig Santos Perez, *From Unincorporated Territory: [guma']* (Oakland: Omnidawn Press, 2014). Citations in the text by page numbers.
18 DeLoughrey, *Roots and Routes*, 26.
19 Yann Martel, *Life of Pi* (New York: Harcourt, 2001), 233.
20 Philip Steinberg, *The Social Construction of the Ocean* (Cambridge: Cambridge University Press, 2001).
21 These four co-authored articles include "Volume and Vision: Toward a Wet Ontology," *Harvard Design Magazine* 39 (2014), 124–9; "A Wet World: Rethinking Place, Territory, and Time," *Society and Space* (2015); "Wet Ontologies, Fluid Spaces: Giving Depth to Volume through Oceanic Thinking," *Environment and Planning D* 33:2 (2015), 247–64; "The Ocean in Excess: Toward a More-Than-Wet Ontology," *Dialogues in Human Geography* 9:3 (2019), 293–307.
22 Jon Anderson, "Relational Places: The Surfed Wave as Assemblage and Convergence," *Environment and Planning D* 30 (2012), 570–87; Jon Anderson, "What I Talk

about When I Talk about Kayaking," *Water Worlds: Human Geographies of the Ocean*, Jon Anderson and Kimberly Peters, eds. (Aldershot: Ashgate Publishing, 2014), 103–18.

23 Kimberly Patton, *The Sea Can Wash Away All Evils: Modern Marine Pollution and the Ancient Cathartic Ocean* (New York: Columbia University Press, 2006).

24 Charles Olson, *Call Me Ishmael* (New York: Grove Press, 1947), 117, 119.

25 A slightly different version of these thoughts on Winton will appear in the journal *SubStance* in 2023.

26 W.H. Auden, *The Enchafèd Flood, or the Romantic Iconography of the Sea* (London: Faber and Faber, 1951). I have been disputing Auden's exclusively Romantic invention of the sea from my earliest writings on oceanic literature; see Steve Mentz, "Toward a Blue Cultural Studies: The Sea, Maritime Culture, and Early Modern English Literature," *Literature Compass* 6/5 (2009), 997–1013.

27 On the sublime from Longinus forward, see Robert Clewis, ed., *The Sublime Reader* (London: Bloomsbury, 2018).

28 Longinus, *On the Sublime*, H.L. Havell, trans., Andew Lang, intr. (London and New York: Macmillan and Col, 1890). Accessed via Project Gutenberg: www.gutenberg.org/files/17957/17957-h/17957-h.htm. Accessed 9 June 2021.

29 Graham Harman, "Unsublime Ecology," *Flash Art* #326, June–August 2019: https://flash---art.com/article/unsublime-ecology/. Accessed 9 June 2021.

30 There is no space here to explore how Shakespeare, Milton, Wordsworth, and Shelley represent mainstays of the sublime tradition, nor to elucidate differences among these writers. Some of their shared qualities—all are white men with powerful conceptions of their own individual genius—may be instructive.

31 Tim Winton, *Breath* (New York: Farrar, Straus, and Giroux, 2008). All quotations given parenthetically in the text by page number.

32 Edmund Burke, *A Philosophical Enquiry into the Origin of Our Ideas of the Sublime and the Beautiful* (London, 1757).

33 See Steve Mentz, *At the Bottom of Shakespeare's Ocean* (London: Bloomsbury, 2009), 96–99.

34 For more in this vein, see Steve Mentz, *Ocean* (London: Bloomsbury 2020), and "Swimming in the Anthropocene," *Public Books*, December 2020: www.publicbooks.org/swimming-in-the-anthropocene/. Accessed 9 June 2021.

35 On Winton's solitary and somewhat macho persona in contemporary Australia, see this profile in the *New York Times*. www.nytimes.com/2018/06/12/books/tim-winton-shepherds-hut-australia-novelist.html. Accessed 8 June 2021.

4 The Roaring South

No ocean is wilder than the Southern Ocean. Largely landless, except for the Antarctic continent at its icy core, and almost entirely uninhabited over human history, it boasts the roughest seas and most destructive winds, roaring around the globe below 60 degrees south longitude, a line that crosses no continent. (Tierra del Fuego, the southernmost tip of South America, sits at around 55 degrees south.) Early European explorers who ventured south of Tierra del Fuego encountered what the British admiral George Anson called "continual terror" in a shelterless sea.[1] These "inhospitable latitudes" were among the last charted by Western hydrographers, and they remain among the most remote waters on the globe. The human histories that provide matter for blue humanities scholarship are comparatively absent here, though the voyages of early mariners from Francis Drake to George Anson to James Cook, as well as the exploits of round-the-globe speed yachtsmen today, give these cold waters human touches. To the extent that oceans represent an alien ecosystem for terrestrial humans, no ocean appears more alien than the waters south of Australia, Tierra del Fuego, and the Cape of Good Hope.

The history of representations of the Southern Ocean emphasizes that alterity, but this history also charts methods to bring humans into physical and metaphorical connections with these spaces. The Ptolemaic tradition, developed alongside the landlocked Mediterranean, imagined the round earth as made up of seas enclosed by land. Thus, in the centuries after the voyages of Ferdinand Magellan, Sir Francis Drake, Bartolomeu Dias, and Vasco da Gama made visible the vast expanses of water south of the Americas and Africa, European mariners engaged in a long search for an unknown Great Southern Land.[2] Hester Blum, in her 2019 study of "polar ecomedia," catalogs many nineteenth-century histories and fictions, including Edgar Allen Poe's *Narrative of Arthur Gordon Pym* (1838), with its "milky, boiling South Polar seas," and Samuel Taylor Coleridge's "Rime of the Ancient Mariner" (1798).[3] These literary texts subtend Blum's capacious reading of "polar ecomedia" as high-stakes Anthropocene writing, which can "offer conceptual and formal devices for describing, comprehending, and, most ambitiously, surviving climatic extremity" (5). Blum's reading of

DOI: 10.4324/9781003166665-4

polar ecomedia as environmental art provides a vivid subset of the "wet" narratives with which blue humanities scholarship engages.[4]

Writing about the Southern Ocean emphasizes Anson's "terror" and the "extremity" that Blum finds in polar ecomedia. In places, however, these texts also engage in what Samuel Baker, describing Coleridge's "Rime of the Ancient Mariner," calls an "acculturating mission."[5] The striking if simple moral of Coleridge's "Rime" holds: "He prayeth well who loveth well/ Both man and bird and beast."[6] But the natural forces of ice and wind, in addition to the poem's supernatural horrors, suggest that while prayer and love may help the mariner endure southern latitudes, they cannot expunge what he has seen and felt. For humans, the Southern Ocean and the Antarctic continent represent our planet's most hostile environments.

View from the South: The Spilhaus Projection

From a nonhuman point of view, the Southern Ocean occupies the core of the water-filled southern hemisphere. Viewing the World Ocean from the perspective of its southern pole organizes the Spilhaus Projection. Designed by the South African-born oceanographer Athelstan Spilhaus in 1942, this projection centers the unified oceans while marginalizing the land. The large continents of the Americas and Asia appear as fringes around the map, and the continents of Antarctica and Australia show as islands in the blue water. Even Africa, which looks island-like in this projection, occupies only a minor place. From a blue humanities perspective, the view from below visualizes the unity of the great waters.

Spilhaus, whose academic career included stints at the Woods Hole Oceanographic Institution in Massachusetts and at the University of Minnesota, created this map in order to emphasize the unity of the watery part of the world.[8] The map inverts more common Northern hemispheric projections, including the famous Mercator projection, that center Afro-Eurasia and North America. No two-dimensional project of the three-dimensional globe is "correct," since all involve distortions to represent curved space on a flat surface. But the Spilhaus projection demonstrates the Southern Ocean's distinctive qualities. While this body of water is perforated by Antarctica and Australia, it represents a blue core at the center of our planet. It presents an explicitly antihuman projection of the globe, in that three of the most populous continents—Asia, Europe, and North America—appear only as ragged fringes. Even Africa, the site of humanity's origins and currently home to its fastest-growing populations, appears slightly off-center.

The Spilhaus Projection provides visual clues to the two most striking physical features of the Southern Ocean: ice and wind. Located below 60 degrees south latitude, these cold waters, and the polar continent, contain large amounts of glacial ice. Most of the land of Antarctica sits below the Antarctic Circle (66 degrees 30 minutes south). The intervening six degrees of open ocean—approximately 450 miles—create space for the fastest and

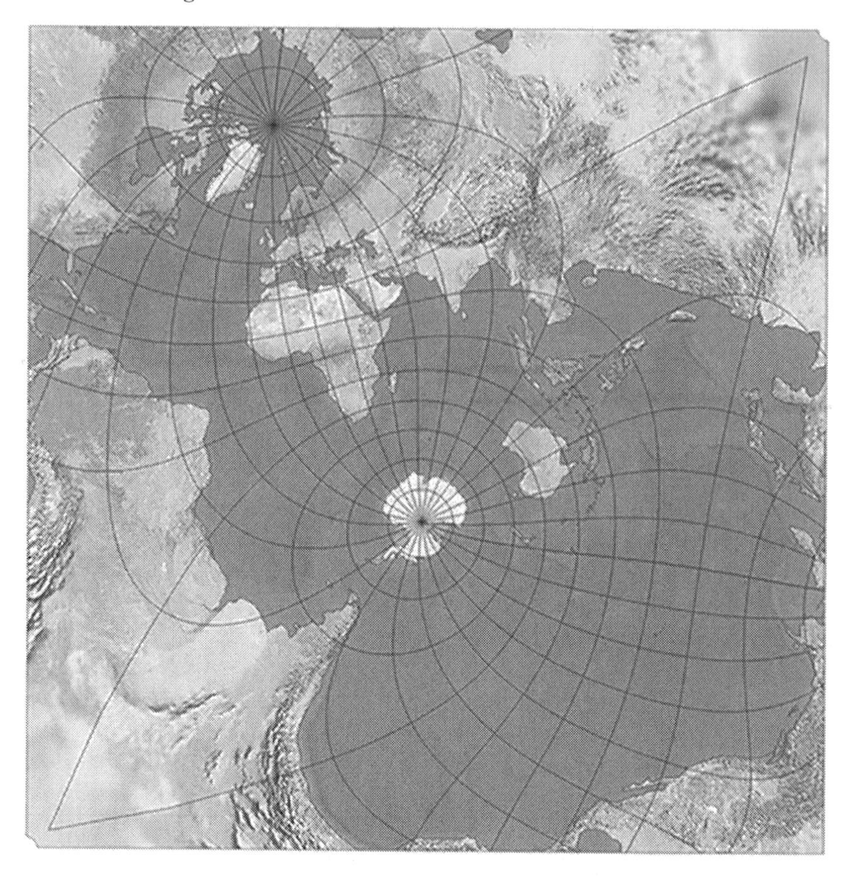

Figure 4.1 The Spilhaus Projection

Source: Courtesy of ArcGIS Pro Project[7]

most violent winds on the planet, which follow the Antarctic Circumpolar Current in a constant raging flow around the curvature of the earth. Unlike the gyre-patterns that circulate in the Atlantic, Pacific, and Indian basins, the Southern Ocean's prevailing currents are never interrupted by encounters with land. Sailors refer to the "Roaring Forties" as the powerful westerlies between 40 and 50 degrees south; these winds carried long-haul sailing ships from Europe to Australia during the Age of Sail, and they power round-the-world yachtsmen today. The winds accelerate as one passes farther south into the so-called Furious Fifties and Screaming Sixties. "Below forty degrees south there is no law," goes the whalemen's saying, "and below fifty degrees south there is no God." The science fiction writer Kim Stanley Robinson has extended the metaphor, so that he concludes, "Below the sixtieth no common sense, and below the seventieth no intelligence whatsoever."[9] Robinson's imagined journey extends onto the frozen lands of the polar continent.

But even the bleak and dry wastes of Antarctica, which have hosted international research stations since the nineteenth century, seem more hospitable than the churning waters and raging waves of the Southern Ocean.

The Antarctic Sublime: Coleridge's "Rime of the Ancient Mariner"

If Tim Winton's Australian surfers capture a warm-water, human-intimate oceanic sublime, the chilly waters of the Southern Ocean present more alienating encounters. For Anglophone writers such as Edgar Allen Poe, voyages to the Southern continent promised encounters with alien landscapes and inhuman seas. In Samuel Taylor Coleridge's verse-parable "The Rime of the Ancient Mariner," first published in 1798, the mariner's doomed excursion into Antarctic waters provides a counter-vision to Winton's tale of risk and bravado. The waters on which the mariner sails remain inhuman, and his own motivations remain opaque, even to himself.

Coleridge's "Rime" has long been considered a mainstay of the Romantic sublime in English poetry, along with mountain poems such as Wordsworth's *Prelude* and Shelley's "Mont Blanc." The poem's stark representations of isolation on a vast sea juxtapose human frailty and inhuman power. From a multiphase blue humanities perspective, the poem depicts multiple encounters with sublime water creatures, including the icebergs of the Southern Ocean, the world-girdling winds of the Roaring Forties, and the inhuman encounter with the albatross. Unlike Winton's surfers or Wordsworth on Mount Snowdon, Coleridge's mariner never recognizes himself in his nonhuman world. Rather, the sublime encounter in this ocean remains opaque, and human agency thoroughly minimized.

The nonheroic sublimity from which Coleridge's mariner speaks represents a variation on the heroic maritime sublime that Winton adapts out of a long tradition of seafaring heroes. In making sense of sublimity in oceanic context, then, it may be helpful to distinguish between a Romantic-egoistic form, often associated with mountain climbing, and a more self-fracturing or even selfless mode, associated with the sea. Winton's heroic surfers, in this respect, resemble mountaineers, but his novel ironizes rather than celebrates their fantasies of accomplishment. The philosopher Emily Brady, in her analysis of an emergent "environmental sublime," suggests that it is possible and necessary to "decouple" the historical and metaphysical traditions of the philosophical sublime from "problematic connections to elitist notions of taste."[10] While Brady observes the human-centered, masculine, and egotistical elements of traditional ideas of the sublime, she suggests that notions such as "the ungraspable" (197) provide a means "to humiliate and humble" (202) a self-aware human subject. Human cognition itself, she suggests, in an analysis largely based on Kant's writings on the sublime, can produce an "aesthetic-moral relationship" (183) between humans and an alien environment. The key emotion for Brady is "distanced fear," which she suggests "prepares the way and presents the ground for a moral attitude toward nature—a route from admiration to respect" (205). Bringing Brady's framework to bear on the supernatural horrors of Coleridge's "Rime" enables an understanding of how the poet recasts oceanic nature as both alien and morally urgent. To encounter the ocean of ice and wind, in this poem, creates possibilities for ethical and spiritual insight.

In treating Coleridge's "Rime" as a case study in anti-egotistical sublime ocean writing, my analysis de-emphasizes the Christian frame in favor of the shock of the encounter with the inhuman. In doing so, I deliberately pass over the "ghost story" figures of Life-in-Death, the zombie crew, and even the Hermit Good who at length rescues the mariner and returns him to human society. Instead, a blue humanities reading of the "Rime" focuses on inhuman powers, especially ice, the albatross, and wind. The frame story locates the mariner in conversation with the Wedding Guest, on the margins of human sociability. Investigating how the poem engages planetary waters requires a plunge into the desolate reaches of the Southern Ocean, including its nonhuman inhabitants.

The most famous symbol in Coleridge's poem is the Albatross, a bird well-known to southern mariners. Adam Nicolson includes the albatross among his list of iconic global seabirds, emphasizing how widely they travel across oceanic spaces.[11] For Coleridge, however, the bird's most visible subtext is Christian. After the mariner shoots the bird, the crew marks him with its corpse: "Instead of a Cross, the Albatross/About my neck was hung" (ll. 137–38). The rhymes make explicit the connection between seabird and Christian symbol. The poet has already seeded this symbolic connection by bringing the words "cross" and "albatross" into proximity twice earlier. When the bird first appears, the word "cross" brings it into contact with the ship: "At length did cross an Albatross" (l. 61). In this initial stanza, the religious metaphor becomes direct, as the mariner continues "And an it were a Christian soul,/We hail'd it in God's name" (ll. 63–64). The mariner's crime, too, invokes the same word as his tool of desecration: "with my cross bow/I shot the Albatross" (ll. 79–80). The poem's quadruple repetition of the word "cross" emphasizes the mariner's sin and the bird's spiritual meaning.

Alongside this Christian symbology, however, the Southern Ocean through which both bird and ship pass provides a less legible background. While the Albatross encourages the reader to understand a familiar typology of human sin and natural vulnerability, the polar icescape invokes a more-than-human cosmology. Ice opens a gateway into a supernatural world less familiar than Christianity. Just before the Albatross appears, icebergs provide a nonhuman soundtrack that alienates and disturbs the mariner and the crew:

> The Ice was here, the Ice was there,
> The Ice was all around:
> It crack'd and growl'd, and roar'd and howl'd—
> Like noises of a swound.
>
> *(ll. 57–60)*

A blue humanities reading emphasizes the Ice and decenters the Albatross. It may be argued that the Ice provides the necessary environmental alienation that enables the arrival of the spirit-bird, but such a reading tends to move past the opaque frozen water to arrive at the legible bird. Instead, reading the ice as Ice opens up the element of oceanic space that was most threatening to eighteenth-century mariners. The crisis of location that icebergs generate by being "here," "there," and "all around" counteracts increasingly successful efforts to map and chart seaways throughout the rest of the globe. Water was navigable; ice was not. The poem's emphasis on unintelligible noises, cracks, growls, roars, and howls makes the ice seem alive, threatening, and alien. The final word of the stanza, "swound," which Coleridge derives from an archaic form of the verb "swoon" or faint, puns on wounds, perhaps even on the Shakespearean form "swounds," which Hamlet uses twice as an oath to refer to God's wounds.[12] The ship surrounded by ice appears wounded, weakened, and entirely out of place, like human bodies in the icescapes of the Southern Ocean.

In suggesting a reading of the mariner's plight that emphasizes alien icescape over bird-murder, I do not aim to dislodge the Christian reading entirely. Rather, the Albatross both tempts the mariner into sin and, initially, delivers the ship from frozen water. After the mariner has killed the bird, the sailors attribute the lack of wind to the killing: "For all averr'd, I had kill'd the Bird/That made the Breeze to blow" (ll. 91–92). But the first consequence of the Albatross's providential appearance was less the "good south wind" (l. 69) than the opening of a way through the solid sea: "The Ice did split with a Thunder-fit/The Helmsman steer'd us through" (ll. 67–68). The opening of the Ice-world immediately precedes the freshening of the breeze. The poem's vision of the polar seas includes supernatural beings and zombified rowers, but its initial challenge is ice. Once the sea becomes scattered with icebergs, the navigational techniques that had enabled British mariners to encircle the globe fail. In these ice-seas the mariner and his ship become vulnerable.

The contrast between the forces of Ice and Albatross suggests that the poem asks us to reconsider the polar environment. The gateway into gothic horror may be as much unfamiliar frozen water as magical bird. It may be possible, in fact, to imagine the relatively intelligible nature of the Albatross-as-Cross symbol as a response to the extreme alienation of a sea covered with ice. Like many Romantic poets, Coleridge aims to disorient his reader, while also providing a route through the strange world he conjures. The proximity in the opening of the poem between the familiar language of Christian symbology and the radical alterity of a frozen sea shows the poet highlighting this contrast. To a blue humanities eye, the mariner's exploration of the Southern Ocean should include not just the ongoing task of mapping remote oceans but also the relatively novel encounter with polar ice. (English mariners had, of course, encountered ice in the Arctic since early modern explorations by John Cabot, Humphrey Gilbert, John Davis, and others, though eighteenth-century voyages toward the southern pole were newer to Coleridge's readers.) The alien world south of Tierra del Fuego and the Cape of Good Hope proves to be home both to magical creatures and vocal but nonliving ice.

The portrait of the Southern Ocean in Coleridge's poem structures itself around the inhuman characteristics of this remote ocean. After ice comes wind. Once the Albatross has been shot and the crew killed, the mariner sloughs off the bird's corpse through his unintentional blessing of the native creatures of the ocean. Finding himself among a "million million slimy things" (l.230) that thrive in the "rotting Sea" (l.232), the mariner connects to his alien environment: "O happy living things! No tongue/Their beauty might declare/. . . . /And I bless'd them unaware" (ll. 274–75, 279).[13] After this blessing, the Albatross/Cross falls off the mariner's neck and "sank/ Like lead into the sea" (ll. 282–83). But while earlier the physical encounter with ice leads to a spiritual encounter with the spirit-bird, in the middle section the order reverses itself. After the spiritual vision that blesses the happy living things, the mariner encounters the naked wind of the Southern Ocean. It is not clear if he sails in the Roaring Forties, Furious Fifties, or farther south, but in whatever case, wind become the dominant environmental feature of this ocean:

> The roaring wind! It roar'd far off,
> It did not come anear;
> But with its sound it shook the sails
> That were so thin and sere.
> *(ll. 301–4).*

Wind replaces ice as material metaphor for alien environment. The central quality of the southern wind is less physical force than "roaring" auditory nature. It is the "sound" of the wind that "shook the sails," not the pressure of the breeze. The threadbare sails, too, seem unable to translate wind into locomotion. Crewless and sail-less, the mariner endures a world overwhelmed by meaningless sound.

That the Southern Ocean is an environment defined by the noise of wind seems true from both modern and premodern sailors' accounts. The background of incessant roaring wind motivates Coleridge's final turns toward supernatural silence. The mariner's return home follows the guidance of mystical seraphs who lead but do not speak: "No voice; but O! the silence sank,/ Like music on my heart" (ll. 535–26). The silence of the seraphs soothes and reverses the endless roar of the Southern Ocean. Even the lasting consequence of the mariner's adventure, his "strange power of speech" (l. 620), becomes audible to the Wedding-Guest (and the reader) only because they (and we) live outside the deafening chaos of the Roaring Forties.

While sea ice and deafening winds are two distinctive features of the Southern Ocean, a third physical element—the polar continent itself—does not appear in Coleridge's poem. The presence of this vast polar landmass distinguishes the southern pole from the northern Arctic Sea, which is water at the pole, though ice-covered during much of the year (at least before rapid global heating). Europeans did not discover Antarctica until 1820, twenty-two years after the publication of Coleridge's poem. Early attempts to reach the south magnetic pole would not bear fruit until the early twentieth century. The presence of this landed "heart" geographically distinguishes the Southern Ocean from the more-traveled Arctic Sea in the north. Many early explorations into the Southern Ocean were made by whalers and sealers looking for fresh hunting grounds. The circum-Antarctic waters would stay teeming with life until the arrival of industrial whaling in the twentieth century.[14] Until then, Coleridge's vision of spirit-birds, floating ice, and roaring winds remained the dominant representation of this least-traveled of the world's oceans.

Polar Fastness: "Will the Whale Diminish?"

Of the speculative, mythic, and faux-historical digressive chapters in *Moby-Dick*, few resonate more powerfully with modern concerns than chapter 105, "Does the Whale's Magnitude Diminish? Will He Perish?" (351–54). Enthusiastic Ishmael, wishing to champion both the symbolic potency of whales and his own experience of the relentless chase, appears caught in his own vise. He recognizes the observable truth that generations of commercial fishermen have relearned time and again: aggressive fishing reduces the population of any fish, whales included.[15] Ishmael sees that this basic pattern creates a dilemma for global whale populations: "the moot point is, whether Leviathan can long endure so wide a chase, and so remorseless a havoc; whether he must not at last be exterminated from the waters, and the last whale, like the last man, smoke his last pipe, and then himself evaporate in the final puff" (352). Ishmael adores whales and whaling, and in the self-obliterating image of the last whale, he entertains the thought that his own practice may consume his objects of worship. Might the whale, like the buffalo, have no place in the wide and remorseless modern world?

Not until whalemen availed themselves of diesel engines and industrial harpoons would this question run to its bloody end. In the days of wooden whaleships and hand-darted harpoons, whale populations preserved some fighting chance. But Ishmael's answer to the pressure of valiant Nantucket whalemen is neither regulation nor restraint. Instead, he celebrates "two firm fortresses" (353), the polar seas north and south, to which Leviathan can retreat. These spaces of resort for threatened whales represent "polar citadels" (353). There, Ishmael avers, whales can retreat, and "diving under the ultimate glassy barriers and walls there, come up among icy fields and floes; and in a charmed circle of everlasting December bid defiance to all pursuit from man" (353). This vision of frozen seas as whale-homes imagines a cetacean Antarctica, a no-kill zone wherein the hunted rest undisturbed. In that sea of ice and isolation, which in some ways resembles Coleridge's Southern Ocean without interloping ships, human violence cannot trespass.

Ishmael's image of whales—the species, as opposed to the unique White Whale with the wrinkled brow—cozily swimming about an impregnable ice palace beneath the poles provides a geographic correlative to the narrator's musings about cetacean immortality. The whaleman does not leave his imagined whales in imagined water but instead insists that "we account the whale immortal in his species, however perishable in his individuality" (354). The distinction relies upon the species' ability to retreat to the planet's polar fortresses. But Ishmael's chapter-closing meditation imagines the whale bursting forth from his ice palace and returning to a drowned world. "In Noah's flood he despised Noah's ark" (354), he asserts. After whales have retreated into the safety of their ice caves, Ishmael draws them back into warmer waters through an imagined second Flood. "If ever the world is to be flooded again, like the Netherlands, to kill off its rats," Ishmael concludes, "then the eternal whale will survive, and rearing upon the top-most crest of the equatorial flood, spout his frothed defiance to the skies" (354). Perhaps the exterminated rats imply the destruction of terrestrial civilizations, as in Noah's flood. The repetition of the word "defiance," which defines the whales' behavior both in their polar fortresses and later in flooded equatorial waters, suggests that what was once confined to the poles may in a postapocalyptic future embrace the center of the globe. Whales represent the anti-terrestrial defiance of oceanic life, spouting disdain at the merely human. For Melville, this basic truth may currently exist only in remote polar seas. But in time, cetaceans will conquer the world ocean in fact as well as symbol. History passed differently, but the vision of icebound whales breaking free in a second Flood captures the ocean-centric catastrophism of *Moby-Dick*. Perhaps Ishmael's catastrophic future anticipates a worst-case sea level rise scenario, in which the whales inherit the earth.

A Global Force: The Circumpolar Current as Planetary Structure

The system of ocean gyres describes the dominant currents that circulate throughout the world's oceans. The North Atlantic and North Pacific gyres rotate clockwise, while the South Atlantic and South Pacific, located in the southern hemisphere, rotate counterclockwise. The Indian Ocean gyre, which spans the equator, shifts direction with the monsoon. In these five cases, ocean currents and prevailing winds double back on themselves because the continents block continuous direct loops about the globe. The blocking force of continental landmasses forces ocean currents into their characteristic loops. (A smaller gyre, the Beaufort Gyre, flows clockwise in the Arctic.) The sole exception to the rule of circular ocean gyres is the Antarctic Circumpolar Current, an endless roaring westerly that wraps around the southern tip of the planet between Tierra del Fuego and Antarctica. While each of the five circular ocean gyres has its own distinctive human history—from the navigators of Oceania riding the Pacific gyre to settle nearly all Pacific islands to the distinctive triangular Europe–Africa–North America pattern that structured the horrors of the transatlantic slave trade from the fifteenth through the nineteenth centuries—only the Southern Ocean's currents run freely about the planet. Other oceans contain sea ice, massive storms, and wild seas, but in none do ocean currents run unimpeded.

The globe-circling power of the Antarctic Circumpolar Current, also called the West Wind Drift, defines the Southern Ocean's difference from the more human-friendly waters of the Atlantic, Pacific, and Indian basins. In Melville's utopian vision, the polar seas represent a home for whales into which humans will never penetrate. Technologies have proved more versatile than Ishmael imagined, but alienation still colors these cold, wild waters. The Southern Ocean, with its ice, wind, waves, and ceaseless currents, represents the least-humanized and least-human-friendly watery environment on the planet. It continues to represent a limit point of human exploration and imagination.

Notes

1 Joy McCann, *Wild Sea: A History of the Southern Ocean* (Chicago: University of Chicago Press, 2018), 7. McCann cites Anson's *Voyage Round the World* (1789).
2 See McCann, *Wild Sea*, 10–27.
3 For a list of histories and fictions, see Hester Blum, *To the Ends of the Earth: The Print Culture of Polar Exploration* (Durham: Duke University Press, 2019), 37.
4 On "wet" and "dry" as narrative categories, see Steve Mentz, *Shipwreck Modernity: Ecologies of Globalization 1550–1719* (Minneapolis: University of Minnesota Press, 2015), 1–24.
5 Samuel Baker, *Written on the Water: British Romanticism and the Maritime Empire of Culture* (Charlottesville: University of Virginia Press, 2010), 27.
6 Samuel Taylor Coleridge, "The Rime of the Ancient Mariner," in *Lyrical Ballads*, William Wordsworth, Samuel Taylor Coleridge, and W.J.B. Owen., eds., 2nd ed. (Oxford: Oxford University Press, 1969), 7–32, ll. 645–46.
7 On the Spilhaus Projection see the ArcGIS project's recent analysis: www.arcgis.com/home/item.html?id=9b2ce7c8179b4744af7bf3ddb86b7804. Accessed 28 November 2022.
8 For a response to the Spilhaus Projection in 2018, see https://bigthink.com/strange-maps/the-spilhaus-projection-ocean-maps/. Accessed August 2022.
9 Kim Stanley Robinson, *Antarctica* (New York: Bantam, 1999).
10 Emily Brady, *The Sublime in Modern Philosophy: Aesthetics, Ethics, and Nature* (Cambridge: Cambridge University Press, 2013), 195.
11 Adam Nicolson, *The Seabird's Cry: The Lives and Loves of the Planet's Great Ocean Voyagers* (New York: Henry Holt, 2018).
12 William Shakespeare, *Hamlet*, Ann Thompson and Neil Taylor, eds. (London: Arden Shakespeare, 2007), 2.2.511, 5.1.263.
13 In later editions of the *Rime*, Coleridge amended the line to a "thousand thousand slimy things."

14 For recent scholarship on Soviet whaling, especially in the Arctic and Antarctic regions, see Bathsheba Demuth, *Floating Coast: An Environmental History of the Bering Strait* (New York: W. W. Norton, 2019); and Ryan Tucker Jones, *Red Leviathan: The Secret History of Soviet Whaling* (Chicago: University of Chicago Press, 2022).

15 On the depletion of North Atlantic fisheries, see W. Jeffrey Bolster, *The Mortal Sea: Fishing the Atlantic in the Age of Sail* (Cambridge: Harvard University Press, 2012).

5 The Human Sea

Networks in the Indian Ocean

Considering the long history of transoceanic voyaging from my own North Atlantic perspective provides a distorting view. The massive footprint of a single voyage, Christopher Columbus's crossing from Spain to the Bahamas between August 3 and October 12, 1492, has convinced generations of Europeans and Americans that oceans represented formidable barriers during early modernity. A rich academic discourse surrounding the "Columbian Exchange" has emerged that considers transatlantic voyaging to be a hinge-point in world history.[1] But a global, rather than North Atlantic, view makes clear that transoceanic voyaging was an ancient human practice long before the European voyages of discovery began in the fifteenth century. Not only had the Vikings crossed the North Atlantic in an earlier era of near-globalization around 1000 CE, but the peoples of Oceania and the Indian Ocean had established transoceanic migration and trade patterns several millennia earlier.[2] The historian Stephen C. Jett suggests that human contact between different continents and ocean basins—an understanding of ancient cross-cultural influences that he terms "diffusionism"—may have been more common than mainstream scholarship suggests.[3] Jett argues that transoceanic contact was feasible and practical, though likely rare, on a very long time horizon. But no matter the exact details of the circulation of human ideas and artifacts among the continents across historical time, it remains clear that since at least the third millennium BCE, the coasts of the Indian Ocean, from East Africa to the Arabian Peninsula to the subcontinent, the peninsula of modern Malaysia, and the islands of modern Indonesia, were connected by sea routes. Ocean historian Michael Pearson argues that "the Indian Ocean is by far the oldest of the seas in history, regular connections between two early civilizations date back over 5,000 years."[4] David Abulafia, in a more recent overview of global ocean history, *The Boundless Sea* (2019), disputes this point, naming the Pacific as the "oldest" human ocean, followed by the Indian Ocean, which he terms "the Middle Ocean," in intentional homage to the Mediterranean.[5] This academic dispute is technical, with Pearson emphasizing transoceanic contact between different civilizations in the Indian basin, while Abulafia reaches back to the initial peopling of southeast Asia and Australia as the earliest human

DOI: 10.4324/9781003166665-5

migrations across watery space. One distinctive feature of the Indian Ocean, in both accounts, is the cultural complexity and resilience of its networks from ancient into modern history.

The physical property of the Indian Ocean that defines and shapes its cross-cultural connections is the seasonal rhythm of the monsoon. These winds shift in a regular pattern along a northeast-southwest axis, facilitating travel in certain directions at certain times of year. As Abulafia explains the geophysical system, the "origin of the monsoons lies in the high air temperatures created in the Asian landmass during the summer; cooler air is drawn northeastwards across the ocean" (51). As the cool air rushes northeast, ships follow from East Africa and the Arabian Gulf toward India. During the winter, the system inverts, so that "September to May was the period of the year when sailing from Gujarat in western India to Aden proved most feasible" (51). Seasonal winds from northeast to southwest follow the same pattern in which cool air rushes toward areas of warmth, because in winter "the landmass cools sharply but the ocean retains its warmth" (51). When Portuguese mariners entered the Indian Ocean trading networks in the late fifteenth century, they encountered well-established trade routes, whose intricacies they were taught by local pilots, as demonstrated in Luis vaz de Camões's sixteenth-century Portuguese epic poem *The Lusíads*. While navigation has a seasonal aspect in many parts of the globe, the stark inversions of the monsoon made Indian Ocean crossings predictable to a greater degree than most other ancient transoceanic voyages. The relationships between ancient cultures, from Sumer and Rome in the west to Ceylon and Gujarat in the East, were structed by reliable shifts of the annual monsoon.

The civilizations of the Indian Ocean, to a greater extent than those of Oceania and even Europe, grew up around great rivers. From the Nile, Tigris, and Euphrates in the West to the Ganges, Indus, and Brahmaputra on the subcontinent, human cultures clung to the banks of massive freshwater arteries. While Karl Wittfogel's nineteenth-century idea of "hydraulic empires" has fallen into disfavor, along with his crude notions about "oriental despotism," the relationship between irrigation and large-scale agricultural civilizations remains unsettled. In James C. Scott's *Against the Grain* (2017), the development of large-scale systems of government appears to have had as much to do with the domestication of animals and subaltern humans, including through slavery, as with irrigation as such—though irrigating practices may have also mattered.[6] More radical reconsiderations of early human communities, such as those championed by David Graeber and David Wengrow in their controversial bestseller *The Dawn of Everything* (2021), suggest that large-scale civilization need not have been only a despotic affair.[7] Intimacy with water marks human cultures everywhere, as Giulio Boccaletti shows in *Water: A Biography* (2021).[8] The lands that surround the Indian Ocean, from the rain-drenched jungles of Southern India to the deserts of Arabia, may be no more river-dependent than the ancient waterscapes of the Mississippi or the Amazon; river valleys are always the best places for farming. In drawing together the pattern of the monsoon with the politics of river valleys, however, I aim in this chapter to sketch some human possibilities and structures typical of the networks of connectivity that span the Indian Ocean.

The first text I explore will be environmental writer Amitav Ghosh's history-as-memoir *In an Antique Land* (1994), which explores a slightly fictionalized history of connections between India and northeastern Africa.[9] After using Ghosh's text to establish patterns of ancient transoceanic voyaging, I turn toward a skeptical reconsideration of the supposed "discovery" of the East Indies by the Portuguese mariner Vasco da Gama. The national epic of Portugal, *The Lusíads*, was published in 1572 to celebrate da Gama's first voyage to India in 1497–99. However, as the poem clearly demonstrates, the Portuguese mariners were guided by masters of the Indian Ocean sailing network, who directed their passage from southeast Africa to India. While European literary tradition and Portuguese national mythology celebrate da Gama as conquering hero, he enters the Indian Ocean as participant in a network, even if European technologies would soon disrupt the region's millennia-old systems. Two visionary moments inspired by the Indian Ocean, "The Grand Armada" in *Moby-Dick* and Salman Rushdie's *Haroun and the Sea of Stories* (1990), provide speculative metaphors for what a pre-European and undisrupted Indian Ocean might have once represented. My effort throughout will be to provide a contrast between the capacious possibilities of an Indian-Ocean-centered history, as opposed to familiar Eurocentric stories of the Mediterranean and the Atlantic, which will in many cases be more familiar to Anglophone scholars.

Amitav Ghosh in Transit: *In an Antique Land*

In his novelistic memoir-cum-history *In an Antique Land*, Amitav Ghosh reanimates the medieval connection between Egypt and the trading port of Mangalore across the Indian Ocean. The key historical figures are Abraham Ben Yiju, a Jewish merchant and writer born in north Africa (modern Tunisia) around 1100, and Ben Yiju's Indian-born slave, whose name is unclear from extant records, but Ghosh reconstructs as Bomma. When Ben Yiju arrives in India, he becomes part of a thriving international community. Ghosh cites the famous Moroccan traveler Ibn Battuta, who spent time in Mangalore some two centuries after Ben Yiju, to describe still-thriving international communities of merchants from Yemen and Persia. For Ghosh, an Indian man doing research in Egypt and India for an Oxford doctorate, the most striking thing about Mangalore in the eleventh and the twentieth century is its close transoceanic connections to wealthy states in the Middle East:

> [Mangalore's] ancient connections with the Arab world have bequeathed it a more useful legacy than a mere collection of artifacts: thousands of

> its residents are now employed in the Persian Gulf, and its suburbs are awash with evidence of the extravagant spending of its expatriates.[10]

The split chronology of Ghosh's book, which oscillates between the stories of Ben Yiju and Bomma in the eleventh century and the author's own experiences in the twentieth century, mirrors the diachronic histories he finds in Mangalore. (Viewers of the 2022 World Cup in Qatar, ongoing as I complete this book, will be aware of some crueler implications of twenty-first century Persian Gulf–South Asian exchange.) Oceanic connections are ancient and contemporary, sometimes recoverable only through rare manuscripts but also still visible on today's streets. The slave Bomma, whose obscure fate animates Ghosh's imagination as well as being the subject of his own scholarly research, represents, as does the modern author, a figure whose fate spans the eastern and western rims of the Indian Ocean.[11]

In Ghosh's scholarship-inspired imagination, Bomma emerges from a local culture on India's west coast. He appears to have been born, according to Ghosh's research, "into one of the several matrilineal communities which played a part in the Bhuta-cult of Tulunad" (254). The lasting connection between Bomma and Ben Yiju thus creates a cultural meeting place, described by Ghosh as "a small patch of level ground" that connects "the matrilineally-descended Tulu and the patriarchal Jew" (263). Ghosh idealizes this mutuality, though he is careful to recall the bonds of slavery and the "formal conversion that Bomma probably had to undergo while in Ben Yiju's service" (263). What catches the writer's eye, however, are hints of human connections between these men, including the possibility that Bomma took over Ben Yiju's mercantile business after the older man died. Ben Yiju appears also to have married an enslaved Indian woman named Ashu, which leads Ghosh further to speculate about what languages the Jewish merchant spoke with Bomma, or indeed with his wife. "It is easy enough to imagine," Ghosh speculates, "that Ben Yiju used a specialized trade language to communicate with his fellow merchants in Mangalore" (281). It is more difficult, Ghosh continues, to imagine "how he and Ashu adapted that argot to the demands of a marital bedroom" (281). In Ghosh's reconstruction of the medieval Indian Ocean world, languages and cultures stretch and adapt themselves to differences that repeatedly come together.

This idyll of transoceanic contact comes to a violent end through the incursions of Portuguese ships and cannon at the end of the fifteenth century. The European celebration of contact and conquest appears in the epic verses of Camões. Ghosh's postcolonial inversion of Camões's early modern celebration, however, is worth quoting to rebut preemptively the early modern poet's idealism. Ghosh's historical narrative is harsher and more accurate:

> Unable to compete in the Indian Ocean trade by purely commercial means, the Europeans were bent on taking control of it by aggression,

> pure and distilled, by unleashing violence on a scale unprecedented on those shores.
>
> (288)

In Ghosh's telling, European violence shattered the relative comity of the Indian Ocean world. In a more recent book, *The Nutmeg's Curse* (2021), Ghosh further suggests that the twenty-first century's environmental crises represent "the globalization of the ecological transformations that were set in motion by the European colonization of much of the world."[12] Today's reaping of what was sown during early modern globalization follows a stark historical pattern. The networks of the Indian Ocean, while not quite as vulnerable to European pathogens as the populations of the Americas and Australia, would prove equally unable to resist the destructive encroachment from mostly European navies traveling across Atlantic, Indian, and Pacific routes.

Luis Vaz de Camões's *The Lusíads:* A Navigational Epic

The narrative poem *The Lusíads* retells the history of the Portuguese nation in an epic that echoes and overgoes Homer and Virgil. Mimicking Homer's structure, the story of the nation appears in the hero's narration of his own history to an idealized audience. In Homer, the site of that retelling is the magical island of Scheria, also called Phaeacia, the last stop on Odysseus's travels before Ithaca and a land whose peaceful inhabitants lack Odysseus's skill in warfare.[13] In place of this utopian island, Camões transforms good King Alcinous of Scheria into the Muslim Sultan of Melinde on the east coast of Africa near modern Kenya. Just as Odysseus receives support from Alcinous as well as a new ship for his final crossing to Ithaca, so da Gama and his men receive sailing directions to cross the Indian Ocean from the sultan. The differences between Odysseus and da Gama in these parallel episodes are instructive. Odysseus arrives alone, half-drowned, and the help he requires includes clothing, a ship, and kingly treasure. Da Gama arrives with an intact fleet, and he requires directions to sail across an ocean that was unknown to him. What in Homer were material gifts become in Camões a navigational key, inviting the Portuguese into the known world of the Indian ocean monsoon.

The fulcrum around which the epic voyage turns is the unnamed figure of the Muslim pilot who guides the Portuguese fleet from Africa to India. This episode, which appears in Canto *Lusíads* 6, tends to be overlooked by commentators. For many readers of Camões, the crucial episodes include the giant Adamastor, a physical representation of the Cape of Good Hope (Canto 5), the anti-maritime curse of the Old Man of Belem (Canto 4), and the erotic fantasy of the Isle of Love (Cantos 9–10) from a promontory on which the sea nymph Tethys shows da Gama "the great machine of the universe" (10.80.1).[14] Compared with these high-drama moments, the pilot's presence in Canto 6 seems somewhat unremarkable. Livelier supernatural action in Canto 6 includes a storm raised by Bacchus, the bête noire of the Portuguese fleet. Concealing a multicultural alliance between the African Muslim pilot and the European Christian fleet beneath feuding classical deities and da Gama's Christian prayers suggests that the route to the East requires a carefully managed multiplicity of peoples, religions, and supernatural powers. This human and more-than-human plurality shows how the Indian Ocean world shapes and is shaped by human and nonhuman histories.

Although the African pilot is the essential guide to the Portuguese fleet, the character appears only three times in Canto 6. These three textual references, however, demonstrate that this nameless figure's expertise enables the voyage. For a time, historians assumed that the historical da Gama's pilot was Ahmad Ibn Majid, the famous Arab navigator, but he appears to have retired in 1465, decades before the Portuguese fleet arrived in Malinde. The canto that floats the European fleet across the Indian Ocean opens with a contrast between the Sultan of Malinde's desire to "entertain the brave mariners" (6.1.2) and the Portuguese captain's desire to depart, "aware he was lingering/too long" (6.3.1–2). The first reference to African navigators connects their services to the stores needed for the voyage; the ships are "supplied with pilots/And fresh provisions from the land" (6.3.3–4). Another reference assures the trustworthiness of these sailing experts: "In his new pilot there was no deceit" (6.5.5). After these cursory references, the pilot does not appear again until the end of the canto, when "cheerfully said their Malindian pilot/'That land ahead is surely Calicut'" (6.92.7–8). Only when the fleet has arrived, and the pilot's expertise is no longer needed, does the poem announce his African origins. To emphasize the epic qualities of the Portuguese heroes, Camões minimizes their dependence on the existing human and oceanic networks of the Indian Ocean.

The center of Canto 6 allegorizes the dangers of alien seas through the hostility of classical gods. Roused by Bacchus, who has long hated the Portuguese, the sea gods assemble on the bottom of the ocean to plot a supernatural blocking storm. In "undiscovered depths" (6.9.1), Bacchus implores the maritime deities to assail the Lusitanian heroes. A noteworthy descriptive passage shows the multiple ways that water functions in Neptune's kingdom:

> And the bright form was also carved
> Of Water, dividing the continents,
> Propagating fish of every species,
> While by moisture flesh prospers and increases.
> *(6.12.5–8)*

The undersea palace combines different phases and forms of water. The salt seas separate the continents, including the relatively unknown (to Europeans) lands of east Africa and southern Asia. These waters teem with alien kinds of fish, but they also support the life of "flesh," including humans, whose bodies prosper because of fresh drinking water and bodily moisture.

Like many poetic epics in early modern Europe, including Ludovico Ariosto's *Orlando Furioso*, Torquato Tasso's *Jerusalem Delivered*, Edmund Spenser's *Faerie Queene*, and John Milton's *Paradise Lost*, Camões's poem balances its debts to classical literary forms against a Christian superstructure. Bacchus and the sea gods represent a lingering threat of non-Christian forces, though the only Muslim figure on the voyage is the friendly pilot. The sea gods strike the fleet with "a sudden, almighty tempest" (6.71.2), in language that Camões adapts closely from Ovid's *Metamorphoses*.[15] Against the storm the Portuguese sailors respond with maritime labor, striking sails and manning the pumps, but a desperate da Gama believes that only the "Divine guardian, merciful providence" (6.81.1) can preserve them. The saving force, however, is not the Christian God but da Gama's patron Venus, who with her nymphs seduces the winds into calm (6.88–91). The heroism of the Portuguese mariners thus does not represent a full synthesis of Christian and classical models, as might be the case in Spenser, nor a strict hierarchy in which Christian values dominate, as in Milton. In Camões, Venus allies herself with the mostly hidden expertise of a Muslim pilot to guide the European heroes to their predestined goal. This epic mixes classical, historical, and geographic systems together to reimagine da Gama's historical voyage in multicultural context.

The storm that threatens the Portuguese fleet also fuels their speedy passage. "This is the land you have been seeking," says the Malindean pilot, "This is India rising before you;/. . . . /Your long task is accomplished" (6.93.1–2, 4). A slight navigational irony subtends this episode, in which Bacchus's hostility encourages the sea gods to raise a storm that ends up driving the fleet the way they always intended to go. Camões, himself an experienced Asian traveler, dramatizes the monsoon itself, the powerful winds that controlled all maritime voyages across the Indian Ocean. While it is typical of classical and early modern epic to have a hero's wanderings ultimately caused by divine forces, as Odysseus is beset by Poseidon and Aeneas by Juno, in da Gama's more historical epic, the storm-raising powers of Neptune and his undersea deities resolve into the material forces of the global ocean-system. In fact, if Venus and her nymphs represent calm weather after the monsoon, both the opposing and supporting figures from classical myth represent geophysical features of the Indian Ocean. In this most structured of oceanic spaces, the hostility that defines the epic hero's experience of the storm becomes assimilated into a knowable system of navigable monsoon winds. To be an Indian Ocean sailor, more than a sailor on the Atlantic or even the Mediterranean, requires knowing and exploiting complex patterns. Or, perhaps, it requires enlisting the aid of experts from African allies.

The Isle of Love: Indian Ocean as Colonialist Fantasy

European colonial expansion into the Indian and Pacific Oceans has always included an unhealthy dose of sexual fantasy and exploitation. From the sex tourism that in the early twenty-first century still imposes itself on local populations from Thailand to Sri Lanka to the brutal sexual politics of the British Raj and Dutch East India Company settlements, European men preyed upon non-European women throughout, and beyond, the colonial era. The culminating episode of *The Lusíads*, in which da Gama and his sailors are entertained by nymphs on the Isle of Love (Cantos 9–10), presents an early modern version of the tropical island fantasy that still motivates the tourist industry. A fantasy island populated by beautiful and loving women has long enticed travelers, including soldiers and sailors, who are far from home. In Camões's mythologized version, the Isle of Love represents a reward for the world-transforming Portuguese fleet. From a wider historical view, this episode epitomizes the eroticized violence of global oceanic colonialism.

The Portuguese fleet encounters the Isle of Love on its return voyage, riding the southwesterly monsoon back toward the Cape of Good Hope. During the journey, Venus reveals that her plan all along has been to hybridize and make oceanic the Portuguese nation. "I wish to populate Neptune's realm," she announces, "with the strong and beautiful" (9.42.1–2). The goddess's procreative focus frames the fleet's landfall on the magic isle in explicitly sexual terms. The island itself, with its anticipations of such *loci amoeni* of early modern verse epic as Spenser's Garden of Adonis and Milton's Eden, eroticizes the relationship between humans and land: "The lovely, verdant island hovered/As Venus wafted it over the waves" (9.52.1–2). The description of the island both dramatizes the way sailors sight distant landfalls at sea and gestures toward an amalgamation of stable land and dynamic ocean. As one of the Portuguese mariners who arrives to find the island populated with beautiful nymphs describes it, "Wonders exist, and marvels are apparent,/Though the world hides this from the ignorant" (9.69.7–8). The Isle of Love combines the magic of the goddess with a sense that only long-haul sailors like da Gama and his men can encounter true knowledge of the sea. The men's reward is fantasy sex, though Venus also has longer term imperial and colonial plans.

That the island's erotic vision also includes conquest and political dominion becomes clear in the coupling of da Gama with the sea-goddess Tethys. In a passage that reaches back to and inverts the endless longing for Tethys of the Titan Adamastor, whose massive body allegorizes the Cape of Good Hope (5.50–59), the sea-goddess gives herself to the captain.[16] Notably, the choice appears to be the goddess's: "Tethys herself, the greatest among them,/. . . . /Took, as he deserved, the captain" (9.85, 1, 6). But the poem emphasizes less the erotic delights of the union than its political promise. Tethys reveals to the Portuguese captain "through prophecy/The still-unmapped continents,/The oceans as yet unsailed,/All bound together in this earthly sphere,/Which Portugal alone deserved to hear" (9/86.5–8). Camões himself sailed to southeast Asia and India between 1553 and 1570, including an infamous, and possibly legendary, shipwreck on the Mekong River, from which the poet supposedly saved only the manuscript-in-progress of *The Lusíads.*[17] The emphasis in Tethys's promise on the "unmapped" and "unsailed" world ocean is, of course, a Eurocentric vision, but by the time the poem was written in the second half of the sixteenth century, quite a few Europeans, including the poet, had sailed Indian and Pacific waters. The close connection between tropical islands, sexual desire, and political conquest that these lines weave, however, would continue to define Europe's violent encounters with the cultures and navigational systems of the Indian Ocean world.

The poet's vision of a Portuguese maritime empire does not end in the waves or beaches of the Isle of Love. Rather, the poem's final canto presents another history lesson from Tethys to da Gama, culminating with the revelation of "the great machine of the universe" (10.80.1), a system that unifies classical and Christian myth as well as the imputed relations between "Christian Europe" (10.92.1), "Africa" (10.92.3), and other parts of the world. Camões's mythmaking constructs a geographical and cultural route that links ocean-facing Portugal to the riches of the East. In addition, the poet imagines a universal hierarchy in which all peoples and places become legible within a comprehensive system. In these stanzas, the poet carefully distinguishes between the epic destiny of the nation, which Camões by the 1570s may well have realized might slip out of Portugal's grasp, and the individual suffering of the poet. Josiah Blackmore has observed that in Camões's ironic vision, shipwreck occupies the same poetic space as empire, "so there is no cause and effect between the two: empire exists alongside shipwreck, alongside its own undoing."[18] In an invocation of himself as author, Camões describes his poem as "these Cantos, snatched/Soaking from sad, wretched shipwreck" (10.128.2–3) and himself as a servant of the crown, "Whose lyre, played with such sweet dexterity,/Will bring him fame, but not prosperity" (10.128–7–8). The bifurcation between suffering poet and triumphant crown barely conceals the anxieties that the courtier has about the future of his nation. Portugal has opened a door onto the wealth and human complexities of the Indian Ocean world, but even its national poet cannot quite believe that its dominion will last. From a longer historical perspective, in fact, what seems most notable about the purported discovery of Indian Ocean networks by da Gama's fleet is less the prospect of conquest than the human and mercantile complexity already in place.

Oceanic Community in "The Grand Armada"

In the voyage of the *Pequod,* the hinge between the Indian Ocean and Ishmael's beloved Pacific, where Moby Dick will at length be encountered and harpooned, appears in a strangely visionary episode in which the whaleship passes through the Sunda Strait, a narrow body of water between Java and Sumatra. In moving through this geographic constriction to seek the White Whale's home waters in the Sea of Japan, the whaleship passes through a narrow path filled with mother whales and calves. Melville, who is seldom shy about his metaphors, emphasizes the gender symbolism in which the *Pequod*, hurling harpoons and lances on all sides, forces its violent way through a narrow gestational space. But the vision of the Armada itself, a gathering of mostly female and infant whales, represents one of the few moments in this oceanic novel's near-circumnavigation in which the whalemen encounter recognizable feminine forces. In the fantasy waters of "young Leviathan amours in the deep" (301), Ahab's crew glimpses maternal power, eroticism, and community. Like the final sojourn of the Portuguese mariners on the Isle of Love, the intrusion of eroticism into a narrative of masculine violence represents one cruel way that Europeans understood the native populations of the Indian Ocean. Whales and women, nymphs and hosts, the inhabitants of this human ocean get constructed as welcoming. The sailors on the *Pequod*, however, even more explicitly than da Gama and his fleet, come bearing barbs.

The description of calves and mother whales provides an intrusion of feminine utopia in Melville's obsessively masculine novel about hunting and queer connections. "But far beneath this wondrous world upon the surface," Ishmael observes as the ship moves into the straits, "another and still stranger world met our eyes as we gazed over the side" (302). The intricate network of calves and mothers, sometimes still connected by "long coils of the umbilical cord of Madame Leviathan" (303), revealed to the violent hunters "the subtlest secrets of the sea . . . in this enchanted world" (303). Newly born whales appear attractively human: "The delicate side-fins, and the palms of his flukes, still freshly retained the plaited crumpled appearance of a baby's ears newly arrived from foreign parts" (303). The hunters stare blindly down into the "exceedingly transparent" (303) waters, as if seeing in this female community something they have themselves lost. The chapter has reminded its readers a few pages earlier that whaleships, since they carry no cargo except oil from whales they kill, pack enough food and water that they do not need to touch land at all during years-long voyages. Ishmael exaggerates, minimizing the risk of scurvy to make a symbolic point about the male hunters' community being sufficient unto itself.[19]

In a pool of maternal love, Ishmael allegorizes, as he likes to do. He sees in the fecund waters a vision that we might describe as an Indian Ocean fantasy, comparable with the frolic of the Portuguese mariners on the Isle of Love. This world is welcoming, supportive, nurturing, and erotic:

> And thus, though surrounded by circle upon circle of consternations and affrights, did these inscrutable creatures at the centre freely and fearlessly indulge in all peaceful concernments; yea, serenely revelled in dalliance and delight.
>
> (303)

The Indian Ocean, which the *Pequod* is in the process of leaving in this chapter, represents a human ocean, with human pleasures and desires, even if in Melville's novel those pleasures are felt by whales. The actual humans in this episode, notably, perform a flurry of violence, trying to stick as many whales as they can, though in the end they are mostly unable to land their prey. Only Ishmael, though he gamely pulls his bow oar, connects fully to the undersea beauty. He rhapsodizes:

> But even so, amid the tornadoed Atlantic of my being, do I myself still for ever centrally disport in mute calm: and while ponderous planets of unwaning woe revolve around me, deep down and deep inland there I still bathe me in eternal mildness of joy.
>
> (303)

Perhaps because Ishmael operates on the margins of the hunt—he raises no whales from the masthead, casts neither harpoons nor lances, and in the final chase of the White Whale gets thrown overboard and left behind—he sees an undersea island of peace. But his collaboration with Ahab's murderous crew, like the violent and racist fantasies that subtend da Gama's sojourn on the Isle of Love, exile the whaleman from this more-than-human ocean community.

Human Oceans and the "Sea of Stories"

In the years immediately following the fatwa issued by Iran's Ayatollah Khomeini in February 1989, Salman Rushdie lived in hiding. The next novel that he published was a children's tale, *Haroun and the Sea of Stories* (1990), dedicated to his son, Zafar. Like most of Rushdie's novels, the tale circles around global Indian diasporic communities, in this case displaced onto imaginary locations such as Alifbay, "a city so ruinously sad that it had forgotten its name."[20] Amid the glorious busyness of the story sits what I take to be Rushdie's most direct symbolic portrait of the Indian Ocean world and its human and narrative complexities. The Ocean of the Streams of Story represents the core source of narrative invention, the mixing of human and nonhuman stories into glorious hybridity. The description of these waters is worth quoting in full, since it represents in symbolic terms the narrative interrelationships that comprise the cultures of the Indian Ocean world:

> He looked into the water and saw that it was made up of a thousand thousand thousand and one different currents, each one a different colour, weaving in and out of one another like a liquid tapestry of breathtaking complexity, and Iff [one of Haroun's guides] explained that these were the Streams of Story, that each coloured strand represented and contained a single tale. Different parts of the Ocean contained different sorts of stories, and also all the stories that had ever been told and many that were still in the process of being invented could be found there,

> the Ocean of the Streams of Story was in fact the biggest library in the universe. And because the stories were held here in fluid form, they retained the ability to change, to become new versions of themselves, to join up with other stories and so become yet other stories; so that unlike a library of books, the Ocean of the Streams of Story was much more than a storeroom of yarns. It was not dead but alive.
>
> (71–72)

Rushdie's idealized polyglot narrative universe assumes the form of an Ocean because oceans are the biggest and most flexible objects on the surface of our planet. The way that ocean currents and mixtures become, in Rushdie's allegory, representations that maximize both difference and connection emerges from long-held ideas about oceans as both barriers and pathways. Rushdie's agglomeration of all stories into a dynamic order of exchange and interpenetration may in some ways oppose Camões's imperial hierarchy and Melville's violent imposition of the order of an American whaleship. But for all these writers, among many others, oceans as such, and the Indian Ocean in particular, capture ways to unite differences without flattening them into sameness.

The great challenge of any fully diversified sea of stories, as readers of Rushdie well know, is comprehension. How can we extract from the network of story streams the exact tale that we need—in Haroun's case, the story that will reunite his mother and father? Since *Haroun and the Sea of Stories* is a fairy tale, the wished-for ending comes true, as rarely happens in Rushdie's allegories of tragic history, from *Midnight's Children* (1981) through *Quichotte* (2019). The structure of Rushdie's happy ending in *Haroun* calls attention to the mechanical nature of the process. A character called the Walrus, whose name of course comes from the Beatles' song, explains to Haroun, "It is precisely because happy ends are so rare" in the world of history that "we . . . have learnt how to synthesize them artificially. In plain language: *we make them up*" (201, emphasis in original). Rushdie is joking and, to some extent, hand-waving his way past the tragic history of Kashmir, the geographic region that shadows the fanciful geography of the novel. But the optimism of this statement suggests how literary fictions can press back against the brute facts of history. The Ocean of the Stream of Stories represents, for Rushdie, a nearly infinite reservoir of possible endings, happy and sad. The process of fictionalizing—of making things up—resembles a form of navigation, choosing paths through dynamic and unknowable seas. That vision of making order represents an essential project of the literary blue humanities, in and beyond the Indian Ocean basin.

Hydrocolonialism at the Dock

Utopian visions and happy endings seldom correspond to the lived experiences of the generations of humans who have lived, sailed, and struggled on or near the Indian Ocean. A book by the South African scholar Isabel Hofmeyer, *Dockside Reading* (2022), theorizes the ways in which the processes through which maritime goods are registered and shipped can provide insight into the networks that shape communities across the Indian Ocean. She emphasises the physical entanglements of objects in densely bureaucratic processes such as copyright and censorship across Indian Ocean spaces. These processes generate two essential ideas, which she calls "the colonization of water and the creolization of water."[21] Both concepts advance the larger project Hofmeyr names "hydrocolonialism," which brings water into the larger discourses of colonial and postcolonial studies, with special attention to the Indian Ocean world.

The notion of "colonized water" operates through the tension between the desire of imperial centers to control their peripheries and the dynamism and instability of watery environments. Hofmeyr cites Siobhan Carrol's work on remote air, water, and ice as challenges to ideas of empire, because these spaces "could not be settled or occupied" (21).[22] The physical structures of port cities struggled against the alien nature of watery space. Hofmeyr notes that South African ports were constructed through "land [being] extended into the sea, either literally through reclamation and submarine infrastructure or by the extension of land-based methods of governance over the ocean" (21). In a conceptual sense, she notes that "port engineering" functions as an "antidote to shipwreck" (21), creating "a founding mythology of port cities themselves" (22). Ports and their mechanisms serve as drying machines, restructuring the dynamic sea as a space of government, order, and human control.

The ideology of centralized rule and terrestrial order never perfectly organizes the port towns of the periphery. The countervailing pressure of unstable water on landed polities appears in Hofmeyr's concept of "creolized water," which includes the incursion of elements of the sea onto the land. These intrusions include physical objects, such as "shipwrecks, collapsed infrastructure, and detritus dumped by ships and port workers" (22). Taking the Southern African port of Durban on the Indian Ocean as her case study, Hofmeyr argues that the port's complex physical and cultural mixtures construct "water itself as cosmopolitan or creolized, containing both the material and imaginative remains of different communities across the port city" (23). She connects this principle of creolization to scholarship on the Black Atlantic and the Caribbean, including work by Christina Sharpe on the legacy of the Middle Passage and the underwater fantasies of Black survival constructed through the music of Drexciya (23).[23] In an "enlarged realm" (23) that includes cultural ancestors from Africa, Asia, and Europe, she interprets Durban's waterfronts through the complex intermingling of the Indian Ocean's global cultures.

Hofmeyr's hydrocolonialist scholarship contests the collectivizing impulses of European figures such as Camões. In the early modern poetic epic, the only possible response to geographic and cultural diversity was the construction of hierarchies, especially religious and racial. Reading *The Lusíads* in the twenty-first century, however, after the dissolution of European maritime empires, exposes the interdependencies and mutual aid the Portuguese fleet receives from peoples and forces outside the imperial center. Da Gama and his mariners need the expertise of the Africa pilot, and through that pilot's knowledge they learn to employ the seasonal monsoon that had been powering intra-Indian Ocean trade for millennia. This moment of collaboration between the peoples and knowledges would lead to horrifying violence as European weapons of war disrupted existing networks. Hofmeyr's postcolonial alliances and entanglements inverts Camonian empire. She rejects the religious and racial hierarchies that animate Camões, but her insight into the interpenetration of cultures and objects constructs an Indian Ocean world that seems structurally related to the underlying truths of that earlier moment of multicultural encounters. The Indian Ocean may not boast the most ancient epic of large-scale maritime migration, which consists of the stories of Oceania and the Pacific, but its millennia-long history of trade and contacts contrasts sharply with the Atlantic, which was only intermittently spanned before the fifteenth century. Future scholarship on connections and conflicts across the Indian Ocean may serve to displace and reorient overly Atlantic-fixated understandings of oceanic history.

Notes

1 The term "Columbian Exchange" was coined by the biologist Alfred Crosby in 1972. On its relationship with early modern globalization, see Steve Mentz, "Wet Globalization: The Early Modern Ocean as World-System," *A Cultural History of the Sea in the Early Modern Age*, Steve Mentz, ed. (London: Bloomsbury, 2021), 1–23.
2 On an earlier phase of globalization around 1000 CE, see Valerie Hansen, *The Year 1000: When Explorers Connected the World—and Globalization Began* (New York: Scribner, 2020).
3 Stephen C. Jett, *Ancient Ocean Crossings: Reconsidering the Case for Contacts with the Pre-Columbian Americas* (Tuscaloosa: University of Alabama Press, 2017), 7.
4 Michael Pearson, *The Indian Ocean* (London: Routledge, 2003), 3.
5 David Abulafia, *The Boundless Sea: A Human History of the Oceans* (Oxford: Oxford University Press, 2019), 43–296. See also Lincoln Paine, *The Sea & Civilization: A Maritime History of the World* (New York: Vintage Books, 2013), esp. 137–66.
6 James C. Scott, *Against the Grain: A Deep History of the Earliest States* (New Haven: Yale University Press, 2017), esp. 116–49.
7 David Graeber and David Wengrow, *The Dawn of Everything: A New History of Humanity* (New York: Farrar, Straus and Giroux, 2021).
8 Giulio Boccaletti, *Water: A Biography* (New York: Pantheon, 2021).
9 For a survey of contemporary postcolonial ocean literature in global context, see Kritish Rajbhandari, "Postcolonial Fiction, Oceans, and Seas," *Oxford Research Encyclopedias, Literature*, published online July 2022. https://doi.org/10.1093/acrefore/9780190201098.013.1376. Accessed 14 September 2022.
10 Amitav Ghosh, *In an Antique Land* (New York: Vintage, 1994).
11 For Ghosh's scholarly research about Bomma, the facts of which inform *In an Antique Land*, see "The Slave of MS H.6," *CSSSC Occasional Papers* No. 125 (Calcutta 1990), published by the Centre for Studies in Social Sciences, Calcutta.

12 Amitav Ghosh, *The Nutmeg's Curse: Parables for a Planet in Crisis* (Chicago: University of Chicago Press, 2021), 167.
13 Possible geographic matches for Scheria include Corfu and Minoan Crete, though some ancient and modern interpreters, including Strabo, place the island out in the Atlantic.
14 Luis vaz de Camões, *The Lusíads*, Landeg White, trans. (Oxford: Oxford University Press, 1997), 213.
15 The passage in Ovid is *Metamorphoses* 11.475–543, describing the shipwreck of Ceyx.
16 On Adamastor as symbol of global oceanic expansion in the early modern period, see Steve Mentz, *Ocean* (London: Bloomsbury, 2020), 43–52.
17 On the importance of shipwreck to Camões's poetic and political vision, see Josiah Blackmore, *Manifest Perdition: Shipwreck Narrative and the Disruption of Empire* (Minneapolis: University of Minnesota Press, 2002).
18 Blackmore, *Manifest Perdition*, xix.
19 On the cultural history of scurvy, including references to *Moby-Dick*, see Jonathan Lamb, *Scurvy: The Disease of Discovery* (Princeton: Princeton University Press, 2017).
20 Salman Rushdie, *Haroun and the Sea of Stories* (New York: Grant Books, 1990), 15.
21 Isabel Hofmeyr, *Dockside Reading: Hydrocolonialism and the Custom House* (Durham: Duke University Press, 2022), 21.
22 She cites Siobahn Carroll, *An Empire of Air and Water: Uncolonizable Space in the British Imagination, 1750–1850* (Philadelphia: University of Pennsylvania Press, 2015).
23 On Drexciya and its artistic legacy, see chapter 5.

6 Surrounded by Land

Mediterranean Examples

In *The Boundless Sea* (2019), his massive history of all the world's oceans, the distinguished Oxford historian of the Mediterranean David Abulafia describes the Indian Ocean as being a "middle ocean" that resembles the landlocked Mediterranean on a larger scale. Exploring the coastal fringes and trading networks that define the Indian Ocean world, Abulafia suggests that many historians have characterized "the Indian Ocean as a sort of Mediterranean, a sea defined by its edges, even if there is no southern edge" (46). Moving from the massive scale of the Indian Ocean, roughly 27 million square miles or more than 70 million square kilometers, to the smaller Mediterranean, which spans just under one million square miles or 2.5 million square kilometers, requires a narrower focus. In Western scholarship, however, the Mediterranean has always had an outsized place. Home to classical Greek culture, the Roman Empire, and religious centers from Rome to Jerusalem to Mecca, the Mediterranean represents many different cultural sources and origins. The maritime habits and structures that developed in this smaller basin would be exported during Europe's early modern surge of colonialism and imperial expansion. For environmental historians, also, the pioneering example of Fernand Braudel's *Mediterranean and the Mediterranean World in the Age of Philip II*, first published in French in 1949, looms large. An influential example of what would become known as the *Annales School* of historiography, Braudel's attention to the *long durée* and to how environmental forces and structures shape human history remains influential in many discourses of environmental history. Although recent scholars have updated and contested Braudel's comprehensive vision, his efforts to bring human history in contact with nonhuman forces such as geography, weather, and nonhuman time scales remains noteworthy.

The physical property of "connectivity" epitomizes the Mediterranean in this chapter because of the long history of physical and cultural movements along and across this body of water. To some extent, connectivity defines all watery bodies, from vast oceans and large rivers to streams and lakes. Mediterranean connectivity distinguishes itself in two ways. This small sea is arguably more culturally diverse and closely connected than larger oceans. The sea sits astride the continents of Africa, Europe, and Asia, and

DOI: 10.4324/9781003166665-6

the region has been the cradle of many civilizations, from Greece, Rome, and the Ottoman Empire to Judaism, Christianity, and Islam. Second, the sea's modest size enables this region to function as a microcosm, and in fact the idea of "a Mediterranean" has become, as Abulafia notes, an exportable scheme among global historians.[1] In using the lattice of connectivity as my key physical property of water in this chapter, I aim to treat the Mediterranean Sea as an exemplary case of a more general aquatic phenomenon, as ocean currents have an exemplary function in the chapter on the Southern Ocean and the monsoon for the Indian Ocean. This chapter's freshwater geography emphasizes the crucial role of lakes and springs in supporting human habitations along the Med's mostly arid coastline. The circulating logic of the region operates through the intersection of rapid movement facilitated by sea travel and the constraining presence of fresh water in only certain places. The historical picture that emerges will resist any comprehensive summary, and I am conscious that my analysis here, which draws in large part from the Western classical tradition that began with Homer, does scant justice to Muslim, Jewish, and other traditions. My hope is that the mechanisms I explore about connectivity, relationships between fresh water and salt water, and human actors as builders, sailors, swimmers, and soldiers may prove exportable to areas beyond my expertise.

Connectivity and the Med-System

In Peregrine Horden and Nicholas Purcell's *Corrupting Sea* (2000), perhaps the most significant single volume written on Mediterranean history since Braudel, the watchwords for the region are "microecology" and "connectivity."[2] These scholars argue that it is only possible "under the sign of the microecology . . . to elaborate a conception of how Mediterranean unity has actually worked" (2). They oppose their system of contrasting but connected microregions to Braudel's simpler and more comprehensive "man and environment" structure (2). In a detailed analysis of "the intricate local patterns throughout the dispersed hinterlands of Mediterranean settlements" (123–72), Hordern and Purcell find "continuities of structure" (464) rather than homogeneity. In their reading, "all is mutability—to a degree that is distinctive, and also that is evident right across the 'pre-modern' centuries" (464). Complexity and connections across differences are the guiding principles in their revitalization of the environmental history of the Mediterranean.

A more lyrical if fundamentally sympathetic conception of the region as defined by connections and differences appears in Predrag Matvejevic's philological memoir *Mediterranean: A Cultural Landscape* (1999). For Matvejevic, the distinguishing characteristic of this region is its multiplicity of both humans and objects:

> The Mediterranean shores have seen not only the silk route but also the crisscrossing of many others: routes of salt and spices, amber and

> ornaments, oils and perfumes, tools and arms, skills and knowledge, arts and sciences. Hellenic emporia were markets and embassies; Roman roads spread power and civilization; Asian soil provided prophets and religions. Europe was conceived in the Mediterranean.
>
> (10)[3]

Although Matvejevic's refrain in this passage leans toward Eurocentrism, his deep familiarity with both eastern and western Mediterranean waters emerges in the lyrical abundance of his prose. "The Mediterranean," he suggests, "is not merely geography" (8). The primary representational modes he explores include abundant reproductions from ancient and modern maps, as well as close attention to sailing routes and languages. There is, he notes, "a long line of links between sailing and writing" (57). To follow his descriptions entails committing to a kind of verbal sea route, crossing from port to port. Considering the growth of world powers beyond the Inner Sea leads him to the melancholy conclusion that the "Mediterranean has maintained its primacy in words, but lost it in everything else" (92). For Matvejevic, the poetic origins of the region sing through the *Iliad*, the *Odyssey*, and Xenophon's *Anabasis*, and he also awaits "a new [poetic] masterpiece dealing with man and the sea" (93). His Mediterranean is literary and melancholy, "acquired not inherited . . . a decision, not a privilege" (93). To claim membership to this geographic community requires repeated acts of transit and poetic invocations. As Claudio Magris notes in his introduction to Matvejevic's idiosyncratic book, the modern author follows his ancient models in partaking of both history and fiction. Mediterranean culture, in Matvejevic's imaginative narration and in Horden and Purcell's analytical eco-history, spills into plural, concentrated forms.

"Loomings" and the View on the Surface

"Meditation and water are wedded for-ever" (19), intones the narrator in the opening chapter of *Moby-Dick*. Except for the opening invitation to "Call me Ishmael," this connection between thought and water may be the novel's most oft-quoted line. In connecting this early pronouncement to the narrow seas of the Mediterranean rather than the global "wonder-world" (22) onto which the *Pequod* will sail, I suggest that the story of Ishmael's "transition . . . from a schoolmaster to a sailor" (20) begins by way of the classical sea. The opening chapter, "Loomings," provides a range of geographic references, mostly from the northeastern United States, from the Saco River to Niagara Falls to Rockaway Beach. The core mystery of the sea as Ishmael presents it, however, emerges from Greek literature, especially the story of Narcissus. In retrospect, the narrator's summary of the myth anticipates the entire tragic course of his doomed quest:

> And still deeper [is] the meaning of that story of Narcissus, who because he could not grasp the tormenting, mild image he saw in the fountain,

> plunged into it and was drowned. But that same image, we ourselves see in all rivers and all oceans. It is the image of the ungraspable phantom of life, and this is the key to it all.
>
> (20)

An anticipation of Ahab's final plunge emerges from the conceit that what humans want from water is a graspable reflection. Water produces a vision of the self, and for such figures as Narcissus and Ahab that near recognition is fatal. For Ishmael, however, the same image lures him in, but not to drown. To approach the phantom, but not grasp it, defines the narrator's quest. He follows Ahab's hunt, but he seeks something quite different.

Ishmael will, as he learns to find honor and glory in whaling, come to adopt the Pacific as his spiritual ocean. But Melville starts his ex-schoolteacher in two very different symbolic watery bodies: with Narcissus in the streams and fountains of Greece, and on the oceanic verge of New York City. Ishmael merges with the crowds at the Battery, for whom "nothing will content them but the extremest limit of the land" (19). As a response to "hypos" and the "damp, drizzly November in my soul," proximity to the water provides a working "substitute for pistol and ball" (18). By suggesting that the water in "Loomings" begins in the Greek Mediterranean before expanding around the watery globe, I imply that *Moby-Dick* initially takes a schoolteacher's attitude toward the cultural history of water. The story begins at the busiest port of the largest city in the nineteenth-century United States, New York City. It also begins with the primal interaction between Narcissus, his reflection, and water's reflective surface. These water-spaces enjoin Ishmael to transform himself from teacher to sailor and from observer to maritime hero. *Moby-Dick* spins a global oceanic story, and so it cannot be the Mediterranean literary "masterpiece" for which Matvejevic pines. But before meeting either Queequeg or the *Pequod*, Ishmael's eyes appear focused on Mediterranean waters and Mediterranean ideas.

Odysseus the Builder

Homer's *Odyssey* occupies the center of the Mediterranean literary tradition. One of the oldest and most-imitated stories in Western literature, the *Odyssey* tells the story of a man skilled in sea travel, violence, and, significantly, building maritime tools. In fact, much of maritime fiction distinguishes itself through its detailed focus on technology, from the obsessive descriptions of the trying-out of whale blubber in *Moby-Dick* to the complex vocabularies of lines and rigging in sea fiction from Joseph Conrad to Patrick O'Brian. The English word "technology," Margaret Cohen has observed, seems to have first appeared in English in a prefatory sonnet to John Smith's book *Sea-Grammar* (1627).[4] As terrestrial mammals, for us to survive and transport ourselves over water, we need to be builders. The skills of Odysseus as fighter, sailor, trickster, and teller of tall tales are familiar to most readers. A closer look at his skills as a craftsman of maritime tools will repay analysis.

Odysseus's first action in Homer's epic is building a boat. When the hero makes his delayed appearance in Book 5, the process, as described in Homer's verse, is painstaking and technical:

> With his bronze axe he cut down twenty trunks,
> polished them skillfully and planed them straight.
> Calypso brought a gimlet and he drilled
> through every plank and fitted them together,
> fixating it firm with pegs and fastenings.[5]
>
> *(5.144–48)*

The hero's first physical actions involve tools: axes, pegs, fastenings, a drill. Odysseus has many skills, including warfare, navigation, and storytelling, but building occupies a special place in the epic as a marker of civilization.[6] In order to return to the human world of Ithaca, the hero must construct his own maritime transportation.

A moment near the end of the epic further reinforces the hero's intimate connection to water-going tools. After reconciling with his wife, Penelope, Odysseus reveals what the prophet Tiresias has said about the day of the hero's death. The mariner's final adventure will take him far from the sea:

> Tiresias foretold that I must travel
> through many cities carrying an oar,
> til I reach men that do not know the sea . . .
> He said that I
> will know I have arrived when I encounter
> someone who calls the object on my back
> a winnowing fan.
>
> *(23.267–69, 272–75)*

This episode identifies the hero with the tools of his sea wanderings and connects death itself to the exhaustion of maritime mobility. Even in his last dry adventure, Odysseus remains marked by ocean. Immediately preceding this moment, the hero has proved his identity to Penelope by recounting the story of having fashioned their marriage bed by hand out of a single living olive tree (23.183–205). After this emphasis on domestic and inland technology, the invocation of the oar as winnowing fan appears designed to reconnect the wandering hero, home at last, with seafaring technology. The man of twists and turns has many skills, but first and last, from his escape from Calypso's island to his final journey, he builds crafts that traverse watery spaces.

Gun Island and the Multispecies Med

In his novel *Gun Island* (2019), Amitav Ghosh also stages a Mediterranean crossing, in this case on a boat filled with Bangladeshi refugees attempting to enter the European Union via Italy. In a climactic scene that recalls the "magic realism" of writers such as Gabriel García Márquez and Salman Rushdie, the refugee ship arrives with a multispecies honor guard of birds, dolphins, and whales. Ghosh had previously written, in *The Great Derangement* (2016), that the fundamental failure of the modern literary novel in the West has been its exclusion of the nonhuman, including above all the increasingly dominant reality of climate disruption. He notes that the "irony of the 'realist' novel' [is that] the very gestures with which it conjures up reality are actually a concealment of the real."[7] The literary novel, like the modern West, remains stuck, in Ghosh's understanding, inside a merely human, anthropocentric point of view. *Gun Island* represents Ghosh's efforts as novelist to write himself out of that dilemma.

In staging the Odysseus-like return of the refugee Tipu in concert with a multispecies "major migration event," Ghosh reimagines the solitary human hero as part of a collective of humans and nonhumans.[8] The novel's feminist academic wisdom figure Cinta has already suggested that narrative itself should be understood as not uniquely human:

> What if the faculty of storytelling were not specifically human but rather the last remnant of our animal selves? A vestige left over from a time before language, when we communicated as other living beings do? Why else is it that only in stories do animals speak? Not to speak of demons, and gods, and God himself? It is only through stories that the universe can speak to us.
>
> (141)

Breaking realist conventions, *Gun Island* lets the voices in. The rescue of Tipu and the other refugees comes through the agency of a "storm of living beings" (307) that act as a collective. The unity of these many different kinds of creatures is less strategic or calculated than coincidental or on a fundamental level narrative. All these agents, from an honorable Italian naval officer to a television crew eager to publicize Tipu's story, act together.

The most symbolically significant nonhuman agents in Tipu's rescue are cetaceans and birds. Species by species, starting with "long-finned pilot whales" (284), every kind of whale and dolphin native to the Mediterranean arrives to escort the refugee boat. The marine mammal behavioral scientist Piya, who throughout the novel always rejects supernatural or artistic explanations, ticks the creatures off one by one: "Sperm whales at three o'clock!" (288), "fin whales . . . bottlenoses . . . they're all there" (301)! Millions of migrating birds pass overhead (306). Even the microscopic dinoflagellates that produce "bioluminescence" (307) make a stunning appearance, as "an unearthly green colour, bright enough that we could see the outlines of the dolphins and whales" (307). Whether this multispecies cornucopia is "a miracle," as Cinta and Admiral Vigonovo insist, or an unexpected consequence of the "intersecting events" of climate change, as Piya hypothesizes, the simultaneous arrival of the collective brings Ghosh's story to a narrative climax by moving beyond realism. His story is largely though not exclusively maritime, populated by cetaceans, seabirds, and sailors.

Utopian rescue replaces the travails of a solitary Odysseus with a multispecies collective. Ghosh's point, however, also includes a critical political point. At the center of the human story are Bangladeshi laborers eager for a new start in Europe. Their plight, according to both Cinta and the Ghosh-like narrator, mirrors the sufferings of unfree laborers from the slave trade to "the indentured workers who had been transported from the Indian subcontinent to distant corners of the globe in order to work in plantations" (303). Unlike the imperial and colonial projects of years past, however, twenty-first century migrants move independently of European desires:

> This entire project [of European control] had now been upended. The systems and technologies that had made these massive demographic interventions possible—ranging from armaments to the control of information—had now achieved escape velocity: they were no longer under anyone's control.
>
> (305)

The "angry young men" flooding into Europe from Asia and Africa represent forces that Old World powers cannot make orderly. Like climate change, and to a large extent fueled by climate change, mass migration rewrites the borders of nations, regions, and cultures. *Gun Island* reconfigures that multiplicity as utopian assemblage. Ghosh's multispecies Mediterranean teems with life, and its waters are open, at long last, to migrants from beyond its borders.

Odysseus, Leadership, and Violence

When the refugee boat crosses the watery border into Italy, the deus ex machina plot device has Admiral Vigonovo recognize the "miracle" (309) of the multispecies movement, disobey his orders, and allow the refugees in. That nonviolent resolution has rarely been common in historical migrations. Violence remains the hero's signature in most Mediterranean narratives. Odysseus, trickster and sailor, starts his post-Troy adventures by destroying a city. As he narrates his adventures to King Alcinous, "The Cicones in Ismarus, I sacked/the town and killed the men. We took their wives/and shared their riches equally among us" (9.41–43). The inverse of Odysseus the builder is Odysseus the killer. This hero, like generations of

European mariners who molded themselves in his image, starts his voyage with blood. Violent ruthlessness appears a baseline requirement for Homer's conception of heroic masculinity. Odysseus is also, as the poet describes him in the first line of his self-narration, "lord of lies" (9.1), but direct violence always looms large among his tactical options.

The culminating bloodbath in the *Odyssey* involves the hero and his son butchering the 108 suitors who have taken over Ithaka and pressured Penelope to forsake her husband and marry one of them. A key plot turn reveals the disguised hero only when he strings his own great bow. The weapon unfurls itself as an instrument of civilization:

> After examining the mighty bow
> Carefully, inch by inch—as easily
> As an experienced musician stretches
> A sheep-gut string around a lyre's peg
> And makes it fast—Odysseus, with ease,
> Strung the great bow. He held it in his right hand
> And plucked the string, which sang like swallow-song,
> A clear sweet note.
>
> *(21.405–13)*

The hero combines musician, mariner, and warrior. Ghosh might emphasize that the Greek hero's slaughter of suitors and Cicones speaks to the fundamental violence of the European colonial drive—but Ghosh's heroes, too, mirror Odyssean complexity. Loving and skilled use of tools defines civilized behavior for Homer's Mediterranean and for global societies that engage with his model. It may be possible, as Ghosh's novel with its bookish and self-effacing hero attempts, to reject elements of the Odyssean package. The heroic structure that unifies music, warfare, and navigation, however, remains potent nearly three millennia after the first circulation of these narratives. To the extent that Odysseus represents the Mediterranean hero par excellence, the project of our age of climate disruption asks us to reimagine and reconstruct this figure for changing times.

Cervantes's Captive and Mediterranean Exchange

The famous knight Don Quixote glimpses the waters of the Mediterranean only near the end of the second volume of his adventures. He and Sancho compare the sea to the inland lakes they know from the dry plains of Montiel: "they saw the ocean, which they had not seen before: it seemed broad and vast to them, much larger than the Lakes of Ruidera that they had seen in La Mancha" (2.62).[9] But Cervantes's prose anti-epic also contains a hero of the maritime Mediterranean, the Spanish Captain Ruy Pérez de Viedma, whose captivity in North Africa mirrors Cervantes's own biographical experience. The scholar María Antonia Garcés, in her study *Cervantes in Algiers*

(2005), suggests that the autobiographical trauma of captivity was central to the author's artistic career.[10] Unfurling the early modern history of the multiculturalism Ghosh highlights in his twenty-first century portrayal of Mediterranean mobility, I suggest that it is possible to find in the Captive's Tale (*Don Quixote* 1.38–41), among other places in the vast corpus of the two-part novel, an indirect argument in favor of religious cohabitation with Islam and a multicultural Mediterranean. That position of cultural sympathy may seem odd coming from a celebrated Spanish author who lived during an era of Spanish imperial greatness. *Don Quixote* was published in two parts, in 1605 and 1615, near the end of the period widely known as the Spanish "Golden Age." That period is generally understood to have commenced in 1492, with the coincident expulsion of Jews and Muslims from Spain and Columbus's first voyage to the New World. María Rosa Menocal's book *The Ornament of the World* (2002) treats the hinge-date of 1492 as a fall from grace, after which the Catholic *Reconquista* crushed the utopian communities of the preceding centuries of *convivencia*.[11] A recent argument by Muhsin al-Ramli, an Iraqi novelist, has reopened the question of the debts of Cervantes to the Islamic-influenced culture from which he emerged. According to al-Ramli's analysis, presented in a doctoral thesis in Madrid, Cervantes values Islam. Cervantes's understandings of irony, history, and cultural mingling appear sympathetic to Muslim culture, as he knew it in both Africa and in Spain. As recently explored in a public humanities essay by Jeffrey Herlihy-Mera, it appears that Cervantes, like Menocal, may have longed for the lost glories of Muslim Spain.[12]

The era of cultural sympathy between the three Abrahamic faiths in the western Mediterranean that Menocal, al-Ramli, and Herlihy-Mera celebrate contrasts sharply with the reality of Christian slavery in North Africa, as experienced by Cervantes between 1575 and 1580 and fictionalized in the story of Captain Ruy Pérez de Viedma. David Quint has observed ways in which Captain Viedma's captivity and redemption parallel not only Cervantes's experiences but also Don Quixote's. The captain, whose military career gets described in rich and accurate historical detail, ends up being redeemed from captivity by the love, money, and faith of the Muslim heiress Zoraida. Quint suggests that the subsequent loss of Zoraida's treasure chest, swept overboard in advance of their escaping galley being boarded by French pirates, enables the novel to put into practice "a narrative trick by which Cervantes is able to back away from and repudiate the troubling implications of the story—and to substitute a Christian resolution in their place. The money that has been the means of action and desire . . . is not allowed to be their end."[13] My reading of the Captive's Tale agrees with Quint that Cervantes deep-sixes Zoraida's money to shift to a religious rather than mercantile frame. In following al-Ramli's conception of Cervantes's semi-hidden affinity for Islam, however, I suggest that the Mediterranean Sea that safeguards Zoraida's gold and jewels represents a multireligious community that the novel embraces, almost overtly.

The Captive, Captain Viedma, is often understood to represent the intrusion of a real hero into Don Quixote's mad quests. His close connection to historical reality appears not only in his detailed descriptions of naval warfare in the Mediterranean (1.39–40), but also, perhaps most directly, in his claim of acquaintance with the author himself, "a Spanish soldier named something de Saavedra" (344) whom Viedma claims to have met in Algiers. According to Quint, the captain's return to Spain and marriage to the now-converted Zoraida restores "a heroic and religious meaning" (88) to his life. (His two brothers, notably, each end up wealthy in Spanish America; only the captain remains in the homeland.) As Quint emphasizes, money represents the social corrosive that breaks down the idealistic world in which Don Quixote wants to live (8). The captain, in this reading, gets the best of both worlds: he uses Zoraida's money to redeem himself and her from captivity, but then avoids overt dependence on it when he arrives back in Spain. He and his newly converted wife will be reunited with the Viedma family and live in Catholic virtue.

Such a reading glosses over both Viedma's dependence upon Zoraida's wealth and her combination of both Christian and Muslim elements in her own person. In the letters she writes to Viedma in Arabic, which must be translated by a Spanish renegade, who will also translate Viedma's Spanish replies into Arabic, Zoraida conflates her two protections, Lela Marién and Allah. Lady Mary speaks to her heart and fires her desire to become a Christian and flee Algiers with Captain Viedma. But at this point, she never really relinquishes Allah. Her first letter to Viedma contains a fully Cervantine set of nested ironies. Zoraida reminds the captain that she is "very beautiful and young" and also that she has "a good deal of money to take with me" (347), thus indicating that the rescue plan follows both a romance and a mercenary plot. She insists that her guiding spirit is Lela Marién, but she easily connects her patroness to the Muslim name for God, Allah. In Cervantes's Spanish, the connection rhymes; Zoraida commits her captain to the protection of "Ella y Alá"—she and God.[14] The emphasis on translation between Arabic and Spanish echoes the larger frame tale in which the novel itself is a translation from the original text of the Arab historian Cide Hamete Benegeli; as Jeffrey Herlihy-Mera observes, many elements of the novel connect to the fantasized memory of "an Islamic-Spanish-Arabic world." The lost age for which the knight of the "triste figura" (literally, "sad face") pines is the make-believe world of Amadis of Gaul. But for the author Cervantes, elements of Moorish Spain also seem worth valuing.

The Mediterranean milieu of Captain Viedma, like that of Miguel de Cervantes, crossed both water and the boundaries of the Abrahamic religions. Cervantes spent five years in captivity in Algiers, and by most reports he was treated well; evidence for a possible love affair with a Muslim woman is thin but tempting.[15] The ravenous capacity of Cervantine irony, however, appears more than capable of including Muslim and perhaps Jewish figures in its gentle grasp, even if Cervantes, like his fictional avatar Viedma, fought against the Ottoman Turks. If, for Ghosh in the twenty-first century, Mediterranean inclusiveness entails bringing birds, whales, and bioluminescence into his multispecies rescue mission, perhaps Cervantes attempts to do justice to his own experience of multireligious exchange in the early modern Med. Even the French pirates who intercept the Captive and Zoraida—and whose actions cause Zoraida's treasure to go into the sea—hail from La Rochelle, making them presumably Protestant, adding to the multi-faith stew. The early modern Mediterranean of Cervantes, as for Shakespeare also, represents an uneasy cultural crossroads, populated by chivalric knights, Jewish moneylenders, and Moorish generals who defend (mostly) Christian Venice against the Ottomans. The conception of sea travel as cultural mixer and hybridizing force, which would dominate Atlantic culture after the early modern period, appears in miniaturized form in the story of Cervantes's Captive as well as his knight.

Odysseus the Swimmer

The fecundity of the multispecies and multicultural Mediterraneans depicted by Homer, Cervantes, Shakespeare, Ghosh, and others suggests ways that this relatively small sea, straddling the borders of the Old World continents of Europe, Africa, and Asia, acts as a kind of world ocean in miniature. Physical, religious, and cultural connectivity across diversity would venture through the Pillars of Hercules first to Atlantic islands such as the Canaries, Azores, and Cape Verde, and subsequently to and beyond the Atlantic. Before shifting to the American side of the globe and considering the many significant consequences of exchanging a short crossing for a much longer one, the interaction of humans and oceans without boats is worth exploring. Karen Eva Carr, in her *Shifting Currents: A World History of Swimming* (2022), has emphasized that swimming prowess was common in ancient warm-water cultures including Egypt, and it is probable that the classical Greeks learned to swim from African tutors.[16] But in Homer's world, Odysseus learns from the White Goddess, Ino. As he is stranded on a raft after Poseidon's storm has wrecked the ship he built on Calypso's island, Odysseus hears the voice of the goddess:

> You seem intelligent. Do as I say.
> Strip off your clothes and leave the raft behind
> for winds to take away. With just your arms
> swim to Phaeacia. Fate decrees that there
> you will survive. Here, take my scarf and tie it
> under your chest: with this immortal veil,
> you need not be afraid of death or danger.
> *(5.342–48)*

The goddess's instructions invert Odysseus's usual reliance on technologies such as ships, bows, or lyres. His act of faith requires him to immerse himself bodily, trusting only his arms and Ino's scarf. The hero is typically suspicious—"But what if the gods are weaving tricks again?" (5.357)—but he recognizes that he has no other option. Notably, however, Odysseus does not immediately follow Ino's advice. He clings to a single long timber as his raft disintegrates, "rode along/as if on horseback" (5.372–73). But soon he splashes naked into the sea, "spreading his arm to swim" (5.375). In this moment, the hero matches himself bodily against the Mediterranean.

Even in this immersive instant, Odysseus is not really alone. Poseidon rages against him, and his divine ally Athena ensures that the winds drive the swimmer to Phaeacia. An epic simile captures alienation from land as a sickness, and the island as redemption:

> As when a father
> lies sick and weak for many days, tormented
> by some cruel spirit, till at last the gods
> restore him back to life; his children feel
> great joy; Odysseus felt that same joy
> when he saw the land.
>
> *(5.393–99)*

In an interesting reversal, Odysseus in this metaphor occupies the place of the relieved children, rather than the sick father. In returning to land, the hero returns to a human world, and also to human dependencies such as family and physical frailty.

To survive in stormy water requires not just the goddess's token but also a heroic excess of inhumanity that connects to Ghosh's multispecies Med. The swimming adventure does not end with the sight of land. The hero must strategize about how to reach shore in the violent surf. "If I attempt to scramble out," he speculates, "a wave/will seize and dash me on the jagged rock" (5.415–16). Athena's protection ends up getting him over the rocks, but another simile, this time a nonhuman one, portrays the struggling swimmer's efforts:

> As when an octopus, dragged from its den,
> Has many pebbles sticking to its suckers,
> So his strong hands were skinned against the rocks.
>
> *(5.432–34)*

To swim safely to shore through the storm, Odysseus must be both relieved child and dislodged octopus, both human happily reunited with his family and sea creature violently yanked out of its element. To be a Mediterranean hero requires both human and inhuman qualities, Homer's similes suggest. To endure watery privation, one must maintain hope in a human reunion.

But when landfall comes at length, the suckers one has grown to survive in the water will be skinned off one's fingers. Humans cannot live in the sea. We long to return to shore. But especially in the warm waters of the Med, there remains something that stays in the water when we return to dry land. Traces of his octopus-identity haunt Odysseus during his long return to terrestrial living.

Notes

1 Many other regions have been described as "archipelagic," even though the term was initially used only of the Greek archipelago. Many regions have also been imagined as "Mediterraneans," including both the Pacific and the Caribbean. For a rereading of American studies in this light, see Brian Russell Roberts, *Borderwaters: Amid the Archipelagic States of America* (Durham: Duke University Press, 2021).
2 Peregrine Horden and Nicholas Purcell, *The Corrupting Sea: A Study of Mediterranean History* (London: Blackwell, 2000).
3 Predrag Matvejevic, *Mediterranean: A Cultural Landscape*, Michael Henry Heim, trans. Claudio Magris, intr. (Berkeley: University of California Press, 1999).
4 The prefatory sonnet by Wye Saltonstall, and Saltonstall's etymological gloss on the unfamiliar Greek word *technology*, appears in Margaret Cohen, *The Novel and the Sea* (Princeton: Princeton University Press, 2010), 42.
5 Homer, *The Odyssey*, Emily Wilson, trans. (New York: W. W. Norton, 2018), 188. Further citations in the text by book and line numbers.
6 On Odysseus as a hero, see Steve Mentz, *Ocean* (London: Bloomsbury, 2020), 21–29.
7 Amitav Ghosh, *The Great Derangement: Climate Change and the Unthinkable* (Chicago: University of Chicago Press, 2016), 23. For a rejoinder to Ghosh's argument that takes seriously the central position of science fiction in modern narrative, see Mark Bould, *The Anthropocene Unconscious: Climate Catastrophe Culture* (London: Verso, 2021).
8 Amitav Ghosh, *Gun Island: A Novel* (New York: Farrar, Straus, and Giroux, 2019), 300.
9 Miguel de Cervantes, *Don Quixote*, Edith Grossman, trans. Harold Bloom, intr. (New York: Harper Collins, 2003), 862. Further quotations given in the text by volume and chapters numbers, as well as page number in this edition.
10 María Antonia Garcés, *Cervantes in Algiers: A Captive's Tale* (Nashville: Vanderbilt University Press, 2005).
11 María Rosa Menocal, *The Ornament of the World: How Muslims, Jews, and Christians Created a Culture of Tolerance in Medieval Spain* (New York: Little, Brown, and Company, 2002).
12 Jeffrey Herlihy-Mira, "Did Don Quixote Long for Muslim Spain?," *Public Books*, 12 August 2021. www.publicbooks.org/did-don-quixote-long-for-muslim-spain/. Accessed 2 September 2022.
13 David Quint, *Cervantes's Novel of Modern Times: A New Reading of Don Quijote* (Princeton: Princeton University Press, 2003), 73.
14 For the Spanish text, see Miguel de Cervantes Saavedra, *Don Quijote de la Mancha, Part I*, Martín de Riquer, ed. (Barcelona: Editorial Juventud, 1995), 410. In her second letter, Zoraida repeats the connection if not the rhyme, referring to "Alá y Marién" (411).
15 Garcés, *Cervantes in Algiers*, 50.
16 Karen Eva Carr, *Shifting Currents: A World History of Swimming* (London: Reaktion, 2022), 19–28, 56–59.

7 In the Caribbean

A suggestive distinction between the classical Mediterranean and the slave-trade-haunted Caribbean appears in the work of the Francophone poet and theorist Édouard Glissant. Contrasting the two seas, Glissant emphasizes that "the Mediterranean . . . is an inner sea surrounded by lands, a sea that concentrates." By contrast, he continues, "the Caribbean is . . . a sea that explodes the scattered lands into an arc. A sea that diffracts."[1] The diffraction that Glissant conjures suggests that the Caribbean represents the polycultural forces of global modernity, as opposed to the classical inwardness of the Mediterranean. The preceding chapter has suggested that the Mediterranean may be best defined by connectivity and multicultural connections, and Glissant's notion of an "inner sea" may not fully capture that complexity. But his focus is primarily on his native Caribbean and the radical changes its cultural mixtures have brought into the world. In the same volume, *Poetics of Relation* (1990), Glissant projects the Middle Passage as a moment of origin, in which the slaver's boat is "a womb abyss" floating above the "next abyss [which] was the depths of the sea" (6). Into a maritime world defined by the violent mixing of American, African, and European populations, Glissant posits the idea of "Relation" as a poetic language to bring differences into contact with each other:

> Relation is not made up of things that are foreign but of shared knowledge. This experience of the abyss can now be said to be the best element of exchange.
>
> (8)

Forged into unity by the violence of the slave trade, Caribbean cultures, in Glissant's poetic imagination, form themselves into historically new amalgamations. The "shared knowledge" that Relation creates results in new forms of social, cultural, and poetic understanding.

A key element of this combination is multilingualism. Glissant, a Francophone writer from Martinique, argues that "Relation . . . is spoken multilingually . . .. Relation rightfully opposes the totalitarianism of any monolingual intent" (19). This hymn to the plural emerges from attention

DOI: 10.4324/9781003166665-7

to the Caribbean as cultural crossroads, a maritime meeting place of peoples, languages, and objects. In *A Map of the Door of No Return* (2001), her memoir of childhood in Trinidad, the poet Dionne Brand emphasizes the visual and symbolic primacy of the sea in Caribbean culture: "Water is the first thing in my imagination. . . . All beginning in water, all ending in water. Turquoise, aquamarine, deep green, deep blue, ink blue, navy, blue-black, cerulean water."[2] From her view in the southeastern Caribbean, near the coast of Venezuela, Brand sees a prismatic blue world. Even before she has traveled far from home, she recognizes in salt water both a promise of movement and the reality of suffering. "Water is another country" (56), she notes later. Her global travels take her to Elmina Castle in West Africa, from which so many European ships sailed west with human cargo, and to her adult home in Toronto. "A map," she concludes, "is only a life of conversations about a forgotten list of irretrievable selves" (224). Alongside Glissant's assertive claims for heroic Relation, Brand's melancholy and intimate voice recalls the human costs of Caribbean dislocations. She speaks for herself and for a region ruptured by history.

In addition to Glissant and Brand, numerous other poets and cultural theorists from the Caribbean have defined this region as central to the way we think about oceanic space in the twenty-first century. Major authors include Aimé Césaire, a Martinican intellectual who wrote *Une Tempête* (1969), a fiery riposte to Shakespeare's drama *The Tempest*.[3] Kamau Braithwaite, a Barbadian poet and critic, devised the prominent trope of "tidalectics" in an effort to assimilate historical thought to the rhythms of Caribbean living.[4] The Nobel Laureate Derek Walcott, an Anglophone poet from St. Lucia, counts among his major literary achievements the post-Homeric epic *Omeros* (1990), which explores the lives of Caribbean fishermen in dialogue with classical models, and the much-quoted poem "The Sea is History" (1979).[5] These figures, among many others, have made the Caribbean a crucial oceanscape for blue humanities thinkers. The geographers Jonathan Pugh and David Chandler, in fact, argue that for island studies scholarship, Glissant's Caribbean epitomizes the relational and ontologically fluid modern ocean.[6] The intersection between theorists such as Pugh and Chandler and poets such as Brand and Glissant suggests that this relatively small region of the western Atlantic will continue to be central to blue humanities thinking for decades to come.

Storms, Swamps, Maroons, and Viscosity

Among the distinctive geographic and meteorological features of the western Atlantic, two of the most noteworthy are hurricanes and humidity. Neither of these properties is unique to this region, though, according to the *Oxford English Dictionary*, the word "hurricane" derives from the Indigenous Taino word *furacan* or *hurucan*, transmitted into Latin and Spanish by early Iberian chroniclers. Peter Hulme, in an important study of early European encounters with the Caribbean, has suggested that one of the most distinctive features of the New World was "that novel and much-feared natural phenomenon, the hurricane."[7] A western Atlantic variation on the Indian Ocean monsoon, albeit less regular and less amenable to commercial trading patterns, the hurricane represents a distinctive and history-shaping structure in the greater Caribbean. As historian Stuart B. Schwartz has explored, the story of how "people, governments, and societies have responded to" hurricanes comprises a full history of the post-contact Caribbean.[8] For Indigenous societies before the arrival of Europeans, hurricanes figured in religious and ceremonial life, though we lack detailed knowledge of individual storms and their histories.

On a more intimate scale, humidity and swamp typify the Caribbean environment from Venezuela to Florida. In taking swamps as the freshwater space of this chapter, I do not mean to exclude the salt marshes that make up large amounts of the area's wetlands. Instead, I emphasize how the human experience of swamp living, with its humid closeness and physical contact with insects and other creatures, was central to Caribbean cultures both Indigenous and creolized. In *Ariel's Ecology* (2013), Monique Allewaert examines what she terms the "American tropics" or the "plantation zone."[9] Describing an environment she calls the "swamp sublime" (36–37), Allewaert suggests that these conditions subject human bodies to complex processes that entangle them with their nonhuman surroundings. Taking as her poetic model Ariel's song of transformation in *The Tempest*, she suggests that the swamp-infused body represents "an emerging minoritarian conception of agency by which human beings are made richer and stranger through their entwinement with the operations of coral and . . . other colonial climatological forces as well as plant and animal bodies" (1). Resembling in some ways a microcosm of the multispecies alliances that Ghosh's *Gun Island* would develop in the migratory Mediterranean, Allewaert's anticolonial hybrid bodies, "largely developed by Afro-Americans" (2), generate what she terms an "alternate materialism of the body" (3). Building on Glissant's ideas of Relation and proposing a model she terms "parahuman," Allewaert integrates the human body into "what we might now call an ecological phenomenon" (9). Her swampy, local, and highly idiosyncratic notion of an Anthropocene human enables the "emergence of a disaggregated conception of the body" (9), whether that body is imagined as purely human, nonhuman, or parahuman. She develops this emerging form of embodiment through the literary figures of Shakespeare's Ariel and Caliban, but her historical examples are almost all enslaved Africans and Indigenous Americans, struggling against bondage.

Beyond Allewaert's theoretical frame, which enables rich eco-materialist analyses of how terrestrial and aquatic environments shape human agency in the Caribbean, the figure of the maroon, while not unique to the Caribbean, provides a powerful symbol of the struggle for freedom in this violent, multicultural region. The *Oxford English Dictionary* states that the English word "maroon," which refers to societies made up of escaped African and Indigenous slaves, emerged from the Spanish word *cimmarón*, a word used to describe cattle in Hispaniola that escaped colonial farms and roamed the backcountry. English readers were introduced to the term via Francis Drake's exploits in Panama when he created an anti-Spanish alliance with *Symerones* living in the hills. The historian Sylviane Diouf, in *Slavery's Exiles: The Story of the American Maroons* (2014), emphasizes that maroons sought, and created, "autonomy" and self-determination.[10] The maroon, living free in the mountains, provides a compelling contrast with European castaways such as Robinson Crusoe, struggling in solitude near the shore.[11] The philosopher Neil Roberts has elaborated *marronage* as a conceptual urge and physical leap towards freedom. "Marronage," Roberts observes, "is a multidimensional, constant act of flight that involves what I take to be four interrelated pillars: distance, movement, property, and purpose."[12] Building, like Allewaert, upon Glissant's theoretical structures, Roberts identifies the "*refugee-immigrant*" as a figure for "a late modern maroon straddling the outward flight into diaspora of genres of grand marronage and macro-visions of another world in the vévé architectonics of the sociogenic imagination" (170). Roberts's word "vévé," sometimes also spelled "VèVè," refers to a Caribbean religious symbol in the system of Vodun or Voodoo. This term suggests that, for Roberts, the structures of marronage and the cultural architecture of maroon societies emerge through a transformational encounter between African bodies and American environments. In the swamps of America, new systems of human living are born.

The earth-infused air and waters of the American tropics are thick and heavy. Sweat represents a physical human response, whether one is in the muddy terrain of the interior of Florida or along the sparkling beaches of the Antilles. To be in that thick and heavy Caribbean air means sweating, often profusely. The visible sweat that appears on working human bodies in this weather represents an equilibrium between the water inside human bodies and the water in the humid air. American writers of the South, including such figures as Eudora Welty and William Faulkner, have explored the distinctive bodily poetics of the sweaty South.[13] In keeping with Allewaert's eco-materialist analysis of the physical porosity of the human body to environmental forces, a blue humanities focus on sweat might consider how watery flows, in which water moves in, over, and out of the body, represent the vexed equilibrium necessary to live in tropical climes. To sweat in the Caribbean means transferring a small sample of one's own bodily water into larger flows of water vapor and liquid. In the exchange of heat and moisture between body and air, Caribbean swamps leave damp marks on human experience.

Pirates and Castaways

If maroons and enslaved laborers represent the working core of the Caribbean plantation system, the region's florid and anarchic outside emerges through the figures of the pirate and the castaway. These figures both would become central to the cultural imagination of the region after first contact. I touch here on some examples of how pirates and castaways might figure in blue humanities thinking through a series of quick portraits of ships and men in the eighteenth-century Caribbean. I start with a short history of four pirate ships, two real and two fictional. From the ships I move to two exemplary pirates, one real and one imaginary, and at length to two eighteenth-century English books, probably only one of which was written by Daniel Defoe. My aim in this brief analysis will be to suggest some reasons we might want to modify our ways of thinking about early modern piracy. Much excellent pirate scholarship in recent decades has built upon a basically human-centered, and often explicitly political, understanding of piratical motives and cultures. By suggesting a blue humanities posthuman addition to this scholarship, I gesture toward nonhuman forces of oceanic circulation and ecological disruption. My hope in reimagining early modern pirates through a blue humanities lens will be to open this figure outward into water-focused discourses. Pirates have long been important historical and cultural figures; I hope to extend study of these oceanic criminals in wet eco-materialist directions.

Maritime piracy, including Caribbean piracy, represents a violent comingling of capitalism, imperial expansion, and ecological violence. The "Golden Age" of European piracy in the eighteenth century brought these forces together alongside the oceanic expansion of European powers into and beyond the New World. Recent scholarship on piracy, including the works of Marcus Rediker, Dan Vitkus, Claire Jowitt, Manushag Powell, and many others, has situated these figures in literary and historical contexts from the transatlantic slave trade to the transmission of classical romance narratives.[14] The pirate may be thought of, in Jowitt's delicate phrasing, as "ambiguously serviceable" to the early modern state (she is thinking about Drake and Elizabeth I), or alternatively, in Rediker's influential formulation, as the leading edge of a "radical democratic social order and culture" (82) whose primary values were "collectivism, anti-authoritarianism, and egalitarianism" (29). Recent scholarship connecting pirates to the slave trade has taken some of the shine off Rediker's political vision, but the sense remains strong that turning pirate represents a radical critique of the establishment. German philosopher Peter Sloterdijk, zooming out to a wide-angle view, understands the pirate and the slave trader both as "foremost manifestation[s] of a naïve globalization criminality."[15] The "anarcho-maritime figure" (113) of the pirate represents "the first entrepreneurial form of atheism" (112). In a world liberated from divine commandments, pirates rule—or at least they represent the leading edge of a future that will become increasingly global, ambivalently secular, unrelentingly violent, and overwhelmingly mercantile.[16] Through a blue humanities lens, however, ships represent more-than-human communities more than human-directed machines. What I call "wet globalization" operates through the overlapping agencies of mariners, empires, ocean currents, and animal, plant, and viral populations.[17] In drawing pirate scholarship into this more-than-human critical conversation, I start not with the pirates but their ships.

Four Ships

Early modern legal systems imagined ships to be floating representations of national sovereignty, though the extent of that sovereignty was always contested by swords and cannon at sea as by pens and lawyers on land.[18] In ecological terms, a ship represents a territorial infringement on the watery environment and a machine that enables land mammals to live, temporarily, outside their element. The implication that a ship brings humans outside our natural place appears common in anti-navigational writings from Hesiod and Plato forward, as well as in the Biblical injunction that paradise will be the place in which "there will be no more sea."[19] If we invert the problem and do not interpret a ship through its failure to be land, we arrive at Michel Foucault's remarks about the ocean-going vessel as "a floating piece of space, a place without a place."[20] Foucault further observes that ships represent the "heterotopia *par excellence*. In civilizations without boats, dreams dry up, espionage takes the place of adventure, and the police take the place of pirates" (27). Foucault's analysis focuses on the ship as object and vessel, a container in which humans and ideas thrive. But his resonant phrasing does not directly address the core eco-materialist question: what, actually, is a ship at sea? If we look closely at this amalgam of wood, rope, tar, metal, humans, plants, vermin, viruses, and other living and nonliving objects, what kinds of unities arrive from all those diversities?

To answer that question, I want to introduce some brief descriptions of early modern ships as diverse human communities. No matter which flag flew from the mainmast, Union Jack or Jolly Roger, all ship's crews included multiple languages, cultures, nationalities, and backgrounds. Even leaving aside nonhuman agents from viruses and bacteria to invasive plant or animal species, early modern ships contained multitudes. A quick survey of four notable pirate ships, two historical and two fictional, will demonstrate this point.

Perhaps the most familiar of these ships is Sir Francis Drake's world-circling *Golden Hind*, a life-scale replica of which floats today on the south bank of the Thames in London. Built in 1574, the ship was originally named *Pelican*, after one of Queen Elizabeth's favorite Christian symbols, and then rechristened *Golden Hind* after passing through the Straits of Magellan—at least according to one manuscript account of the voyage. The ship's multiple names, which apparently also included the *Francis*—though perhaps that was just Drake's hopeful idea—gesture toward the vessel's symbolic pliability, its ability to be reimagined for new patrons. Drake's crew, as far as we can tell, was mostly drawn from his West Country extended family and community; the names we know from the surviving records sound very English.

In addition to multiple Drakes and Hawkinses, we have John Fry, Robert Winterby, "a seaman named Oliver" and several others.[21] What seems crucial about the men who set sail with Drake in 1578, however, is that many were dead when the ship returned to England in 1580; around half of the sailors did not return.

To contrast with Drake's pirate-or-privateer's vessel, I offer a nineteenth-century American whaleship: Melville's *Pequod.* This boat is technically fictional, though it closely mirrors the *Acushnet,* on which Melville himself sailed on a whaling voyage that left New England in 1841. One advantage of taking the *Pequod* as my example is that Melville's novel provides a detailed who's-who of the crew. The whaleship is ruled by a tyrannical Nantucket captain, controlled by a trio of white male officers, but populated by a multiethnic crew that includes Parsees, Manxmen, Lascars, United States citizens from both South and North, Native Americans, African Americans, Africans, and crewmen described as Dutch, French, Icelandic, Maltese, Sicilian, Long-Island, Tahitian, Portuguese, Danish, English, St. Jago, and Belfast sailors—not to mention a chatty schoolteacher from upstate New York and a tattooed superhero from the mythic island of Kokovoko. The *Pequod* floats the world.

To these two ships I add two more vessels, another each in the historical and fictional categories. Both ships appear in *A General History of the Pyrates* (1724), the popular compilation of pirate histories once erroneously attributed to Defoe. These ships are the historical Captain Henry Avery's *Fancy* and the fictional Captain James Mission's ship *Victoire.* In part 1 of the *General History*, the author attacks celebratory depictions of Avery, including one that was probably written by Daniel Defoe in *King of the Pirates* (1720). As Frederick Burwick and Manushag Powell have observed, the mythology of Captain Avery at the turn of the eighteenth century recapitulated legends of Elizabethan sea dogs like Drake a century earlier (28). The *General History* rejects this mythology, at least when it writes about Avery.

In the case of Captain Mission, however, we can recognize an effort to restructure the pirate myth. The multinational identity of Mission's ship and crew seems especially important. Mission himself is French; his free-thinking anticlerical right-hand man Seignior Caraccioli is Italian, and the crew they assemble on the *Victoire* becomes increasingly global as their adventures proceed. Their ship may not boast quite as many named nationalities as the *Pequod*, but their adventures in the West Indies and Madagascar witness Mission and his crew freeing African slaves, who join the ship (403). They later defeat Dutch (406) and English ships (408), some of whose crewmen also join the pirates. They finally intermarry with the Indigenous community of Johanna Island (modern Anjouan in the Comoro Islands) near Madagascar, with whom they establish the pirate utopia of Libertalia.[22] In a significant passage about that imagined nation, Mission asks his people to reject their former identities in favor of the new name of "*Liberi* . . . [he] desiring that in that [name] might be drown'd the distinguish'd Names of

French, English, Dutch, Africans, &c" (417). The utopian project aims to erase the crew's pre-pirate terrestrial nationalities by forging a new political identity. To some extent this recalls, in a utopian rather than tragic key, the claim Marcus Rediker makes in *The Slave Ship* (2008), that the violence of the Middle Passage occasioned the transformation of "a multiethnic collection of Africans" into a somewhat unified body of African Americans (10).[23] For pirates and slavers, Sloterdijk's twin symbols of maritime modernity, multiplicity plus violence, create community. It seems plausible that narrative collections, including large collections such as *A General History of the Pyrates* and smaller one such as *King of the Pirates*, might be themselves undertaking a conceptual suturing-together through violent melodrama to create the "pirate" as collective symbol.

These four ships and their crews demonstrate that the pirate-as-symbol rejects nations such as England or France or later the United States. Maritime criminals become global figures, but more particularly they appear blue and oceanic. The blue turn from land to sea clarifies our vision, because the ocean covers most of our blue planet. Humans live almost entirely on atypically dry patches on the surface of the world. Pirates and saltwater castaways, I suggest, get represented as a leading edge in placing human history in oceanic context.

Ecotheoretical scholarship aims to replace human-centered narratives with posthuman or not-only-human perspectives. Turning to ecotheory does not mean ignoring humans, which would be obtuse ecologically during the Anthropocene and conceptually impossible in any case. Posthuman and posthumanist theory, however, enables other actors, from ocean currents to the Coriolis effect, to become meaningful actors. Humans remain on board, but not at the helm. We need not give up our favorite pirates, either as historical/literary figures or symbols of maritime anarchy. Whether we follow Rediker's democratic idealism or the more politically ambivalent paths of Powell or Jowitt, pirates as representations of antisystemic forces remain potent. Turning pirates blue and posthuman may douse some of the more heroic claims about them, in particular claims about individuality and absolute freedom. But getting them wet puts these figures in contact with larger, less anthropocentric, and more material forces in historical change.

The Music of Deep History: *The Mermaid of Black Conch*

The massive surge of Caribbean culture onto the global stage that followed late-twentieth century writers such as Glissant, Brand, Césaire, Walcott, and Brathwaite has transformed Caribbean fiction into a global phenomenon. An award-winning novel by Trinidadian writer Monique Roffey, *The Mermaid of Black Conch* (2020), braids together multiple human and nonhuman cultures on a remote island. The animating figure of the novel is Aycayia, a mermaid who had centuries before been an Indigenous Taino woman, cursed by other women for her beauty and driven into the sea from pre-contact Cuba. When this supernatural figure of Indigeneity emerges from the sea, she disrupts the creole community of the island, including the Black fisherman David Baptise, who falls in love with the mermaid; the white landowner Arcadia Rain, who speaks Black Conch patois and loves a Black man; and even a pair of Yankee fishermen from Miami who hook the mermaid and drag her onto the dock. The allegorical structure that Roffey builds seems simple, though she is attentive to mixtures, as represented by figures such as Arcadia Rain's multiracial deaf son Reggie, whose Black father returns to the island in the course of the novel. Aycayia, whose verse monologues punctuate the text, appears fascinated by what Reggie tells her about mixing and the modern Caribbean:

> I learn from Reggie
> He tell me that Bob Marley
> love a white woman
> and hate his white father
> Bob Marley is half and half
> Reggie is half and half
> He have white mother
> And he half and half too
> None of them half fish[24]

As Aycayia comes to understand the island, she recognizes that her own hybridity, her fish-ness, exceeds what the human system can tolerate. The Yankee fishermen, and some of the local islanders, believe the mermaid too valuable a prize not to sell. David, who falls in love with Aycayia, and Reggie, who learns to communicate with her in sign language, see in her hybrid form something missing in the island.

From her first appearance, the mermaid represents the ancient and mostly unknown human history of the Caribbean. David spies her one early morning when he is out fishing:

> She was a red woman, like an Amerindian. Or anyway, her top half was red. He had seen her shoulders, her head, her breasts, and her long black hair like ropes, all sea mossy and jook up with anemone and conch shell. A merwoman.
>
> (4)

The Indigenous body takes on physical qualities from the undersea world, decorating herself with anemone and conch. Aycayia connects, with her red skin and tattoos, the late-twentieth-century world of Black Conch to a pre-European past. The ropey dreadlocks in her hair, however, gesture toward the modern Rasta culture for which Reggie's boom box provides the Bob Marley soundtrack. Aycayia, whose name, meaning "lovely voice," comes from a Taino folktale and combines all elements of Black Conch's cultural stew except European and Yankee latecomers.

As she sheds her tail and returns to human form, Aycayia recognizes the cruelty that structures the hybrid worlds of Black Conch, past and present. Arcadia Rain tells her the sordid truths of colonial history:

> I ask why everybody in Black Conch is black-skinned
> She told me how black people came
> I ask here where are the red people like me
> She told me they were mostly all dead and gone, murdered
> I learn from Miss Rain
> how the Castilian admiral
> MURDER all my people in a very short time
>
> *(113)*

The brutality of a half-millennium of colonial history becomes miniaturized into a childlike poem. Roffey's anticolonial vision lacks some of the fierceness of the generation of Césaire and Glissant, but she is more attentive than they were to feminist questions. The Black community of the island divides around the mermaid, with only David and Arcadia appearing uninterested in the money promised by the Yankee interlopers. The novel represents masculine violence through the Yankee fisherman and a corrupt local police officer who attempts to sell the mermaid's body. Both these figures embody a mercenary lust for control that none of the island's songs, neither the mermaid's nor David's nor even Bob Marley's, can dispel. The Caribbean that Roffey's novel describes bears the scars of colonial violence, with consequences that neither music, love, nor sympathy can erase.

An environmental feature of the Caribbean, the hurricane, wipes the slate partly clean and creates new possibilities for the future. The novel's culmination brings a storm to the island that Roffey names "Huracan Rosamund." As David notes in retrospect in his journal, "I hardly know what to say about the time of Rosamund, 1976, Still just about the most devastating storm ever to hit Black Conch" (206). Under cover of the storm, Aycayia returns to the sea, the Rain family's colonial house gets ripped from its foundations, Arcadia's former lover decides to stay with her and their son, and the Yankee fisherman's son admits his bisexuality to his domineering father. Rosamund destroys in order to rebuild: "The storm was sweeping things away in its path; that was its grand design, its meaning for them all" (224). The strongest natural force in the Caribbean, the novel implies, is the storm wind, which makes possible new futures. The supernatural mermaid must return to the sea, dooming David to a life of loneliness and maritime visions. But the destruction of the old colonial house and the reunification of the Rain family represent new possible futures for the "half and half" culture growing up on the island.

Aycayia herself, having regrown her tail and returned to the sea, represents a glimpse back into the primordial human history of the Caribbean. The last song she sings as they drive her down to the water captures a precontact world that neither descendants of slaves nor of colonizers has glimpsed before:

> They could just hear Aycayia singing, a sound like Africa, like the Andes, like old Creole hymnals, like shamanic icaros from a time when people healed themselves with simple herbal wisdom, when they understood all the kingdoms of the earth.
>
> (219)

The global vision of the mermaid's voice brings together the cultures of Africa and South America through the Amazonian songs, "icaros," that continue to be used today in ayahuasca ceremonies. Aycayia's global South, however, is not just Afro-Amazonian; it also includes the "old Creole hymnals" of the Black Christianity that took root in the New World. Above all, however, the mermaid's song captures a lost moment of human unity, a time "when they understood all the kingdoms of the earth," that counteracts the shattering violence of colonial modernity. For Roffey, as with other twenty-first-century Caribbean writers and artists, the region speaks to a global future.

The Limits of Interpretation: "Queequeg in his Coffin"

This chapter on the Caribbean ends with a brief consideration of Indigenous tattoos. Although Melville's Queequeg is a Pacific Islander, not Carib or Taino, he like the mermaid of Black Conch is covered with obscure tattoos. Melville explores the tattoos at the end of a chapter that focuses on the harpooner's mysterious illness and equally mysterious recovery. Having had a coffin, which he calls "a canoe like those of Nantucket" (362), built for him during his sickness, Queequeg upon recovery occupies himself by reinscribing onto the coffin the "twisted tattoos" (366) that mark his own flesh. Tattoos represent an ancient practice of nearly all human cultures, but in Melville's nineteenth century, the ornate decorative tattoos of Pacific Islanders were especially fascinating to Anglophone readers. Like Aycayia's tattoos, her singing, and her Indigenous gods in *The Mermaid of Black Conch*, Queequeg's tattoos represent radical cultural difference generated through intimate physical connection to the ocean. Unlike Aycayia, the harpooner from Oceania is only a metaphorical merman. But the art that covers his body suggests that the practices of Indigenous cultures have special abilities to construct a mutually supporting relationship between human bodies and oceanic space.

Queequeg's tattoos represent absolute knowledge and basic illegibility. They resemble the hidden truths of ocean as well as Ishmael's fundamentally religious understanding of the sperm whale. When Ishmael considers his desire "to read the awful Chaldee of the Sperm Whale's brow," he implies his own, and the reader's, inevitable failure of comprehension: "Read it if you can" (275). Similarly, Queequeg's tattoos, written by a "departed prophet and seer of his island" (366), represent "a complete theory of the heavens and the earth, and a mystical treatise on the art of attaining truth" (366). On the beautiful male body of the harpooner appears universal truth. Ishmael reports that Queequeg is "a riddle to unfold; a wondrous work in one volume; but whose mysteries not even he himself could read" (366–67). The interpretive dilemma emphasizes the opacity of Queequeg's skin-text, unknown even to himself, not to mention his bosom companion and metaphorical spouse. The art of tattoos, in *Moby-Dick* as in *The Mermaid of Black Conch*, represents a deep historical insight unavailable to modern humans. For both Melville and Roffey, the art of the sea-novel entails visualizing that knowledge, even if it cannot be fully interpreted.

In the oceanic vision of *Moby-Dick*, the total knowledge that the tattoos represent does not remain above the waves to be interpreted. Because Queequeg goes down with the *Pequod*, his tattoo-text gets consigned to the whale's road. Even before the islander's fate is known, however, Ishmael emphasizes that the human body is itself ephemeral, so the secrets inscribed on Queequeg's flesh "were therefore destined in the end to moulder away with the living parchment whereon they were inscribed, and so be unsolved to the last" (367). Aycayia's immortality—"I am now and forever/I will be here for the whole of time" (177), she sings—means that her secret text will never decay, though it also remains beyond human understanding. While Ishmael the whale-lover appears to have the closest insight into the mysteries of the maritime body, his narrative grants to Ahab the whale-killer the closing response to Queequeg's tattoos: "Oh, devilish tantalization of the gods!" (367). The mixed supernatural nature of the tattoos, which Ahab understands as devilish and divine, frustrate interpretation. Queequeg represents Indigeneity as mystery and oceanic connection. Faced with the inaccessible, both Ishmael and Ahab, despite their powerful contrasts throughout the novel, remain equally stymied.

The lingering desire to comprehend the universal knowledge of the Indigenous world captures an important feature of the modern Caribbean. It seems noteworthy that, of the major oceans and seas, the Caribbean is one of few whose English name emerges from a native American language. The cultural mixing that Glissant calls Relation creates new creole hybrids out of ingredients from many locations in Africa, Europe, and both Americas, with Asian influences arriving only slightly later. In the spaces of human history and humidity, of swamps and sweat, the Caribbean represents the shock of transoceanic modernity, with its cruelty, disruptions, and transformative amalgamations. The global resonance of this relatively small corner of the western Atlantic seems likely to remain powerful in coming decades.

Notes

1 Éduoard Glissant, *Poetics of Relation*, Betsy Wing, trans. (Ann Arbor: University of Michigan Press, 1997), 33.
2 Dionne Brand, *A Map of the Door of No Return: Notes on Belonging* (Toronto: Vintage Canada, 2001), 6.
3 Aimé Cesairé, *Une tempête* (Paris: Éditions de Seuil, 1969). For an English translation, see Aimé Cesairé, *A Tempest*, Richard Miller, trans. (New York: Theatre Communications Group, 2002).
4 On contemporary thinking around tidalectics including Braithwaite's celebrated poem "Dream Haiti," see Stefanie Hessler, ed., *Tidalectics: Imagining an Oceanic Worldview Through Art and Science* (Cambridge: MIT Press, 2018).
5 Derek Walcott, *Omeros* (New York: Farrar, Straus and Giroux, 1990, and Derek Walcott, "The Sea Is History," *Selected Poems*, Edward Baugh, ed. (New York: Farrar, Straux and Giroux, 2007), 137–9.
6 Jonathan Pugh and David Chandler, *Anthropocene Islands: Entangled Worlds* (London: University of Westminster Press, 2021), 17 and *passim*.
7 Peter Hulme, *Colonial Encounters: Europe and the Native Caribbean, 1492–1797* (London: Methuen, 1986), 94. On English literary responses to New World storms, see Steve Mentz, "Hurricanes, Tempests, and the Meteorological Globe," *The Palgrave Handbook of Early Modern Literature and Science*, Howard Marchitello and Evelyn Tribble, eds. (London: Palgrave Macmillan, 2017), 257–76.
8 Stuart B. Schwartz, *Sea of Storms: A History of Hurricanes in the Greater Caribbean from Columbus to Katrina* (Princeton: Princeton University Press, 2015), xvii.
9 Monique Allewaert, *Ariel's Ecology: Plantations, Personhood, and Colonialism in the American Tropics* (Minneapolis: University of Minnesota Press, 2013), 1–9.
10 Sylviane Diouf, *Slavery's Exiles: The Story of the American Maroons* (New York: New York University Press, 2014), 2.
11 On these figures in dialogue, see *Maroons and the Marooned: Runaways and Castaways in the Americas*, Richard Bodek and Joseph Kelly, eds. (Jackson: University of Mississippi Press, 2020).
12 Neil Roberts, *Freedom as Marronage* (Chicago: University of Chicago Press, 2015), 9.
13 For a brief discussion of sweat and humidity in Faulkner and Welty, see Steve Mentz, "Ice/Water/Vapor," *The Cambridge Companion to the Environmental Humanities*, Jeffrey Jerome Cohen and Stephanie Foote, eds. (Cambridge: Cambridge University Press, 2021), 185–98, 187–88.
14 Marcus Rediker, *Villains of All Nations: Atlantic Pirates in the Golden Age* (Boston: Beacon Press, 2004); Dan Vitkus, *Piracy, Slavery, and Redemption: Barbary Captivity Narratives from Early Modern England* (New York: Columbia University Press, 2001); Claire Jowitt, *The Culture of Piracy, 1580–1630* (London: Routledge, 2010); Frederick Burwick and Manushag Powell, *British Pirates in Print and Performance* (London: Palgrave Macmillan, 2015).
15 Peter Sloterdijk, *In the World Interior of Capital: Towards a Philosophical Theory of Globalization*, Wieland Hoban, trans. (New York: Polity Press, 2013), 112.
16 On this topic, see a new book by the late anarchist scholar David Graeber, *Pirate Enlightenment, or the Real Libertalia* (New York: Farrar, Straus and Giroux, 2023).
17 Steve Mentz, *Shipwreck Modernity*, xxix.
18 Richard J. Blakemore. "Law and the Sea," *The Routledge Companion to Marine and Maritime Worlds, 1400–1800*, Claire Jowitt, Craig Lambert, and Steve Mentz, eds. (London: Routledge, 2021), 388–425.
19 On this injunction, see Christopher Connery, " 'There Will Be No More Sea': The Supersession of the Ocean, from the Bible to Hyperspace," *Journal of Historical Geography* 32:3 (2006), 494–511.

20 Michel Foucault, "Of Other Spaces," *Diacritics* 16 (1986), 22–27, 27. 1967 lecture, published in French 1984.
21 Harry Kelsey, *Sir Francis Drake: The Queen's Pirate* (New Haven: Yale University Press, 1998), 137.
22 [Daniel Defoe], *A General History of the Pyrates*, Manual Schonhorn, ed. (Mineola: Dover Maritime, 1999). Modern scholarship rejects Defoe's authorship of this collection.
23 See also Stephanie Smallwood, *Saltwater Slavery: A Middle Passage from Africa to American Diaspora* (Cambridge: Harvard University Press, 2008).
24 Monique Roffey, *The Mermaid of Black Conch* (New York: Alfred A. Knopf, 2022), 74.

8 Northern Visions

While the Southern Ocean presents the least humanized of the world's waters, a dynamic system of ice, water, and unimpeded winds, with an until-recently unpopulated continent at its core, the north polar regions, encircled by the northern tips of America, Europe, and Asia, comprise pure water. For much of the year, at least until recent global heating, the Arctic Ocean is covered by ice, across which Indigenous peoples travel and hunt. Ice-breaking ships also traverse this region, in recent years through the formerly impassable Northwest and Northeast Passages that link the North Atlantic and North Pacific basins. Beyond being its physical opposite—the north pole is a watery center surrounded by land, the south pole a land core surrounded by water—the Arctic region distinguishes itself from the Antarctic region through robust human presence. New evidence, as detailed in Jennifer Raff's *Origin: A Genetic History of the Americas* (2022), has pushed the earliest arrivals of Homo sapiens into Alaska and the Pacific coast back to around 20,000 years ago, substantially before the end of the last Ice Age.[1] The arrival of Viking voyagers around the year 1000 CE preceded by nearly half a millennium early modern efforts to find passages to Asia. The northern polar regions have long been central pathways for human migration. While efforts to pioneer maritime routes to Asia have, until now, been failures, the massive wealth of the north has come in fish—primarily cod, but also whales, pollack, crab, and many other commercial catches. The northern tip of the world has represented, at least since the sixteenth century, the wealthiest fishing grounds in the world.

Compared to the south, then, the north polar regions represent a human ice sea. The ancient presence of Eskimo–Inuit peoples preceded several distinct surges of non-native migrants, from the Norse around 1000 to Europeans after the mid-sixteenth century. Most of those Europeans came for fish, though fantasies of easy access to China and northern gold lured early modern explorers, including Sir Humphrey Gilbert, who drowned returning from Newfoundland in 1583, carrying with him a cargo of minerals he wrongly believed were gold. Gilbert, a major booster of Elizabethan colonization in Ireland and the New World, typifies early modern European colonial rapacity.[2] The alien icescape of the Arctic frustrated him. Floating sea

DOI: 10.4324/9781003166665-8

ice, which briefly fractures into open water during the short polar summer before clamping shut in the fall, represents the landscape's nonhuman actors. As Julie Cruikshank notes in *Do Glaciers Listen?* (2005), Indigenous oral traditions assert that "glaciers take action and respond to their surroundings" (1).[3] As this concept has been expanded by ecotheorist Lowell Duckert, the agency of ice appears not strictly metaphorical but articulates an "icespeak" that influences humans.[4] In this model, the "Ice Age is never over" (149) because the solid water landscape of the far north remains constantly in motion. Bathsheba Demuth's *Floating Coast* (2019), an exploration of the human and nonhuman ecologies of the Bering Sea, focuses on the "power of people's ideas to change the Earth" while also noting that humans are themselves shaped by "rules whose origins were not only human." Demuth further wonders, "What is the nature of history when nature is part of what *makes* history?"[5] In the Arctic the "nature" that is making history today includes rapid climate change, which occurs in the high latitudes much faster than the temperate zones.

The Arctic for these different writers represents a dynamic and deeply human land- and seascape. A front line in the changing climate, as well as a final frontier for resource extraction as the Northwest and Northeast passages open in the wake of melting sea ice, there is reason to believe this region will become increasingly visible to the global community in the twenty-first century. Scholarship by the geographer Phil Steinberg, who was appointed Chair of Political Geography at the University of the Arctic in January 2022, has been spearheading multiple initiatives on Arctic legal systems and geographies.[6] Blue humanities scholarship should attend to the diverse human and animal populations that occupy the region and engage with the dynamic ruptures currently being driven by climate change.

Hugh Willoughby, the Seafarer, and Ice

The English explorer Sir Hugh Willoughby froze to death in the winter of 1553–54 while his ship *Bona Esperanza* overwintered in Novaya Zemlya in what is now the Russian Arctic. None of his shipmates survived the winter either, though the Russian fishermen who found the ship the following spring recovered Willoughby's journal. The final days of this expedition represent a brutal, mortal encounter between humans and ice. To make sense of what the northern icescape represents, I juxtapose Willoughby's account with an Old English poem written during the tenth century about northern sea travel, "The Seafarer," which survives in one copy in the Exeter Book manuscript. The author and exact date of the poem remain unknown. I bring together a historical figure, Willoughby, and a literary figure, the Seafarer, because understanding extreme environments requires the combined resources of historical facts and poetic imagination. Ice as these two figures encounter it is solid fact and poetic gleam together, each figuration informing the other.

Water in its liquid state comprises the fundamental building block of life on our blue planet. Our bodies and our globe are equally aqueous. But the phase shift from liquid to solid reveals perhaps the single most important chemical anomaly that shapes terrestrial life. When water freezes, it expands and becomes less dense, so that solid ice floats in liquid water. Since a general rule of physics is that things shrink when cooled, this property of frozen water is unusual. The expansion of ice enables underwater life to survive even in low temperatures. The positively charged hydrogen atoms in ice crystals form a network of bonds with each other, linking molecules of ice together. The lattice of these bonds holds open space that causes an assemblage of frozen water molecules to expand slightly compared to the liquid state. In an ecological context, this property of ice enables the biological survival of creatures beneath a frozen surface. Floating ice also facilitates hunting by humans, polar bears, and other large predators. The paradoxical structure of ice subtends its deep allure and its function as both catastrophic limit and aesthetic ideal. We love ice and some humans depend on it, but it does not love us.

My literary figure, the narrator of "The Seafarer," voices a lyrical description of frozen northern waters as sites of physical, cultural, and spiritual alienation. In his telling, "ice-cold waves" ("iscaldne waeg" 19a) represent human exile, even though they may eventually give way to a promised reward from God in heaven ("Faeder on heofunum" 115a).[7] By contrast, my historical figure, Willoughby, treats ice as obstacle. The confluence of poetic alienation and historical encumbrance suggests that ice represents an environmental limit that humans translate into cultural symbol. Willoughby confronts a killing icescape that resists being transmuted into symbol, but nonetheless he, like the Old English poet, makes ice into metaphor. These two responses suggest that it is not finally possible to separate ice as barrier from ice as idea. Human understandings of ice emerge by mixing these perspectives.

I juxtapose the experiences of these two men, one historical and the other fictional, in relation to three experiences that characterize premodern encounters with the frozen north: ice as discovery, ice as mystery, and ice as catastrophe. Willoughby's words come from historical records gathered and published in Elizabethan London by Richard Hakluyt, an early advocate for transatlantic colonial expansion. Willoughby's death was one of many disasters Hakluyt needed to explain away in order to build support for colonialism. These two figures together show how ice provides a glimpse into the risks of transforming environmental dangers into symbolic tokens as well as the human compulsion to perform those transformations.

Willoughby explains that his task as captain general of the Muscovy Company's voyage was "to goe to countries to them heretofore unkonwen, as well to seeke such things as we lacke, as also to cary unto them from our regions, such things as they lacke" (2:210).[8] The ultimate goal was a Northeast Passage that would open trade with "the mighty empire of Cathay" (2:209). The animating vision was "universal amitie" (2:210), in which "every man desireth to joine friend with other" (2:209). Willoughby sailed as merchant and discoverer, and his surviving writings epitomize a culture that imagined no distinction between these identities.[9] His chief pilot, Richard Chancellor, on board a slightly larger ship, survived the winter and arrived the following spring at Ivan the Terrible's court. Willoughby encountered ice instead of Russia.

The seafarer's itinerary is less geographically precise. He speaks of his "food-weary soul" ("merewerges mod" 12a) and the prison it makes his body: "My feet fettered with ice, clasped by cold, bound with frost" (8b–10b). He expresses no illusions about human amity. He travels with and to ice, rather than encountering it along the way. The seafarer follows his cold path into the whale's home, "hwaeles ethel" (60a), where he hears the cries of birds. He takes pleasure from them but wishes they were human:

> At times the swan's cry pleased me,
> The gannet's noise and curlew's voice
> Substituted for human laughter.
> Still the gulls sang
> While others drink mead.
>
> *(19b–22b)*

The seafarer speaks of being lured toward ice-mountains and seeing colors in the sky. He ventures forth:

> And now my spirit twists outside,
> Bursts from the locker of my heart onto the flood.
> Spanning the whale's home it soars wide
> Across the wet surface of the curving earth . . .
>
> *(58a–61a)*

Soul-flight is the seafarer's goal. He seeks neither the gold of Cathay nor mercantile profit, but only mystery and the touch of icy waters, alien and insistent.

Willoughby also found mystery but was not looking for it. He became confused when he sailed past Iceland and around the north cape of Norway into the cold waters we now name the Barents Sea, after another dead explorer. "The land lay not as the Globe made mention" (2:221), he wrote in his journal. When he found a harbor, he wrote, "The water was so shoale, where was very much ice also" (2:221). In this haven, Willoughby's ship sat, and ice surrounded it. Willoughby never recorded the experience in words, but he must have felt something inside the frozen-in *Bona Esperanza* in January 1554. Catastrophe was no fiery apocalypse but rather a slow freezing, a drowsy half-step struggle to burn anything that could slow down the slowing down. Each day he became a little more like the ice around his ship. The last thing he wrote in his journal, describes when he was pleased to have found good anchorage at 72 degrees north latitude in six fathoms of water. His final encounter with ice began with bounty:

> The haven runneth into the maine [land], about two leagues, and is in bredth half a league, wherein were very many seale fishes, & other great fishes, and upon the maine we saw beares, great deere, foxes, with divers strange beasts . . . and such other which were to us unknowen, and also wonderful.
>
> (2:223)

Here, he reports, "we thought best to winter" (2:223). Hakluyt's marginal note in the printed text records the consequence: "In this haven they died" (2:223). Dying Willoughby may well have thought about ice in those final days, inside the trapped ship, waiting as everything slowed and their bodies did too.

The seafarer's insight is sharper and more pointed. "Fate is greater," he writes, "the Maker mightier, than any thoughts of men" (115b–116b). We can imagine the two dead men silently holding hands, encountering the frozen element together. The contemporary poet Caroline Bergvall voices the harsh lesson of ice in her book *Drift* (2014), which is in part a translation of "The Seafarer": "Let the tides shake your life" (110).[10] The seafarer reminds us "there is no man on earth" who has not encountered "sea-sorrow." Sometimes this vision is doomed, as in Willoughby's innocent phrase, "we thought best to winter there" (2:223). The encounter with ice never fails to change us. Living near ice invites an alien presence into our experience of this watery planet. It burns when we touch it.

The Ocean from an Island: Melville's "Nantucket"

Mariners such as Willoughby, like many others who sought the Northwest and Northeast passages through the Arctic, aimed to make the north pole a global crossroads. The fantasy of transoceanic connection finds powerful voice in the early chapter "Nantucket" in *Moby-Dick*. In describing an island off the Massachusetts coast, today a playground for millionaires and vacationing American presidents, Melville transforms the small rock into a maritime gateway. By connecting "Nantucket" to the Arctic Ocean, I suggest that Melville's oceanic vision better resembles the polar north than coastal New England.

In Melville's vision, Nantucket barely can be categorized as land at all. "Look at it," he exclaims, "a mere hillock, and elbow of sand, all beach, without a background" (64). The most basic feature of land—that it provides a habitat for vegetation—does not hold here, since "they have to plant weeds there, they don't grow naturally" (64). Occupying this barren elbow, both the Indigenous inhabitants and their Quaker whaleman inheritors—Melville strategically blurs the histories of these two groups—"pushed off in boats and captured cod" (65), before moving on to bigger prey. In the nineteenth-century present of the novel, the watery kingdom of Nantucket whalemen rivals the violent conquest of new lands for the American nation:

> Let America add Mexico to Texas, and pile Cuba upon Canada; let the English overswarm all India, and hang out their blazing banner from the sun: two thirds of this terraqueous globe are the Nantucketer's.
>
> (65)

The whaler's island has dominion over the sea. By comparison, terrestrial conquests, however vast, count little.

Nantucket globalism embraces all the seas of the world, but there is reason to suspect that Melville remains partial to polar extremes. He emphasizes that Nantucket ships have "put an incessant belt of circumnavigations round" (65) the globe, but more particularly he observes that these sailors have "peeped in at Bhering's Straits" (65), between Alaska and Siberia. In the rousing peroration of the short chapter, Melville invokes the Biblical Flood, stating that, for the Nantucketer, "a Noah's flood would not interrupt" (66) business on the great waters. The phrase "Noah's flood" appears several other times in *Moby-Dick*, notably in "Brit" ("Noah's flood is not yet subsided" 224) and "Will the Whale Diminish?" ("In Noah's flood he despised Noah's ark" 354). Both these chapters, along with "Nantucket," imagine whalemen penetrating high north or south latitudes. For *Moby-Dick*, the center of the world may be the island of Nantucket, but the goal of the mariners' wanderings appears as the farthest and coldest reaches of the polar seas.

A Brief History of Atlantic Cod

Melville's whale-focused rhapsodies should not obscure the primary source of wealth for Europeans in the waters around Newfoundland: the millennium-long harvest of codfish from the Grand Banks. Beginning around the year 1000 CE, by which point Europe's freshwater streams and lakes had already been substantially depleted, European ships sailed north and west into this abundant fishery. Mark Kurlansky's bestselling history *Cod: A Biography of a Fish that Changed the World* (1997) chronicles the thousand years of European cod fishing, from the early voyages of Vikings and Basque mariners, followed by the English and many others, through to the Canadian codfish moratorium in 1992 after the fish population had crashed.[11] Marine biologist Callum Roberts argues in *the Unnatural History of the Sea* (2007) that the story of cod represents the norm rather than an exception: human fishing always depletes fish stocks, after which point fishermen change technologies, locations, target species, or all of these.[12] The story of North Atlantic cod follows the familiar pattern of resource depletion on a millennial timescale. Between the Viking arrival into the North Atlantic around 1000 CE and the moratorium by the Canadian government in 1992, millions of tons of codfish emerged from the sea floor to feed humans around the North Atlantic and the world.

A detailed analysis of the long history of northern Atlantic and Arctic fishing appears in W. Jeffrey Bolster's *The Mortal Sea: Fishing the Atlantic in the Age of Sail* (2012). Bolster emphasizes that reports of American abundance that were brought back to early modern Europe by mariners such as John Smith are considered by ecologists and marine scientists to emerge from the contrast with locally depleted fishing grounds in and near Europe. "American abundance," Bolster observes, "reflected European depletion."[13] While it was long common to assume that Smith's portraits of teeming wildlife in North America were exaggerations or utopian fantasies, the current consensus is that early modern Europeans had never seen a non-depleted ecosystem. Bolster notes that "when Renaissance seamen and naturalists such as Anthony Parkhurst, John Smith, and James Rosier were describing lush boreal estuaries on the American shore, the assault on European boreal estuaries, rivers, and coastal seas had persisted for centuries" (31). The massive surge of fishing in northern waters preceded the continental settlements in Jamestown, Quebec, and Plymouth. By the seventeenth century, Bolster estimates "as many as 200,000 metric tons of cod per year (live weight) were leaving Newfoundland for Europe" (47). That abundance of protein, and wealth, was in the long run unsustainable, as the late-twentieth-century crash shows. Bolster further documents, however, multiple efforts by early modern leaders, including such prominent figures as Governor William Bradford of Plymouth Colony, to restrict fishing to preserve fish populations. Ultimately, these efforts would not keep up with changes in fishing technology, most destructively the bottom trawl, and economic pressure. The story of the northern codfish, like that of whales and many other fish stocks, continues to be one of failure, at least in the long run.

Dark Traffic: Joan Naviyuk Kane's Melting Arctic

The final textual example describing the human relationship with the Arctic comes from the contemporary Inupiaq poet Joan Naviyuk Kane. Kane, whose family comes from King Island (Ugiuvak) and Mary's Igloo in northwestern Alaska, is an award-winning poet and faculty member at the Institution of American Indian Arts. Her book *Dark Traffic* (2021) contains a series of poems that reflect upon the changing nature of water in Alaska's Bering Sea coast. I will focus primarily on the title poem of the collection. Climate change disrupts the frozen surfaces across which Indigenous people have traveled for centuries. Kane's poem recognizes the rupture of this twenty-first-century moment, and she observes the human burdens of persistence and adaptation. Her verse, in the title poem and throughout the collection, responds to the fracturing of the Arctic climate by evoking pervasive loss, exploring forms of adaptation, and imagining possibilities for new relationships with a changing place. As new texts for blue humanities scholarship, the poems in *Dark Traffic* open windows onto a remote and changing icescape.[14]

Increased temperatures, which have come faster in the Arctic than most other places, have led to literally unsettling losses of stability. Where land and sea were once solid and frozen, they now melt into water and mud. As the Inuit activist Sheila Watt-Cloutier observes in her book *The Right to Be Cold* (2015), "The world I was born into has changed forever."[15] Loss of sea ice and Indigenous languages, among other things, has contributed to the "what seemed permanent begin[ning] to melt away" (2). In response to this physical and cultural loss, Kane's poems memorialize transformation. In "Dark Traffic," the title poem of her book, the poet fixes on physical loss; she sees only "water/over water where once we found ice."[16] The absence of once-solid ice also represents cultural loss. "There is no day without a symptom" (5), Kane observes. The "Dark Traffic" that the poem describes refers obliquely, as do many of the poems in the volume, to the out-migration of people, especially women, from traditional lands. "*I thought her gone already*," the poem observes in italicized right-justified lines, "*that she had gone/to neglect the late migration*" (5, emphasis in original). The poem bears witness, in its spare lines and fragmented syntax, to the shattering of a system.

Later poems in the book, including "I Am Chopping Ivory or Bone" and "Dark Passage," respond to climate disruption via imagined dialogues. As Craig Santos Perez's poems embrace the Indigenous languages of Oceania, Kane's verse memorializes and employs Inupiaq words throughout her book. Her poems demonstrate how human vocabularies capture moments of crisis in dynamic environments, including basic changes in things such as the presence or absence of ice, liquid water, birds, and animals. Faced with loss and radical change, humans adapt, often in painful ways. Kane's poems present complex processes of adaptation. The sea that once was solid ice melts and collapses into formlessness. Birds and marine mammals can no longer survive this new waterscape. The poet bears witness to the end of an ecological system binding together humans, animals, and the ocean.

The story Kane's poems tell is tragic, but her act of telling constructs new relations between humans and nonhumans. Especially in poems such as "The Sea" and "Rehearsal for Surveying the Ruins," she engages with changing Arctic water- and icescapes. Like all environmental art in the Anthropocene, these poems witness suffering and imagine ways to endure. An Indigenous environmental poet of the north, Kane represents loss, adaptation, and the pain of recreating a life in a place that is not what it once was. As the twenty-first-century Arctic continues its rapid changes, voices such as Kane's are essential to remember the human past and prepare for an uncertain future.

Notes

1 Jennifer Raff, *Origin: A Genetic History of the Americas* (New York: Twelve, 2022).
2 On Gilbert's last doomed voyage, see Steve Mentz, "Hakluyt's Oceans: Maritime Rhetoric in *The Principal Navigations*." *Richard Hakluyt and Travel Writing in Early Modern Europe*, Daniel Carey and Claire Jowitt, eds. (Aldershot: Ashgate, 2012), 283–94.
3 Julie Cruikshank, *Do Glaciers Listen?: Local Knowledge, Colonial Encounters, and Social Imagination* (Vancouver: UBC Press, 2022), 1.
4 Lowell Duckert, *For All Waters: Finding Ourselves in Early Modern Wetscapes* (Minneapolis: University of Minnesota Press, 2017), 102.
5 Bathsheba Demuth, *Floating Coast: An Environmental History of the Bering Strait* (New York: W. W. Norton & Company, 2019), 3. Italics in original.
6 On Steinberg's appointment, see www.durham.ac.uk/research/current/thought-leadership/the-university-of-the-arctic-uarctic-appointed-prof-philip-steinberg-as-chair/. Accessed 19 October 2022.
7 "The Seafarer," *A Guide to Old English*, Bruce Mitchell and Fred C. Robinson, eds., 5th ed. (London: Blackwell, 1992), 276–82. Cited by line and half-line in the text. All translations from the Old English text of "The Seafarer" are mine. The most famous modern translation is by Ezra Pound in 1911. Other modern versions appear in Michael J. Alexander, ed. and trans., *The Earliest English Poems*, 2nd ed. (New York: Penguin, 1977), 63–79, and Craig Williamson, trans., *The Complete Old English Poems*, Tom Shippey, intr. (Philadelphia: University of Pennsylvania Press, 2017), 467–71.
8 Richard Hakluyt, ed., *The Principal Navigations Voyages Traffics and Discoveries of the English Nation*. Vol. 12 (New York: AMS Press, 1965).
9 On English exploration and trade, see Richard Helgerson, *Forms of Nationhood: The Elizabethan Writing of England* (Chicago: University of Chicago Press, 1994).
10 Caroline Bergvall, *Drift* (Brooklyn: Nightboat Books, 2014), 110.
11 Mark Kurlansky, *Cod: A Biography of the Fish that Changed the World* (London: Walker Books, 1997).
12 Callum Roberts, *The Unnatural History of the Sea* (London: Shearwater, 2007).
13 W. Jeffrey Bolster, *The Mortal Sea: Fishing the Atlantic in the Age of Sail* (Cambridge: Belknap Press, 2012), 41.
14 Joan Naviyuk Kane, *Dark Traffic* (Pittsburgh: University of Pittsburgh Press, 2021), 5. Further citations given in the book by page number.
15 Sheila Watt-Cloutier, *The Right to Be Cold: One Woman's Fight to Protect the Arctic and Save the Planet from Climate Change*, Bill McKibben, intr. (Minneapolis: University of Minnesota Press, 2018), 1.
16 "Dark Traffic" from *Dark Traffic* by Joan Naviyuk Kane. ©2021. Reprinted by permission of Pittsburgh University Press.

9 The Tornadoed Atlantic

In modern world history, the Atlantic circulates in a loop, from Europe and Africa westward through the tropics, up into the Caribbean, and northeast along the coast of North America before returning to Europe. Similar loops, spinning counterclockwise, connect southern Africa and South America. Following the winds and currents of the North and South Atlantic gyres, these circles fueled the "triangular trade" that brought millions of enslaved Africans across the ocean into plantation slavery, while returning raw materials from the New World back to European economies. In the half-millennium of the slave trade's mercantile orbit, these gyres shaped Atlantic history and launched European maritime empires onto the World Ocean. In the opening essay of *Poetics of Relation*, Éduoard Glissant observes that the transatlantic trade in humans and the slave ship he calls a "womb abyss" represent violent birth:

> Imagine two hundred human beings crammed into a space barely capable of containing a third of them. Imagine vomit, naked flesh, swarming lice, the dead slumped, the dying crouched. Imagine, if you can, the swirling red of mounting to the deck, the ramp they climbed, the black sun on the horizon, vertigo, this dizzying sky plastered to the waves.[1]

The modern Caribbean as Glissant and others have imagined it took shape during the Middle Passage. His striking description constructs the modern Atlantic as less the parent of the Caribbean basin than its discontinuous appendage. To be Atlantic after Glissant means to poise oneself between the creole cultures of the New World and the imperializing visions of Old Europe.

A slightly less Caribbean-centric vision of this transoceanic movement appears in the Black Atlantic as theorized by Paul Gilroy. In his book *The Black Atlantic* (1993), Gilroy emphasizes the sea's engendering of mobility and exchange. The "central organizing symbol" for Gilroy is "the image of ships in motion across the spaces between Europe, America, Africa, and the Caribbean."[2] The historian Stephanie Smallwood, in her *Saltwater Slavery* (2007), emphasizes how oceangoing voyages "challenged African

DOI: 10.4324/9781003166665-9

cosmologies, for the landless realm of the deep ocean did not figure in precolonial West African societies as a domain of human (as opposed to divine) activity."[3] Transportation to the New World was not exclusively westbound—Africans and Native Americans traveled both east and west across the Atlantic during the early modern period—but for the majority of the transported, the journey was one way. The forging of new identities and cultures in the Americas emerged in dialogue with African social orders, but the New World differed radically from the old.[4] When scholars such as the eco-Marxist Jason W. Moore and the earth systems scientists Simon Lewis and Mark Maslin both finger transatlantic slavery as the origin point of modernity and the Anthropocene, they turn to the horrors Glissant, Smallwood, Gilroy, and many others have excavated.[5]

In linking the Atlantic to the physical feature of polarity, which represents water's tendency to function as a universal solvent, I treat the dissolving violence of the Middle Passage as the defining global event of modernity. Just as a polarized water molecule, with its asymmetry between positive hydrogen and negative oxygen charges, breaks down and eventually dissolves any substance placed inside it, so the Atlantic system dissolved and recreated the human cultures who mixed along its waterways after the fifteenth century. Many scholars, including Smallwood and Rediker, have emphasized how the slave trade remade the plural cultural identities of African nations and tribes into a semi-collective "African-American" identity on the far side of the ocean.[6] Many regional and national identities, from Chile and Argentina to Canada and the United States, have been formed out of the combination and mutual dissolution of disparate cultures after the transatlantic encounter. The results of Atlantic polarity and human dissolution have been a group of polyglot and polyethnic societies built atop the dispossession of most of the hemisphere's Indigenous inhabitants. In highlighting polarity and dissolution in Atlantic and transatlantic context, I emphasize the forced transportation of Africans as the core of modernity's transformation, while also recognizing that many other peoples and cultures were dissolved in the globalizing stew.

Among efforts to conceptualize and respond to the legacy of transoceanic violence, the works of Saidiya Hartman and Christina Sharpe stand out. Hartman, in a series of literary-historical works that respond to lives about which established archives rarely do justice, describes in *Lose Your Mother* her experience as an African-American academic in Ghana, from whence so many slave ships sailed. "I, too," she writes, "am the afterlife of slavery."[7] Sharpe takes the present tense as conceptual challenge and impossible task: "How do we memorialize an event that is still ongoing?"[8] To theorize an answer, Sharpe creates what she calls "wake work" (21). Among the relevant meanings of the word "wake" for her theory, blue humanities scholars might be especially interested in "the track left on the water's surface by a ship, the disturbance caused by a body swimming, . . . a region of disturbed flow" (21)—as well as the non-maritime meanings of a ritual of mourning and to become awake, or fully conscious (21). Following Sharpe, the fluid presence of the Atlantic seems essential to understand the realities of Black life and multiracial societies of the modern Americas.

The Atlantic also, as readers of this book's Preface may recall, represents the ocean down the street from my house in New England. Older and, in many ways, dated academic histories of "Atlantic history" were built explicitly alongside the Anglo-American alliance and the North Atlantic Treaty Organization.[9] The scientific lyricism of Rachel Carson, the founding mother of American environmentalism, emerged from her lifelong connection to the Atlantic seaboard. The stark contrast between the horrors of slavery, as explored by figures such as Hartman, Sharpe, and Dionne Brand, and the lyrical evocation of the Atlantic shore, as described by Carson among others, poses a theoretical challenge. How can we love the same sea that covers, in Glissant's phrase, "those balls and chains gone green"? (6). Few writers or thinkers can hold simultaneously the truths of slavery and of oceanic experience. Perhaps Melville's manic vision of whiteness, alterity, and violence comes close.

Demonism, Whiteness, Whales: Melville's Oceanic View

The core enigma of *Moby-Dick* is whiteness. Published in 1851 and drawing on Melville's maritime experiences in the 1840s as well as the legend of the albino whale Mocha Dick, which sunk the whaleship *Essex* in 1820, Melville's novel transforms the whale's unusual color into a dynamic metaphor for unstable American identities.[10] Published a decade before the Civil War, the novel engages with the whiteness of white supremacy in the United States. In dividing his novel's focus between murderous Ahab and mystical Ishmael, Melville responds ambivalently to ideas about whiteness as dominion. Ishmael himself, not his captain, spends an entire chapter ruminating on "The Whiteness of the Whale." Even though other interpretations of the novel seem viable, especially those that follow C.L.R. James in focusing on the multiracial crew of the *Pequod*, the mystery of whiteness sits near the book's heart.[11] "It was the whiteness of the whale," Ishmael intones, "that above all things appalled me" (159). Rarely one to undersell his anxieties, the narrator continues that "in some dim, random way, explain myself I must, else all these chapters might be naught" (159). To define whiteness as fear and obsession represents Ishmael's intellectual goal. The narrator himself never arrives at clarity—but perhaps, in dialogue with longer view of Atlantic and literary history, it may be possible to clarify his befuddlement. Whiteness represents an urge to dominate. Ahab seeks to slay whiteness as a trophy. Ishmael, perhaps like his author Melville, hopes to comprehend it.

When the narrator explores the color white as historical and physical feature of "vague, nameless horror" (159), he elaborates a cultural system that centers whiteness while also etherealizing it. After cataloging white figures from the albatross to Jove as a white bull, Ishmael settles on the "Albino man" (161) as the key. The Albino resembles other men but is rejected by them:

> The Albino is as well made as other men—has no substantive deformity—and yet this mere aspect of all-pervading whiteness makes him more strangely hideous than the ugliest abortion? Why should this be so?
>
> (161)

The repeated trope of "The Whiteness of the Whale" is the rhetorical question. As in Ishmael's opening-chapter interjection "Who ain't a slave?" (21), these questions explore but do not fully engage with racial categories. The Albino, like the poor Yankee schoolteacher turned whaleman, is white but does not fully embrace the position of whiteness, in the sense of social and cultural dominion. To be an albino, like Moby Dick and his historical model Mocha Dick, means to arrive at whiteness through absence. "Not so much a color as the visible absence of color" (165), as Ishmael sums up the paradox. The "colorless, all-color of atheism" (165) represents not social and racial hierarchy but a stripping away of all markers of power and identity. It seems meaningful that the name Moby Dick is, of course, not what the whale would call himself.

The white-churn of identity crisis that defines the White Whale as well as Ishmael's ambivalent relationship to his own white ancestry expresses itself through multiple kinds of white water. In exploring how whiteness serves as horror-booster, accentuating the "terror of objects otherwise terrible" (163), Ishmael first considers, from the point of view of a sailor at sea, the "roar of breakers" (163) and the "midnight sea of milky whiteness" (163) within which a ship nearing land might find itself. The "hideous whiteness" (164) of the surf calls up the heart-striking vision of snow on distant peaks, such as the Andes above Lima. That unreachable whiteness, "the eternal frosted desolateness reigning at such vast altitudes" (164), causes the narrator to consider "what a fearfulness it would be to lose oneself in such inhuman solitudes" (164). While white racial identity asserts itself as social power, in and after antebellum America, Melville's novel conjures whiteness in waterforms, especially surf and snow, as corrosive of identity. Whiteness drives Ishmael back to the imagined suicidal illness—the "hypos"—of his opening chapter. Perhaps, he wonders, "this white-lead chapter about whiteness is but a white flag, hung out from a craven soul: thou surrenderest to a hypo, Ishmael" (164). Whiteness can neither protect nor solidify the narrator's self.

This plotless, discursive chapter about whiteness does not fully clarify Ishmael's self-understanding, though it does emphasize how his education as whaleman, most of which takes place after the voyage in search of Moby Dick, attempts to fill a hollow core. As retrospective narrator, he builds to a frenzy of white-meanings, finding in whiteness "the great principle of light, [which] for ever remains white or colorless in itself" (165). In a dominion of universal whiteness, Ishmael imagines himself a snowbound Laplander, who "gazes himself blind at the monumental white shroud that wraps all the prospect around him" (165). Melville will use the same word, "shroud," to identify endless liquid water in the last line of the novel's last chapter, when he refers to the "great shroud of the sea" (427). Ice or surf or sea, all "demonism in the world" (164) colors itself white. The devotion that Ishmael feels for the ocean and its godlike whales entwines itself with demonic whiteness. The tragic shape of *Moby-Dick* encompasses more falls than just that of the captain. In identifying himself with sea creatures and oceanic space, Ishmael casts himself off from shore. What hope for a solitary mariner in a world of whiteness?

Rachel Carson's Coastal Encounters

Alongside Ishmael, rhapsodist of the nineteenth-century deep ocean, I counterpose Rachel Carson, poet–scientist of the beach in the twentieth century. Turning from Melville to Carson means shifting gender and genre. Carson's distinctive environment, the beach, enables this shift. On the most basic level, beaches transition. One side is land, and the other sea. Either environment can be as extensive as continent or ocean or as sliver-thin as barrier island or tidal inlet. In all cases, the beach marks the shift, the abrupt and unstable conversion of land to sea or sea to land.

For blue humanities scholars, beaches can be imagined as material arguments, in which land's stability and its nominal support of human culture struggle against the sea's alien motion. In treating this space as a conflict, I speak to both a physical process, in which the incessant friction of sea reduces rocks into grains of sand, and to a metaphorical structure, in which contrasting environments rub against and disturb each other. Among other dualities, of which land/sea, still/moving, and dry/wet remain the most meaningful, the word argument appears to be a divisible term. It refers to the sea's frothing argument with static land and to the arguments we advance in academic discourses. Blue humanities thinkers argue with words as the sea argues with the beach.

Rachel Carson is arguably the most important American sea writer in the twentieth-century after Melville. It seems important that she is a beachcomber, not a deep-water sailor. "In the sea," she writes in *The Edge of the Sea* (1955), "nothing lives to itself."[12] Her lyrical presentation of biological ideas can be extended to the history of human encounters on beaches. Together these two processes enable the physical intermixing of water and land to trigger interpretations that treat beaches as conceptual and physical engagements. Using *The Edge of the Sea* as structural inspiration, I briefly explore the idea of beach as template for an argument between land and sea.

This analysis draws on the thriving sub-discourse of beach studies. In a 2021 special issue of *Comparative Literature* on "Beaches and Ports," Hannah Freed-Thall discusses these locations as "a confluence of bodies, sand, and cargo boxes, and as a matrix of literary and cinematic form."[13] Drawing inspiration from recent work in "oceanic and maritime studies" (131) as well as on the half-dozen substantial articles in the special issue, Freed-Thall explores the meanings attributed to places where land and sea meet. Inspired, like me, by Carson's *Edge of the Sea*, she also explores what Roland Barthes has called the "beach effect" (136). Drawing on thinkers from Allan Sekula to John Gillis, Elsa Devienne, Margaret Cohen, Michael Taussig, Jean-Didier Urbain, and others, she zeros in on the twenty-first-century beach.[14] Her key examples are the artificial Paris Plages that appeared along the Seine in the summers starting in 2002, which she terms an "apt emblem of Anthropocene-era 'nature': colonized, commoditized, artificially-engineered, bombed, trashed—and all the while, intensely fetishized" (135). John Gillis emphasizes that the twenty-first-century beach is rapidly changing during accelerated sea-level rise and coastal development.[15] The sand may be located at the physical margin of the "blue" of the blue humanities, but many scholars recognize this rich ecotone and cultural contact zone as a key environment for human histories and futures.

When Carson described beaches as presenting "the unifying touch of the sea" (249), she was relying on a conception of ocean as substantially beyond human trespass. Comparative religion scholar Kimberly Patton has noted in *The Sea Can Wash Away All Evils* (2006) that ancient and enduring beliefs about the sea as infinitely purifying sit uneasily alongside our global pollution and warming.[16] By the 1950s, Carson had already noticed a "general warming-up" (23) trend that has become increasingly destructive. For Carson, as for many coastal writers and thinkers before the past quarter-century, the ocean represents a "universal truth that lies just beyond our grasp" (250). In making beaches into arguments, I aim to bring these ancient ideas into conversation with contemporary realities. Anthropocene entanglements will abrade but not entirely disfigure Carson's lyric vision. Partly it seems that Carson, with her keen insight into dynamism, was already almost there before we gave the Anthropocene its name. I also emphasize, drawing inspiration from colonial historians such as Greg Dening, that beaches always host conflict.[17] Physical waves grind physical rocks into tiny granules. Different humans meet on beaches with often violent consequences. Arguments are made, sometimes convincingly, and other times less so.

In thinking about beaches as arguments, I draw on three resonant phrases, all of which appear on the opening page of *The Edge of the Sea*. First, Carson insists that "unrest" (1) represents the defining quality of this place. Its incessant motion refuses all stasis. Next, she claims that this quality of beaches unsettles human dreams of historical continuity. "For no two days," Carson intones, "is the shoreline precisely the same" (1). She further asserts that "the shore has a dual nature" (1), which faces equally both the sea and the land. Beaches, in this compact argument, represent a key environment for dynamism and disruption. Carson's beaches can further be imagined as Anthropocene spaces, previewing on microscales the things that will change and how some things may yet endure.

These three phrases characterize what can be learned from spaces where the water meets the shore. The "dual nature" of these spaces remains essential. You can always find at least one more creature on the beach beside you. Unrest itself, perhaps, becomes a foundation. The Bible advises us not to build our houses on sand, but when we look around at our oceanic globe, the edge of the sea seems clearly where humans want to build. Unrest, not stability, marks the foundation when land and sea meet. We cannot escape it. Perhaps we should embrace it. Taking up the question of temporal instability, or what we might term, in Carson's phrase, the "no two days" phenomenon: whatever happens on the beach one day will not happen again. The sea–land interface teaches instability in time and dynamism in place. These are painful and abrasive lessons for terrestrial mammals who live in time. These truths abrade the rocks that are ground into grains of sand. To live with friction, to love nonhuman pressures, to engage oneself with change as it, and we, change—these are the beach's closing arguments.

Equiano's *Interesting Narrative* and the Black Atlantic

In recent decades, driven in part by the scholarship of editor and biographer Vincent Carretta, the abolitionist writer and mariner Olaudah Equiano has become a central figure in Anglophone literary studies.[18] His autobiography, *The Interesting Narrative of the Life of Olaudah Equiano, or Gustavas Vassa, the African*, published in London in 1789 and New York in 1791, represents a major text in the transoceanic circulation of antislavery ideas, texts, and networks, as well as a fixture of Gilroy's Black Atlantic. The most famous section in the autobiography, Equiano's narrative of the Middle Passage, provides the only extant first-person narrative of this horror. His close description of being "put down under the decks," including the emphasis on "such a salutation in my nostrils as I had never experienced in my life" (56), contributes to the power of the text, both to late-eighteenth-century abolitionists and to twenty-first-century readers. Carretta's discovery of documentary evidence concerning Equiano's early life casts some doubt on the *Narrative*'s claim that its author was born in Africa in 1745; he may have been born, according to baptismal records, in South Carolina. Scholars continue to debate this evidence.[19] In Carretta's view, Equiano, whether born in America or Africa, is best understood as "Afro-British" by choice, like other prominent writers of African descent including Ignatius Sancho and Ottobah Cugoano (xviii). In becoming "British by acculturation and choice" (xviii), Equiano participates in British abolitionist politics. Without taking a position on the larger question of the author's biographical origins, my presentation of Equiano as a key blue humanities figure emphasizes his maritime experiences and their shaping role in his life and writing. As Carretta observes, for Equiano maritime life provided "an almost utopian, microcosmic alternative to the slavery-infested great world, in the little world of the ships of the British Royal Navy and merchant marine" (xxiii–xxiv). The slave ship that may have transported this particular African across the Atlantic is of course not one of these utopian vessels. Instead, Equiano, like other mariners of African descent who used their skills to find freedom and political agency, including American whalemen Paul Cuffe and William Sherman, joined in a community of maritime Africans.[20]

The ship, with its interoceanic mobility and need for skilled, independent labor, becomes an idealized counter-representation of the slave system. Gilroy, who draws extensively on Equiano, emphasizes that "ships occupy a primary symbolic and political place" (27) in his theory of the Black Atlantic. Michel Foucault's earlier celebration of the ship as "heterotopia par excellence" further connects ships to assertions of freedom.[21] Equiano's autobiography contains many moments in which maritime skills enable him to assume agency over his life. When he is sold to the West Indies, about which he says that "every part of the world in which I had hitherto been seemed to me a paradise in comparison of the West Indies" (119), he tells his owner that "I knew something of seamanship" (100). Maritime skills, eventually, enable Equiano to become, along with the captain of his ship, "nearly the most useful men in my master's employment" (115). Seamanship earns him money—funds which Equiano eventually used to purchase his manumission in 1766, though he continued to work on ships owned by his former master for around two more years.

In a closely narrated episode, a slaveholding ship on which Equiano sails is wrecked in the Bahamas and the crew survives only through his heroism and leadership. This episode, which begins with Equiano dreaming "that the ship was wrecked amidst the surf and rocks, and that I was the means of saving everyone on board" (148), brings to light the leadership capacities of the former slave. Paul Gilroy, in his 2019 Holberg Prize lecture, suggests that this episode symbolically constructs a "hydrophanic ethics in which meaning is revealed through the mediating agency or presence of water."[22] Equiano's narration follows a literary structure typical of shipwrecks, from the premonitory dream to his own fears and self-condemnation at the moment of crisis. "All my sins stared me in the face," he writes, "and especially I thought that God had hurled his direful vengeance on my guilty head for cursing the vessel on which my life depended" (149). This shipwreck, with its parallels to literary wrecks such as the openings of Virgil's *Aeneid* and Shakespeare's *Tempest*, becomes a moment of symbolic rupture and transformation.[23] Equiano, whose narrative shapes itself as Protestant redemption narrative rather than classical epic or Renaissance drama, asserts that "my sin was the cause of this" (149) and then goes on to bring "all on board safe to shore" (151). His heroic behavior contrasts sharply with the cowardly drunkenness of his fellow sailors, "for not one of the white men did anything to preserves their lives; and indeed they soon got so drunk that they were not able, but lay about on the deck like swine" (151). Whether the classical allusion to Odysseus's men transformed into pigs by Circe is intentional or not (*Odyssey* 10), Equiano's heroic stature is clear.[24] He becomes "a kind of chieftain amongst" the survivors. He transformed himself, through skilled labor in a moment of crisis, into a figure of authority.

The Bahamas wreck marks a fork in Equiano's life and career. After successfully completing his former master's voyage to Georgia, and nearly being kidnapped back into slavery there, he breaks with the Caribbean and sails for England. The latter half of his maritime career includes voyages to the Arctic in *HMS Racehorse* in 1773 and to the Mosquito Coast in Central America. By the 1780s, Equiano settled in London and made connections with the abolitionist movement. He would publish his *Interesting Narrative* in 1789 in London, by subscription to prominent abolitionists.[25] While, for some readers, the image of Equiano as transoceanic victim—the enslaved body in the stinking hold of the slave ship—remains his dominant meaning, Equiano's writing emphasizes his self-creation as self-directed maritime hero. In blue humanities context, his example captures the agency of maritime labor circulating in the eighteenth-century Atlantic. Equiano did not defeat slavery himself, and he, several times before and after his freedom, worked with slave traders. But his self-determination and political advocacy were fueled by his seamanship.

Humidity and Slavery

Whether born in Africa or South Carolina, Equiano spent much of his early life in Europe, enslaved to a Royal Navy lieutenant, in whose company he was present for major encounters in the Seven Years' War during the 1750s. During this time, he appears to have come to identify with England as well as Christianity. Equiano was baptized, with the permission of his then-owner, at St. Margaret's Church in Westminster in 1759.[26] When he was sold into slavery in the Caribbean around 1763, he saw the climate as a symbol of degradation. "I had been so long used to an European climate," he writes, "that at first I felt the scorching West Indian sun very painful, while the dashing surf would toss the boat and the people in it frequently above the high water mark" (99). The climate in the Americas, both in the Caribbean and the southern colonies of the mainland, shocked and injured European bodies, or those that, like Equiano, wished to imagine themselves Europeanized.[27] The humid air on the western side of the Atlantic represented, to Equiano and many others, the suffocating climate of slavery.

Equiano understood the cool air and fog of England as morally superior to the heat and humidity of the New World. In fact, he associates the climate in America with that of Africa. In detailing the horrors of West Indian slavery, Equiano mentions the high mortality of slaves in Barbados—"this island requires 1000 negroes annually to keep up the original stock, which is only 80,000" (106)—as he emphasizes that the climate itself cannot be the cause, since Africa is also tropical. "The climate here" in the West Indies, he writes, "is in every respect the same as that from which they are taken [Africa], except in being more wholesome" (106).

In Equiano's view, the cooler air of Europe, as well as the Christian and abolitionist communities into which he became assimilated, represented freedom. His vision of a post-slavery future does not include independence for the colonies in North America or greater power for the nations of Africa. Instead, he imagines that the English will lead a "commercial intercourse with Africa [that] opens an inexhaustible source of wealth to the manufacturing interests of Great Britain" (234). In this alternative history, Africa becomes the cotton-exporting engine of global trade that in historical fact would be supplied by the slave economy of the American South. "Cotton and indigo," Equiano notes, "grow spontaneously in most parts of Africa" (235). An Anglo-African trade that would effectively cut off the Americas appears to Equiano "a most immense, glorious, and happy prospect" (253), precisely because the manufacturers of England will have as their market "a continent ten thousand miles in circumference" (235). In Equiano's view, the humid Americas and transatlantic trade were horrors to be avoided. Settling in England, where he married in 1792 and died in 1797, Equiano championed both abolitionism and the cause of African Christians, including Black Americans who were Loyalists during the American Revolution and were later resettled, first in Nova Scotia and later in Africa by the Sierra Leone Company in 1792. He remained, to his own end, a loyal British subject.

The Deep and the Undersea Vision

Equiano's vision of an Anglo-African alliance never came to pass, but intercontinental trade networks in humans and goods would continue to shape the Atlantic world. Among the most intriguing mythic elements of the Black and Blue Atlantic is the vision of Drexciya. First invented by the Detroit techno duo of James Stinson and Gerald Donald in a series of recordings in the 1990s in Detroit, the Drexciyan mythos was rejuvenated in 2017 by the hip-hop song "The Deep" recorded by clipping, a group featuring Daveed Diggs, Jonathan Snipes, and William Hutson, and a 2019 novel *The Deep* written by Rivers Solomon in collaboration with clipping.[28] The Drexciyan story, originally elaborated in liner notes and on record albums, describes pregnant African women thrown overboard from slave ships whose children, born underwater, develop the ability to breathe and survive beneath the waves. As John Eperjesi has observed in an essay linking Drexciya to the blue humanities, the haunting music of albums such as *Bubble Metropolis* (1993) generates "a futuristic, aquatopia fantasy of escape—keeping in mind the dual meanings of utopia as both 'better place' and 'no place.'"[29] Connecting the Drexciyan musical experiment to cultural influences including Jules Verne, Jimi Hendrix, and Rachel Carson, Eperjesi suggests that the music creates "an alternative vision of what a marine environmentalism can look, feel, and most importantly, sound like" (137). As clipping's song and Solomon's novel expand the Drexciyan world in the twenty-first century, they transform the underwater soundscape into an expansive utopian vision.

Not a music expert, I will focus on Solomon's novel *The Deep*, bearing in mind that her story draws on both the original Drexciyan soundtrack from the 1990s and on clipping's 2017 reimagination of that music. *The Deep* creates an Atlantic mythos for the Drexciyan story that reimagines the history of the slave trade. The central figure in the novel, a Drexciyan named Yetu, carries in her mind the memory of the tragic origins of the species, which she shares with her community in an annual ritual known as the Remembrance. "Our mothers were pregnant two-legs thrown overboard while crossing the ocean on slave ships," Yetu begins the ritual. She continues, "We were born breathing water as we did in the womb. We built our home on the seafloor."[30] Most wajinru, as the Drexciyans call themselves, live without long-term memories—the implication being that as half-fish, they have only animal memories—but Yetu as Historian recirculates the society's collective memories in an annual ceremony inside an artificial womb. The history of the wajinru has three phases: an air-breathing beginning, in which the first mothers are thrown into the sea; a deep-sea middle, in which the immersed babies learn to survive underwater; and a mid-ocean ending, in which an underwater society emerges. In between their deep past as two-legged Africans and their present as wajinru, the key helping hands for undersea survival, Yetu reveals, were provided by cetaceans. Ventriloquizing her species history, she intones:

> We lived only by the graciousness of the second mothers, the giant water beasts we've years and years later come to call *skalu*, whales, who feed us, bond with us, and drag us down to the deepest depths where we are safer. Sperm whales, blue whales, whales that are now extinct, whales so rare there are only one or two left of their kind.
>
> (42–43)

The whale interlude bridges the violent immersion of the first mothers and the ongoing undersea lives of the wajinru. This cross-species alliance places the wajinru in a symbolic position resembling whales today—nonhuman but not entirely alien figures of near extinction and vulnerability that are under threat but remain powerful images of majesty and melancholy.[31] To be saved by whales rather than, as with contemporary humans, failing to save the whales creates the wajinru as a bridge between humans and nonhumans and between land and sea.

The final stage of the history of the wajinru unfolds through the agency of Waj, an adult human woman who, when rescued, names the creatures "zoti aleyu," which means "strange fish." This phrase, which recurs in the novel as the way humans describe all wajinru, echoes two lines from Shakespeare's *Tempest*. King Alonso, who fears that his son has drowned, laments, "O thou mine heir/. . . . /what strange fish/Hath made his meal on thee?"

(2.1.112–14).[32] In the following scene, the clown Trinculo describes the monster Caliban as "a strange fish!" (2.2.27). These two lines, which Solomon may echo intentionally, construct the wajinru as drowned princes and part-humans, a combination of Ferdinand and Caliban. To be zoti aleyu entails being strangely fish and strangely human, living between worlds. Waj, whose name means "chorus or song" (48), gets lost in a storm, but at a crucial inflection point whales bring futurity to the people through a vast mouth full of "pups that look like miniature versions of us. Little *zoti aleyu*. Strange fish" (51). Scouring the ocean for pregnant first mothers, and raising all the pups they locate, the wajinru build a population, discover sex, and name the first historian (54). As they form themselves into a community of memory and forgetting, they take a new name: "*Wajinru*. We are not zoti aleyu. We are more vast and more beautiful than that name implies. We are song, and we are together" (64). The transformation nurtured by the whales has become its own independent music.

The liner notes to Drexciya's 1997 record *The Quest* suggest that the "aquatically mutated" descendants of drowned Africans would eventually swim up the Mississippi to the Great Lakes of Michigan to make music and liberation in Black Detroit.[33] Solomon's novel imagines a more personal and individual rapprochement between underwater wajinru and their two-legs relatives. Overwhelmed by history, Yetu flees her community and encounters a solitary human fisherwoman named Oori. The interspecies love between Yetu and Oori bears a family resemblance to mermaid love stories such as *The Mermaid of Black Conch*, but the key obstacle in Solomon's novel is the historical rupture created by the slave trade. Yetu has abandoned her role as wajinru Historian because the tragic stories have become unbearable. Oori, lone descendent of a decimated West African human community, nurses the injured Yetu back to life, as David does Aycayia in Roffey's novel. The break between human and sea creature in Solomon's story comes because of history. Yetu wants to forget, but Oori wants her new companion to help recover memories of her lost people. "You are nothing but a silly fish," Oori snaps at Yetu, ". . . you wouldn't understand the importance of having a history" (95). The ancestral history that Yetu still bears, however, includes the deep history of Oori's people, as represented by a carved wooden comb given to Yetu by her mother. "It had belonged to one of the foremothers," Yetu realizes. This historical artifact, whose carvings resemble the tattoos on Oori's body (86), reconnects two lines of African descendants, one terrestrial and the other aquatic.

Solomon's novel ends with multiple reunions and possible futures. Yetu recovers her wajinru community, but now everyone shares the burden of historical memory. She also swims to "a small island in the backward C-shaped cradle of the African continent" (152) in a final effort locate Oori, who has gone missing in the massive storm conjured up by the Historianless wajinru. The markings on the ancient comb, it turns out, tell the story of efforts to form community out of solitude. Yetu's mother, who had previously been unable to access long-term memories, dredges the words from her ancestral memory:

> *Strange fish, strange fish, why do you jump around in my belly like a fish out of water?*
>
> (151)

The fetus in a liquid womb represents the common ancestor of Yetu and Oori, wajinru and human. Returning to the alienating phrase "strange fish," from which ancestral memory had delivered Yetu's people into their wajinru collective, this song shows the former Historian how to create a future for herself. Now that all wajinru can collaborate in a shared act of memory, Yetu swims into her own future.

Few mermaid stories, as imagined from Hans Christian Anderson to Monique Roffey, end happily. The unbridgeable disparity between land and sea usually molds these narratives into tragic shape. Solomon's story, notably, refuses to split her lovers. "Stay with me," invites Yetu, "and we will make a new thing" (152). She does not remake Oori as wajinru, but instead brings her beneath the ocean as a breathing human, "just as she'd breathed in the womb" (155). Both Oori and Yetu now can "breath on land and in the sea" (155). The magic transformative word is invitation. The first wajinru were hurled into the sea by slavers, but "this time, the two-legs venturing into the depths had not been abandoned to the sea, but invited into it" (155). A new human–ocean bond emerges through that invitation.

Dissolution and Atlantic Vectors: Alexis Pauline Gumbs's *Undrowned*

The vision of the future that ends *The Deep* imagines the erotic unity of Yetu and Oori producing a rejuvenated undersea community. That is not the Atlantic world we live in today. More's the pity. But Solomon's tantalizing invocation of whales as transitional figures in the wajinru story suggests a different way to connect to the undersea in the present. Alexis Pauline Gumbs's book *Undrowned: Black Feminist Lessons from Marine Mammals* (2020) asserts, from its title forward, an essential kinship between the Black Atlantic experience and the plight of marine mammals. "I identify as a mammal," Gumbs writes. She continues, "I identify as a Black woman ascending with and shaped by a whole group of people who were transubstantiated into property and kidnapped across an ocean."[34] Whales like Black women bear a shared history of suffering, not to mention dark skin. To Gumbs, the connection is more than merely circumstantial:

> I can't help but notice how marine mammals are queer, fierce, protective of each other, complex, shaped by conflict, and struggling to

> survive the extractive and militarized context our species has imposed on the ocean and ourselves.
>
> (9)

Identifying with marine mammals through what she terms a "*Marine Mammal Apprenticeship*" (7, her emphasis), enables Gumbs to craft something like the multispecies solidarity that in *The Deep* emerges from the relationship of Yetu and Oori. Embracing shared mammalian attributes and cultivating sympathies, Gumbs finds in sea creatures ways to endure a hostile environment.

At the heart of Gumbs's apprenticeship is a practice of breath, an action common to whales, dolphins, and humans. "We are still undrowning" (2), she insists, emphasizing that we, like marine mammals, must defend ourselves against environments that seek to stop our breaths. In a series of twenty lessons, from "listen" and "breathe" through "rest" and "take care of your blessings," Gumbs crafts practices that will enable Black feminists, and all humans, to survive a hostile environment. She connects, perhaps metaphorically, the near extermination of the Atlantic gray whale to the slave trade (118–19). She finds in the typical actions taken by marine mammals—"go deep" (127–30), "stay black" (131–40)—inspiration for human activism. Especially when she considers extinct or nearly extinct species such as the Atlantic gray whale, she worries about dissolution: "And what happens if we just let go?" (121). But by connecting the lessons of marine mammals to Black feminist authors such as Toni Cade Bambara and Audre Lorde (151), Gumbs creates through apprenticeship an oceanic mode of resistance. She never becomes a deep-sea dweller like Drexciyans or wajinru. Instead, she recognizes a fundamental continuity that grows more urgent as the seas rise: "we will all be marine mammals soon" (117). That cross-species link, built on suffering and honed through endurance, represents the possibility of a new Atlantic story, built on the half-millennium of tragedy the follows "in the wake," to borrow Sharpe's term, of the slave trade. The oceanic, terrestrial, and terraqueous shapes that can be crafted out of Gumbs's act of solidarity remain to be practiced.

Notes

1 Éduoard Glissant, *Poetics of Relation*, Betsy Wing, trans. (Ann Arbor: University of Michigan Press, 1997), 5–6.
2 Paul Gilroy, *The Black Atlantic: Modernity and Double Consciousness* (Cambridge: Harvard University Press, 1993), 4.
3 Stephanie Smallwood, *Saltwater Slavery: A Middle Passage from African to American Diaspora* (Cambridge: Harvard University Press, 2007), 124.
4 For a reading of violence in Jamaica in dialogue with African cultural legacies, see Vincent Brown, *Tacky's Revolt: The Story of an Atlantic Slave War* (Cambridge: Harvard University Press, 2020).
5 Jason W. Moore, *Capitalism in the Web of Life: Ecology and the Accumulation of Capital* (London: Verso, 2015); Simon Lewis and Mark Maslin, *The Human Planet: How We Created the Anthropocene* (New Haven: Yale University Press, 2018).

6 Rediker, *The Slave Ship: A Human History* (New York: Viking, 2007); Smallwood, *Saltwater Slavery*.
7 Saidiya Hartman, *Lose Your Mother: A Journey Along the Atlantic Slave Route* (New York: Farrar, Straus and Giroux, 2007), 6.
8 Christina Sharpe, *In the Wake: On Blackness and Being* (Durham: Duke University Press, 2016), 20.
9 See, for example, Bernard Bailyn, *Atlantic History: Concept and Contours* (Cambridge: Harvard University Press, 2005), and Jack Greene and Philip Morgan, eds., *Atlantic History: A Critical Appraisal* (Oxford: Oxford University Press, 2008).
10 On the *Essex*, see Nathaniel Philbrick, *In the Heart of the Sea: The Tragedy of the Whaleship Essex* (New York: Penguin, 2001).
11 C.L.R. James, *Mariners, Renegades, and Castaways: The Story of Herman Melville and the World We Live In*, Donald E. Pease, intr. (Hanover: University Press of New England, 2001).
12 Rachel Carson, *The Edge of the Sea* (Boston: Mariner Books, 1998).
13 Hanna Freed-Thall, "Beaches and Ports," *Comparative Literature* 73:2 (June 2021), 131–49, 132.
14 Allan Sekula, *Fish Story*; John Gillis, *The Human Shore*; Elsa Devienne, *La ruée vers le sable: Une histoire environnementale des plages de Los Angeles au XXe siècle* (Paris: Ed. Sorbonne, 2020); Margaret Cohen, *The Novel and the Sea*; Jean-Didier Urbain, *At the Beach*, Catherine Porter, trans. (Minnesota: University of Minnesota Press, 2003).
15 John Gillis, *The Shores around Us*, 2015.
16 Kimberly Patton, *The Sea Can Wash Away All Evils: Modern Marine Pollution and the Ancient Cathartic Ocean* (New York: Columbia University Press, 2006).
17 Greg Dening, *Islands and Beaches: Discourses on a Silent Land, Marquesas 1774–1880* (Berkeley: University of California Press, 1988).
18 See Olaudah Equiano, *The Interesting Narrative and Other Writings*, Vincent Carretta, ed., rev. ed. (New York: Penguin, 2003); Vincent Carretta, *Equiano, the African: Biography of a Self-Made Man* (New York: Penguin, 2005).
19 See, for example, Paul E. Lovejoy, "Autobiography and Memory: Gustavus Vassa, Alias Olaudah Equiano, the African," *Slavery & Abolition* 27 (2006), 317–47.
20 See W. Jeffrey Bolster, *Black Jacks: African American Seamen in the Age of Sail* (Cambridge: Harvard University Press, 1997). Bolster emphasizes that Equiano and others constituted "an international black community" (37). On William Sherman, who descended both from Africans and from the Golden Hill Pauguessett Indigenous community in Connecticut, see Charles W. Brilvitch, *A History of Connecticut's Golden Hill Paugusset Tribe* (London: The History Press, 2007).
21 Michel Foucault, "Of Other Spaces," Jay Miskowiec, trans., *Diacritics* 16 (1986), 22–27.
22 Paul Gilroy, "Never Again: Refusing Race and Salvaging the Human," 2019. Holberg Prize lecture. www.youtube.com/watch?v=Ta6UkmlXtVo. Accessed 20 September 2022.
23 On the narrative structures of shipwreck, see Steve Mentz, *Shipwreck Modernity: Ecologies of Globalization, 1550–1719* (Minneapolis: University of Minnesota Press, 2015).
24 Carretta emphasizes that Equiano places his entire narrative, including the early chapters in Africa, in a "Judeo-Christian framework" (xxvi).
25 Carretta's edition includes the list of subscribers to the first (London) edition (317–22) and also to the New York edition (323–25). All nine subsequent editions (through 1794) were also published by subscription (xvi).
26 A plaque memorializing his life was dedicated at St. Margaret's Church on 13 March 2009. See https://blackpresence.co.uk/memorial-plaque-dedcated-to-laudah-equiano/. Accessed 20 September 2022.

27 On European responses to American climate, see Karen Ordahl Kupperman, "Fear of Hot Climates in the Anglo-American Experience," *The William and Mary Quarterly* 41 (1984), 213–40, and Karen Ordahl Kupperman, "The Puzzle of the American Climate in the Early Colonial Period," *The American Historical Review* 87 (1982), 1262–89.

28 The song was released on 18 August 2017, by Sub Pop Records. A video is available on YouTube: www.youtube.com/watch?v=yybfqEfuxPc. Accessed 21 September 2022.

29 John Eperjesi, "Imagined Oceans: Drexciya's *Bubble Metropolis* and Blue Cultural Studies," *Journal of Popular Music Studies* 34 (2022), 118–40, 129.

30 Rivers Solomon, *The Deep*, with Daveed Diggs, William Hutson, and Jonathan Snipes (New York: Saga Press, 2019), 28.

31 For an examination of whales as "both symbol and symptom" for contemporary modernity and melancholy, see Graham Huggan, *Colonialism, Culture, Whales: The Cetacean Quartet* (London: Bloomsbury, 2018), ix.

32 William Shakespeare, *The Tempest*, Virginia Mason Vaughan and Alden T. Vaughan, eds. (London: Bloomsbury, 2011), 213. Citations in the text by act, scene, and line numbers.

33 "The Quest," Drexciya, Submerge, 1997. For an online copy of the liner notes, see www.discogs.com/release/12117-Drexciya-The-Quest. Accessed 21 September 2022. The liner notes emphasize the possibilities for mammals to breathe underwater, following experiments pioneered by Jacques Cousteau and others. On the broader fantasy of *homo aquaticus*, see Helen Rozwadowski, "'Bringing Humanity Full Circle Back into the Sea': *Homo aquaticus,* Evolution, and the Ocean," *Environmental Humanities* 14 (2022), 1–28. doi:10.1215/22011919-9481407.

34 Alexis Pauline Gumbs, *Undrowned: Black Feminist Lessons from Marine Mammals* (Chico: AK Press, 2020), 5.

10 Conclusion

Touching Moisture

Scalar disjunction defines the central image of solitary swimmer in planet-girdling ocean. The small human thing appears tiny, but this body, like the fluid in which it floats, contains around two-thirds salt water. The image and the experience of oceanic immersion together represent the physical and metaphorical challenge of bridging the disconnect between individual and environment, weather and climate, human and world. The ocean swimmer focuses ideas about living in a watery environment during today's climate emergency.

Ocean swimming can serve as embodied ecological meditation and prompt for critical thinking for the Anthropocene. Oceanic immersion teaches through feeling. In touching the great waters, we feel something. The feeling combines both visceral physical sensation and something more capacious, like the "oceanic feeling" rhapsodized by poets and psychologists.[1] Feeling of and for the ocean lures us into the water and sometimes frightens us away.

Swimming is only a seminatural practice for terrestrial humans. At our best, we engage the water slowly, awkwardly, and at considerable personal risk. Western literary culture in its earliest stages confined swimming to superheroes such as Beowulf or Odysseus, whose exceptional prowess emphasizes the inability of most humans to endure water. The rise of ocean swimming as popular recreation during the second half of the twentieth century has changed the relationship between human and ocean. In plunging our bodies into an inhospitable environment, we encounter an alien presence, soothing and dangerous at the same time. Swimming has a history, but that history points incessantly forward into our changing environmental present.[2]

Swimming occupies a key node in the network of blue humanities thinking as a site of intimate contact and risk. The long human history of swimming—from the so-called "aquatic ape" hypothesis, which argues that Homo sapiens evolved in an aqueous land- and seacape, to the prowess of superhuman athletes like Lynne Cox and Ian Thorpe—tells a story of love and practice. An essential early text for Anglophone swimmers is Everard Digby's illustrated 1587 how-to-swim manual *De arte natandi*, which pictures

DOI: 10.4324/9781003166665-10

humans swimming like dogs, frogs, ships, and dolphins.[3] Literary depictions of swimming range from Homer and Shakespeare to the contemporary swim-memoirs I explore in this conclusion. From the shipwrecked swims of Odysseus and Robinson Crusoe to the immersive poetry of Lord Byron and Walt Whitman, swimming captures the tactile sensation of environmental alienation. The swimmer's entrance into the great waters embraces ecological uncertainty. The ocean swimmer captures environmental risk and human vulnerability. Those experiences are coming increasingly to define the human relationship with our Anthropocene environment.

My swim-thinking has developed through collaborations with academics, artists, surfers, swimmers, assorted other watery fellow travelers, and perhaps most intensely with several bodies of water. This conclusion touches contemporary swim-writing by Roger Deakin, Charles Sprawson, Leanne Shapton, James Hamilton-Paterson, Lynne Cox, Philip Hoare, and Vanessa Daws. Mixing these writers and swimmers together, and unifying my own archival and immersive practices, will flesh out what I call a "swimmer poetics."[4] To devise a critical, poetic, and active language for immersion, I follow the old Wordsworthian song in which we "half-create" what we also "perceive" about the environment around us.[5] But I remain suspicious of that Romantic vision, for what it excludes and what it occludes. I do not want to be guided just by the things that are easiest to see. One of the best things about swimming, to my mind, is its sensory deprivation. The extreme swimmer Diana Nyad, the only person to have swum without a shark cage the hundred miles between Cuba and the United States, observes that swimming's senselessness provides space for physical meditation.[6] We cannot hear or see or smell very much with our faces underwater. The vast salt universe resolves into an acrid taste and encompassing touch. Perception narrows into feeling, and that feeling expands as far as we can think it, or perhaps farther.

The central term for "swimmer poetics" is, in fact, feeling, as in both the physical feeling of salt water on skin and the oceanic feelings and speculations that emerge from immersion. Many modern writers emphasize "feel for the water" as the special talent of skilled swimmers. As a supplement to feeling, I explore form as a means of surviving and thriving in an alien environment. Splashing back and forth between early modern and early twenty-first-century swimmers provides examples of how feel for the water and laboring forms can characterize swimming as both a symbolic and a practical way of thinking and being in the Anthropocene. The feeling/form binary informs two more outward-facing terms, experience and allegory, that provide suggestions for how the blue humanities can speak to literary and cultural studies writ large.

Watery feeling animates these conclusions. When we immerse our small bodies into our globe's watery skin, we feel something. Nothing like control or mastery animates the swimmer, but rather a physical intuition or connection, a planetary tug, a reminder that one's own water-filled flesh also has tides, also responds to the moon's gravitational embrace, also swims in fluid connections atop a nearly spherical rock in the void. As Astrida Neimanis observes in *Bodies of Water*, an essential project in our increasingly threatening environment will be to "learn to swim."[7] This conclusion literalizes that metaphor. What might it mean to learn to swim in the unfriendly and polluted waters of rising Anthropocene seas?

First Swimmer: Charles Sprawson

The lineup of swimmers starts with Charles Sprawson, author of the wonderfully mad *Haunts of the Black Masseur: The Swimmer as Hero* (1992). Sprawson emphasizes the mystical and heroic elements of water-feeling. His swimmer becomes a determined "individualist" who practices a "lonely, meditative" labor that resembles "a continuous dream of a world under water."[8] Sprawson traces swim mysticism from classical poetry to Romantic figures such as Algernon Swinburne, who rhapsodizes that "to feel that in deep water is to feel—as long as one is swimming out . . .—as if one was in another world of life." Sprawson's book idiosyncratically mixes the words of Olympic champions, poets, and his own experiences to pursue the "ichthyosaurus ego" imagined by John Cowper Powys and the immersive figures of "pagan myth" conjured by Rupert Brooke. The "black masseur" of Sprawson's enigmatic title, which reference he never clarifies in the text, alludes to a shockingly racist story by Tennessee Williams in which a weak white man enters into violent and ultimately fatal erotic communion with a powerful black masseur. The water's touch combines ecstasy with disturbing violence. Sprawson's eagerness launches swimmer poetics, but his enthusiasm for aquatic solitude sometimes moves in painful directions. His final "work" before he died in 2020 was a BBC radio program from January 2019 that provides a melancholy image of the aging swimmer falling into dementia, trapped in a dry facility, isolated from the sea.[9]

Second Swimmer: Everard Digby

In addition to feeling, we need form. One of the clearest images of the formal aspects of human swimming is proffered by Digby in *De arte natandi* (1587). Digby's text speaks to a surge of interest in swimming in early modern Europe. In the ancient Mediterranean, as Nicholas Orme notes in *Early British Swimming* (1983), swimming had been primarily a survival practice and military skill, a way of moving armies across rivers and other bodies of water.[10] Early modern Europe saw a flood of new interest in swimming. Orme points to new and revised translations of ancient and Biblical texts that made them seem less hostile to immersion, as well as a surge in maritime trade and travel as elements that reinvigorated swimming as metaphor and practice. Encounters with African, Native American, and Pacific Islander communities who included strong swimmers also impressed

European sailors and adventurers, in particular when they were establishing pearl fisheries and other maritime colonial projects.

Digby's *De Arte Natandi*, translated into English by Christopher Middleton as *A Short introduction for to learne to Swimme* (1595), represents swimming as a formal skill, suitable for young gentlemen being educated at Cambridge. In a dedicatory epistle directed to Master Simon Smith, Middleton, Digby's translator, describes swimming as among "commendable exercises tending to profitable ends."[11] The main text emphasizes the value of swimming to "preserveth the precious life of man" and also "to purge the skin from all external pollutions or uncleanness" (sig. A3). The outstanding features of Digby's and Middleton's editions (reprinted in Orme) are woodcut illustrations that demonstrate different styles of swimming and aquatic maneuvers. Humans even exceed fish, in Digby's understanding, because of our felicity in "diving down to the bottom of the deepest waters and fetching from thence whatsoever is there sunk down" (sig. A4). The swimmer performs miracles of art and mobility, "sitting, tumbling, leaping, walking" (sig. A4), mimicking the features of "a frog" (sig. A3v), "a dog" (sig. F4), and even "a dolphin" (sig. K4v). Among uniquely human abilities, Digby notes our capacity for " 'swimming upon the back'—a gift which [Nature] has denied even to the watery inhabitants of the sea" (sig. C2). Treating a (male) human body as the measure of all things may be a typical Renaissance affectation, but Digby's portrait of how bodies engage with watery environments gestures toward a growing awareness of swimming as art and experience.

Digby was a Fellow at St. John's College, Cambridge, and the images in his book resemble local haunts along the River Cam. He was not, apparently, a saltwater swimmer. Ocean swimming as recreational practice did not arrive on British shores until around the eighteenth century, during which time Alain Corbin has documented the rapid expansion of "the sea bathing fashion . . . out of a therapeutic objective."[12] Swimmers, often women, were dunked into cold sea water to rebalance bodily humors. Global beach tourism, underwater photography, scuba, and surf culture would reshape the lived relationship between humans and the sea in the twentieth century. Sea level rise and warming-fueled storms today suggest that the twenty-first century desire to live and play near the shore is coming into conflict with the dynamic instabilities of environmental crisis.

Third Swimmer: Leanne Shapton

Turning to the twenty-first century brings us to feeling. Leanne Shapton emphasizes that she was not a real Olympian swimmer but "only went as far as the Olympic trials" for Canada in 1988 and 1992.[13] Her book *Swimming Studies* (2012) traces the scar of her competitive career into a life of recreational immersion. "I still dream of practice," she writes, "of races, coaches and blurry competitors" (6). Her "studies" include watercolor sketches. In both images and prose, she pinpoints what swimming feels like. When a human body submerges in water, we feel disorientation and buoyancy, which translate into vulnerability and sometimes also power. We cannot live in water; we love being in water. Shapton explains that she "feels [her] body acutely in the water." Physical feeling generates understanding: "It's a knowledge of watery space, being able to sense exactly where my body is and what it's affecting, an animal empathy for contact with an element." Her phrase "animal empathy" suggests both that feel for the water is fellow-feeling or connection and that such a bond must be not very human. Later in the book, describing her years of elite competition, she writes, "Watching a good swimmer is the visual equivalent of patting a dog's smooth head—something naturally, wondrously sweet and perfect" (254). The physical ease with which fast swimmers cleave the water must be, in Shapton's understanding, animal in the positive sense: physical, unfettered, unselfconscious. "Here my mind is the plus one," (254), she continues. Swimming, she insists, represents pure physicality. Thinking, as opposed to swimming, is the excess.

Fourth Swimmer: James Hamilton-Paterson

For some swim-writers, the out-of-place-ness of humans in water becomes a Romantic trope and vision of the world. James Hamilton-Paterson, an English writer whose passion for water drew him to spend an entire year living on an uninhabited island in the Philippines, sees in the "hypocrite swimmer" an image of dissolution: "He only has existed as three-tenths and that fraction is melting into water."[14] Immersion brings physical sensation together with an intuitive grasp of vastness and motion. Swimming means feeling the hyperobject ocean against bare skin. As our Anthropocene environment grows more dynamic and unsettled, the swimmer's practice of partial order amid constant threats may become a dream of partial accommodation. For Hamilton-Paterson, immersive practice represents a biological and historical return. The swimmer for him is physical philosopher, spanning worlds with flesh and practice:

> The illusory line separating air from water, dividing the lighter swirl of molecules from the denser, merely compounds the fiction of two worlds dwelling apart, the one inimical to the other. Yet what could be better proof of their radical contiguity than the gallant life force pervading both? Not in a mystical sense, either; but because life originated from below, some of it adapting to permanent exile and some of it staying put. We are colonials. What we have in common with our ancestors is the sea and not the air.
>
> (*Seven-Tenths*, 341)

Throughout *Seven-Tenths*, the inset narrative of an ocean swimmer who has lost his boat and thinks he may drown recurs like a chorus in the larger text.

The swimmer fears death but seems drawn to dissolution. "His entire body is dissolving," Hamilton-Paterson writes (289). Playing on the roughly seventy percent of our planet's surface that is covered by water and the nearly seventy percent of our bodies comprised of water, Hamilton-Paterson seeks the wet visionary encounter. He may get there, but he cannot keep what he finds. "Not being fish," he writes, "we mourn things, the present especially" (391). The salt touch lingers, but eventually dries.

Fifth Swimmer: Lynne Cox

The American cold-water specialist and best-selling author Lynne Cox provides the perspective of an elite competitive swimmer. Cox is most famous for swimming the Bering Sea between the United States and the Soviet Union in 1987, though she has a cluster of first crossings on her resume, from the Cape of Good Hope to Antarctica. The text I engage here, however, is Cox's second book, *Grayson*, published in 2006.[15] The story chronicles one morning when she was a teenage open-water swimmer in southern California who helped a lost gray whale calf find his mother. Like Shapton and Hamilton-Paterson, Cox represents her swimming self as a bridge between humans and the marine inhuman. She starts in darkness at 5 a.m. off Seal Beach, "swimming on pace, moving at about sixty strokes per minute, etching a small silvery groove across the wide black ocean" (1–2). In this featureless world, the gray whale's son, who she names "Grayson" (81), becomes her companion. "You can't swim to shore," a fisherman admonishes her. "If you swim into shore, he'll follow you. He'll run aground" (36). The scenario remakes ocean swimming as immersive human and nonhuman collaboration. Cox swims with Grayson until his massive mother at last returns. Their shared swim represents a fleeting trans-species connection. "Treading water," Cox writes, "I watched the baby whale. I couldn't take my eyes off him" (39). In an adventure story that features sea turtles, Pacific sunfish, jellyfish, dolphins, fishermen, spectators on the pier, and losing and finding whales large and small, Cox inverts the human versus leviathan plot of *Moby-Dick*. The swimmer posits her emotional connection to the whale: "I believed we would find Grayson's mother in the vast ocean" (97). When Grayson at last swims off with his mother they vanish forever, "growing smaller and smaller by the minute as the sea expanded behind him" (143). In what becomes half parable and half children's book, Cox's *Grayson* represents a happy encounter between human and ocean that is only possible if you can swim fast for several hours in frigid salt water.

Sixth Swimmer: Philip Hoare

The English writer Philip Hoare has produced a trilogy of saltwater memoirs: *Leviathan, or The Whale* (2008), *The Sea Inside* (2013), and *Risingtidefallingstar:*

In Search of the Soul of the Sea (2018).[16] The experience of immersion is his obsessive practice and object. In *The Sea Inside*, he writes:

> The sea defines us, connects us, separates us. Most of us experience only its edges, our available wilderness on a crowded island—it's why we call our coastal towns "resorts," despite their air of decay. . . . Perpetually renewing and destroying, the sea proposes a beginning and an ending, an alternative to our landlocked state, an existence to which we are tethered when we might rather be set free.
>
> (7)

Hoare's prose registers a chosen intimacy that transforms into dependency. "I feel claustrophobic if I am far from the water," he writes, "Summer and winter, I plan my time around the tides" (*Leviathan* 4). Extending this idea, he writes in *Risingtidefallingstar* that "for me every day is an anxiety in my ways of getting to the water" (13). When he goes on to wonder, "If there were no oceans, would we have our souls?" (13), he pinpoints a watery entanglement that combines feeling and form.

By his own account, Hoare is not a prodigy like Lynne Cox. Tossed into the municipal pool in Southampton as a child, he splashed and struggled, observing that "the far side [of the pool] was as unattainable as Australia" (*Leviathan* 3). Hiding his inability to swim through his teens, Hoare finally taught himself when he was thirty, living alone in London. Learning to support his body in the water, he discovered "the buoyancy of myself" (3). The practice that would become the mature writer's obsession began as "the idea of going out of my depth, allowing something else to take account for my physical presence in the world, being part of it and apart from it at the same time" (3). As he tells it across three books, swimming becomes a way of experiencing the world. The alien element creates buoyancy, which in turn enables art.

Seventh Swimmer: Vanessa Daws

Swimming as artistic practice introduces the last nonfictional swimmer in this conclusion: swim-artist Vanessa Daws, whose painting "Pluralize the Anthropocene!" appears in chapter 2. If Philip Hoare represents the case of a writer whose swimming generates a poetics of immersion, Daws, who makes video-art from footage she captures while wearing a GoPro in the water, focuses even more directly on the feel and experience of the water. Her adventures include a failed attempt at swimming the English Channel in September 2019 as well as multiple swims in the Swimming a Long Way Together Project, ongoing since 2021.[17]

In an earlier project developed during a three-week residency in Santa Barbara, California, in October 2014, Daws developed a "pyschoswimography" or an exploration of a place "through the art of swimming." Interacting with local swimmers, including a group that calls themselves the "Ocean Ducks," as well as aqua-academics gathered for a conference, Daws produced a small art book that captures her encounter with an unusually warm Pacific and California sea-culture. She organized a joint swim during the conference that brought the Ocean Ducks into contact with enthusiastic academic conference-goers. Stacy Alaimo, a plenary speaker at the conference who swam with us, described the experience in Daws's book:

> It felt like an experiment with becoming a medium for art. To be ourselves in the interchange with the ocean, to be aesthetically overcome by the blues and greens of the water. I won't say the event "elevated" swimming to an art, because elevation would place us above the practice and what is most beautiful to me is to think of how swimming—the immersion of the human in water—releases us from transcendent perspectives, unmoors us as terrestrial creatures, allows us to hover in other ways of being that are, perhaps, less separate from the substances of the world.[18]

I also wrote a short note for *Psychoswimography*:

> When land mammals enter the ocean, buoyancy makes things possible. Swimming is flying, almost, and I love its singular touch. But what I remember most about Santa Barbara is the second thing: how artistic practice made swimming into community. We were surrounded by swimmers, Ocean Ducks, surfers, scholars of premodern literature and critical theory, all together in the ocean. To be in that translucent alien world but not alone in it: the gift of art.

In remembering those swims in Santa Barbara, I imagine that we were all part of a collaboration of which immersion was the physical core, a collaboration between ocean and human, salt water and thinking flesh, global fluidity and individual fragments. We were thinking about the ocean, but not only thinking. Sometimes even academics and artists need to be overwhelmed.

Last Swimmer: Ishmael

The final image of *Moby-Dick* finds our narrator alone after the White Whale has sunk the *Pequod*. In the novel's short "Epilogue," Ishmael floats "for almost a whole day and night, . . . on a soft and dirge-like main" (427). Like Pip, he faces the isolation of a solitary human body in the vast ocean. But with the physical aid of Queequeg's coffin–life buoy, which pops up to the surface from the sinking ship, he preserves himself until another whaleship rescues him. In the last word of the novel, Melville names Ishmael an "orphan" (427), indicating his separation from whaleship and human companions as well as his fundamental alienation from the World Sea.

The tragic isolation of the narrator after the ship goes down can be reimagined as a story of oceanic endurance. Unlike Pip, Ishmael does not fall into madness, nor does he drown with all his companions. Introduced with an epigraph from Job—"And I only am escaped alone to tell thee" (Job 1: 14–19)—Ishmael will go on, the novel has already told us, to a long and varied whaling career. As blue humanities avatar, Ishmael's obsessions with whales and whalemen, seas and ships, capture the discourse's efforts to expand beyond the merely human. The posthuman networks that Ishmael embraces never solve the mysteries of the White Whale, but they enable him to endure oceanic intimacy, at least for a time. Like Ishmael, blue humanities scholarship aims to immerse itself in planetary water, to survive the experience, and to come to understand its meanings.

Experience and Allegory

This book ends with two mantras that have surfaced over years of exploring swimmer poetics and the blue humanities. The first, "Experience is better than knowledge," I borrow from the early modern French mariner Samuel de Champlain. The second, "Always allegorize!," I adapt from Fredric Jameson's *The Political Unconscious*. These two phrases extend the feeling/form binary by turning outward toward the world.[19]

Champlain's version of feel for the ocean comes from his *Treatise on Seamanship* of 1632.[20] The aphorism sounds better in French: "l'experience passé science."[21] The echoing rhyme of *experience* and *science* emphasizes the mutual exchange between these terms. Champlain's *experience* captures both a human desire to touch the world and the way thought cannot escape materiality. This kind of experience exceeds disembodied knowledge, as Champlain's marginal note explains: "Not trust in his own judgment alone."[22] Pure abstraction cannot do everything, as the abundant materiality of the sea helps demonstrate. The pressure of immersive experience and the incessant communication between our bodies and our environment have their own teaching. Experience, the sum of connected feelings, precedes, though perhaps does not fully supersede, intellectual analysis. Tension between experience and knowledge, feeling and form, underwrites the blue humanities.

The second mantra, "Always allegorize!," plays on Fredric Jameson's famous imperative to "Always historicize!," the opening slogan in his influential book *The Political Unconscious: Narrative as a Socially Symbolic Act* (1981).[23] For Jameson as Marxist literary critic, the play between the act of historicizing, which directs attention to the past, and the revolutionary insistence that the critic must "always" labor in the present is precisely the paradoxical point. By replacing Jameson's history with allegory in my version of the mantra, I emphasize the importance of form to understanding. Swimming strokes, in this analysis, allegorize the experience of terrestrial bodies in an alien environment. Attention to form makes survival possible in that fluid world, at least for a time. Allegory interprets form to make meaning, at least temporary meaning, in the world.

These swimmer-poetics mantras enable us to combine the over-fullness of oceanic experience and the lunging formal grasp toward allegorical understanding. I want the feeling of being in the water and the comprehension that flashes out from a well-crafted sentence. I want to be in the moving ocean and to be thinking about it—both at the same time. Experience and allegory, feeling and form, together. Wet and surging.

Notes

1 On the oceanic feeling, see Steve Mentz, "Is Compassion an Oceanic Feeling?," *Emotions: History, Culture, Society* 4:1 (2020), 109–27.
2 For a recent one-volume world history of swimming, see Karen Eva Carr, *Shifting Currents: A World History of Swimming* (London: Reaktion, 2022).
3 Everard Digby, *De arte natandi* (London, 1587).
4 See Steve Mentz, "Swimming Lessons," *Hypocrite Reader*, 2016. www.hypocritereader.com/61/swimming-lessons. Accessed 10 October 2022. I also mention "swimmer poetics" in "After Sustainability," *PMLA* 127:3 (2012), 586–92.
5 William Wordsworth, "Lines Composed a Few Miles Above Tintern Abbey." www.poetryfoundation.org/poems/45527/lines-composed-a-few-miles-above-tintern-abbey-on-revisiting-the-banks-of-the-wye-during-a-tour-july-13-1798. Accessed 10 October 2022.
6 Diana Nyad, *Other Shores* (New York: Random House, 1978).
7 Astrida Neimanis, *Bodies of Water: Posthuman Feminist Phenomenology* (London: Bloomsbury, 2017), 33.
8 Charles Sprawson, *Haunts of the Black Masseur: The Swimmer as Hero* (Minneapolis: University of Minnesota Press, 2000).
9 "Searching for Swimming Pools," *BBC Radio* 4, 23 January 2019. www.bbc.co.uk/programmes/m00024pw. Accessed 10 October 2022.
10 Nicholas Orme, *Early British Swimming, 55 BC—AD 1719* (Exeter: University of Exeter Press, 1993).
11 Everard Digby, *A Short Introduction for to Learne to Swim*, Christopher Middleton, trans. (London, 1595) sig. A2.
12 Alain Corbin, *The Lure of the Sea: The Discovery of the Seaside in the Western World, 1750–1840*, Jocelyn Phelps, trans. (New York: Penguin Books, 1995).
13 Leanne Shapton, *Swimming Studies* (New York: Blue Rider Press, 2012), 3.
14 James Hamilton-Paterson, *Seven-Tenths: The Sea and Its Thresholds* (London: Hutchinson, 1992); James Hamilton-Paterson, *Playing with Water: Passion and Solitude on a Philippine Island* (Amsterdam: New Amsterdam Books, 1987).
15 Lynne Cox, *Grayson* (Boston: Mariner Books, 2008).
16 Philip Hoare, *Leviathan, or The Whale* (London: Fourth Estate, 2009); Philip Hoare, *The Sea Inside* (New York: Melville House, 2014); Philip Hoare, *Risingtidefallingstar: In Search of the Soul of the Sea* (Chicago: University of Chicago Press, 2018).
17 www.swimmingalongwaytogether.com/. Accessed 24 October 2022.
18 Vanessa Daws, *Psychoswimography*, privately printed, 2014. Unpaginated.
19 For a more on the first mantra, see Steve Mentz, "Experience is Better Than Knowledge: Premodern Ocean Science and the Blue Humanities," *Configurations* 27:4 (2019), 433–42.

20 Samuel de Champlain, *Epitome of the Art of Navigation; or a Short, Easy and Methodical Way to become a Compleat Navigator*, rev. and corrected by William Mountaine (London: William Mount and Thomas Paige, 1744), 262.
21 Quoted in Margaret Cohen, *The Novel and the Sea* (Princeton: Princeton University Press, 2010), 35.
22 Champlain, *Epitome*, 262.
23 Fredric Jameson, *The Political Unconscious: Narrative as Socially Symbolic Act* (Ithaca: Cornell University Press, 1982), 1.

Works Cited

David Abulafia. *The Boundless Sea: A Human History of the Oceans*. Oxford: Oxford University Press, 2019.

Stacy Alaimo, ed. *Bodily Natures: Science, Environment, and the Material Self.* Bloomington: Indiana University Press, 2010.

Stacy Alaimo, ed. *Exposed: Environmental Politics and Pleasures in Posthuman Times.* Minneapolis: University of Minnesota Press, 2016.

Stacy Alaimo, ed. "Science Studies and the Blue Humanities." Special Issue of *Configurations* 27, 4 (2019).

Nicholas Allen, Nick Groom, and Jos Smith, eds. *Coastal Works: Cultures of the Atlantic Edge*. Oxford: Oxford University Press, 2017.

Monique Allewaert. *Ariel's Ecology: Plantations, Personhood, and Colonialism in the American Tropics*. Minneapolis: University of Minnesota Press, 2013.

Jon Anderson. "Relational Places: The Surfed Wave as Assemblage and Convergence." *Environment and Planning D* 30 (2012): 570–87.

Jon Anderson. "What I Talk about When I Talk about Kayaking." *Water Worlds: Human Geographies of the Ocean*. Jon Anderson and Kimberly Peters, eds. Aldershot: Ashgate Publishing, 2014: 103–18.

Anonymous. "The Seafarer." *A Guide to Old English*. Bruce Mitchell and Fred C. Robinson, eds. 5th ed. London: Blackwell, 1992: 276–82.

Anonymous [Captain Johnson]. *A General History of the Pyrates*. Manuel Schonhorn, ed. London: Dover, 1999.

Anonymous. "Account of the Very Remarkable Loss of the Great Galleon *S. João*." *The Tragic History of the Sea*. Josiah Blackmore, trans. C.R. Boxer, ed. Josiah Blackmore, for. Minneapolis: University of Minnesota Press, 2001: 3–26.

Noelani Arista. *The Kingdom and the Republic: Sovereign Hawai'i and the Early United States*. Philadelphia: University of Pennsylvania Press, 2019.

Aristotle. *The Rhetoric and the Poetics of Aristotle*. Friedrich Solmsen, ed. and trans. New York: Modern Library, 1954.

David Armitage. "Literature and Empire." *The Oxford History of the British Empire, vol. 1: The Origins of Empire*. Nicholas Canny, ed. Oxford: Oxford University Press, 1998.

W.H. Auden. *The Enchafed Flood, or the Romantic Iconography of the Sea*. London: Faber and Faber, 1950.

Bernard Bailyn. *Atlantic History: Concept and Contours*. Cambridge: Harvard University Press, 2005.

Samuel Baker. *Written on the Water: British Romanticism and the Maritime Empire of Culture*. Charlottesville: University of Virginia Press, 2010.

Ian Baucom. "Hydrographies." *Geographical Review* 89, 2 (1999): 301–13.
Caroline Bergvall. *Drift*. Brooklyn: Nightboat Books, 2014.
Josiah Blackmore. *Manifest Perdition: Shipwreck Narrative and the Disruption of Empire*. Minneapolis: University of Minnesota Press, 2002.
Richard J. Blakemore. "Law and the Sea." *The Routledge Companion to Marine and Maritime Worlds, 1400–1800*. Claire Jowitt, Craig Lambert, and Steve Mentz, eds. London: Routledge, 2021: 388–425.
Hester Blum. *The View from the Masthead: Maritime Imagination and Antebellum American Sea Narratives*. Chapel Hill: University of North Carolina Press, 2008.
Hester Blum. "The Prospect of Oceanic Studies." *PMLA* 125, 3 (2010): 670–77.
Hester Blum, ed. "Oceanic Studies." *Atlantic Studies* 10 (2013).
Hester Blum. *The News at the Ends of the Earth: The Print Culture of Polar Exploration*. Durham: Duke University Press, 2019.
Hester Blum, I. Liang, M. Eyring, and B.R. Roberts, eds. "Archipelagos/Oceans/American Visuality." Special Issue of *Journal of Transnational American Studies* 10, 1 (2019).
Richard Bodek and Joseph Kelly, eds. *Maroons and the Marooned: Runaways and Castaways in the Americas*. Jackson: University of Mississippi Press, 2020.
W. Jeffrey Bolster. *Black Jacks: African American Seamen in the Age of Sail*. Cambridge: Harvard University Press, 1997.
W. Jeffrey Bolster. *The Mortal Sea: Fishing the Atlantic in the Age of Sail*. Cambridge: Harvard University Press, 2012.
Daniel Botkin. *Discordant Harmonies: A New Ecology for the Twenty-First Century*. Oxford: Oxford University Press, 1990.
Mark Bould. *The Anthropocene Unconscious: Climate Catastrophe Culture*. London: Verso, 2021.
Emily Brady. *The Sublime in Modern Philosophy: Aesthetics, Ethics, and Nature*. Cambridge: Cambridge University Press, 2013.
Dionne Brand. *A Map to the Door of No Return: Notes to Belonging*. Toronto: Vintage Canada, 2001.
Kamau Brathwaite. *Black + Blues*. New York: New Directions, 1995.
Fernand Braudel. *The Mediterranean and the Mediterranean World in the Age of Philip II*. 2 vols. Sian Reynolds, trans. New York: Harper and Row, 1972. Orig. French 1949.
Daniel Brayton. *Shakespeare's Ocean: An Ecocritical Exploration*. Charlottesville: University of Virginia Press, 2012.
Charles W. Brilvitch. *A History of Connecticut's Golden Hill Paugusset Tribe*. London: The History Press, 2007.
Vincent Brown. *Tacky's Revolt: The Story of an Atlantic Slave War*. Cambridge: Harvard University Press, 2020.
Edmund Burke. *A Philosophical Enquiry into the Origin of Our Ideas of the Sublime and the Beautiful*. London, 1757.
Frederick Burwick and Manushag Powell. *British Pirates in Print and Performance*. London: Palgrave Macmillan, 2015.
Kerry Bystrom and Isabel Hofmeyer, eds. "Oceanic Routes." Special Issue of *Comparative Literature* 69, 1 (2017).
Luis vaz de Camões. *The Lusíads*. Landeg White, trans. Oxford: Oxford University Press, 1997.
Alexandra Campbell and Michael Payne, eds. "World Literature and the Blue Humanities." Special Issue of *Humanities* 9, 3 (2020).
Karen Eva Carr. *Shifting Currents: A World History of Swimming*. London: Reaktion, 2022.

Vincent Carretta. *Equiano, the African: Biography of a Self-Made Man*. New York: Penguin, 2005.

Siobahn Carroll. *An Empire of Air and Water: Uncolonizable Space in the British Imagination, 1750–1850*. Philadelphia: University of Pennsylvania Press, 2015.

Rachel Carson. *The Sea around Us*. New York: Oxford University Press, 1951.

Miguel de Cervantes Saavedra. *Don Quijote de la Mancha, Part I*. Martín de Riquer, ed. Barcelona: Editorial Juventud, 1995.

Miguel de Cervantes Saavedra. *Don Quixote*. Edith Grossman, trans. Harold Bloom, intro. New York: Harper Collins, 2003.

Aimé Cesairé. *Une tempête*. Paris: Éditions de Seuil, 1969.

Aimé Césaire. *A Tempest*. Richard Miller, trans. New York: Theatre Communications Group, 2002.

Samuel de Champlain. *Les Voyages la nouvelle France Occidentale . . .* Paris: Claude Collete, 1639.

Samuel de Champlain. *Epitome of the Art of Navigation; or a Short, Easy and Methodical Way to become a Compleat Navigator*. William Mountaine, ed. London: William Mount and Thomas Paige, 1744.

Joyce Chaplin. *Round about the Earth: Circumnavigation from Magellan to Orbit*. New York: Simon and Schuster, 2012.

Cecilia Chen, Janine MacLeod, and Astrida Neimanis, eds. *Thinking with Water*. Montreal: McGill-Queens University Press, 2013.

Thomas Churchyard. *A Discourse of the Queenes Maiesties Entertainement in Suffolk and Norffolk*. London, 1578.

Andy Clark. *Being There: Putting Brain Body, and World together again*. Cambridge: MIT Press, 1996.

Robert Clewis, ed. *The Sublime Reader*. London: Bloomsbury, 2018.

Clipping. *The Deep*. Detroit: Sub Pop Records. 2017.

Jeffrey Jerome Cohen, ed. *Prismatic Ecology: Ecotheory beyond Green*. Minneapolis: University of Minnesota Press, 2013.

Jeffrey Jerome Cohen. *Stone: An Inhuman Ecology*. Minneapolis: University of Minnesota Press, 2015.

Margaret Cohen, ed. "Chronotypes of the Sea." *The Novel, Vol. 2*. Franco Moretti, ed. Princeton: Princeton University Press, 2007: 647–66.

Margaret Cohen, ed. *The Novel and the Sea*. Princeton: Princeton University Press, 2012.

Margaret Cohen, ed. *A Cultural History of the Sea*. 6 vols. London: Bloomsbury, 2021.

Margaret Cohen and Killian Quigley, eds. *The Aesthetics of the Undersea*. London: Routledge, 2020.

Samuel Taylor Coleridge. "The Rime of the Ancient Mariner." *Lyrical Ballads*, William Wordsworth, Samuel Taylor Coleridge, and W.J.B. Owen, eds. 2nd ed. Oxford: Oxford University Press, 1969: 7–32.

Christopher Connery. "*There Was No More Sea:* The Supersession of the Ocean, from the Bible to Hyperspace." *Journal of Historical Geography* 32, 3 (2006): 494–511.

Alain Corbin. *The Lure of the Sea: The Discovery of the Seaside in the Western World, 1750–1840*. Jocelyn Phelps, trans. New York: Penguin, 1995.

Lynne Cox. *Grayson*. Boston: Mariner Books, 2008.

Julie Cruikshank. *Do Glaciers Listen? Local Knowledge, Colonial Encounters, and Social Imagination*. Vancouver: University of British Columbia Press, 2022.

Lorraine Daston. "Cloud Physiognomy: Describing the Indescribable." *Representations* 135 (2016): 45–71.

John Davis. *The Voyages and Works of John Davis the Navigator*. Albert Hastings Markham, ed. London: Routledge, 2016.

Vanessa Daws. *Psychoswimography*. Dublin: Private Printing, 2014.

Vanessa Daws. "Pluralize the Anthropocene!" *Watercolor Painting*. Dublin, 2018. Image reproduced by permission of artist.

Vanessa Daws. Swimming a Long Way Together. *Durational Art Project*. www.swimmingalongwaytogether.com/. Accessed 20 November 2022.

Elizabeth DeLoughrey. *Roots and Roots: Navigating Caribbean and Pacific Island Literatures*. Ann Arbor: University of Michigan Press, 2007.

Elizabeth DeLoughrey. *Allegories of the Anthropocene*. Durham: Duke University Press, 2019.

Bathsheba Demuth. *Floating Coast: An Environmental History of the Bering Strait*. New York: W. W. Norton, 2019.

Greg Dening. *Islands and Beaches: Discourse on a Silent Land: Marquesas, 1774–1800*. Los Angeles: Dorsey Press, 1988.

Elsa Devienne. *La ruée vers le sable: Une histoire environnementale des plages de Los Angeles au XXe siècle*. Paris: Ed. Sorbonne, 2022.

Emily Dickinson. *The Poems of Emily Dickinson*. Ralph W. Franklin, ed. Cambridge: Belknap Press/Harvard University Press, 1999.

Jeffrey R. Di Leo, ed. "Blue Humanities." Special Issue of *symploke* 27, 1 (2019).

Sylviane Diouf. *Slavery's Exiles: The Story of the American Maroons*. New York: New York University Press, 2014.

Sidney Dobrin. *Blue Ecocriticism and the Oceanic Imperative*. London: Bloomsbury, 2021.

Drexciya. *The Quest*. Detroit: Submerge Records, 1997.

Lowell Duckert. *For All Waters: Finding Ourselves in Early Modern Wetscapes*. Minneapolis: University of Minnesota Press, 2017.

Lars Ecstein and Anja Schwarz. "The Making of Tupaia's Map." *The Journal of Pacific History* 54 (2019): 1–95.

Philip Edwards. "Edward Hayes Explains Away Sir Humphrey Gilbert." *Renaissance Studies* 3–4 (1992): 270–86.

John Eperjesi. "Imagined Oceans: Drexciya's *Bubble Metropolis* and Blue Cultural Studies." *Journal of Popular Music Studies* 34 (2022): 118–40.

Olaudah Equiano. *The Interesting Narrative and Other Writings*. Vincent Carretta, ed., rev. ed. New York: Penguin, 2003.

Andrew Fitzmaurice. *Humanism and America: An Intellectual History of English Colonization, 1500–1625*. Cambridge: Cambridge University Press, 2003.

Michel Foucault. "Of Other Spaces." *Diacritics* 16 (1986): 22–27, 27 (1967 lecture. French 1984).

Anne-Lise Francois. "Ungiving Time: Reading Lyric by the Light of the Anthropocene." *Anthropocene Reading: Literary History in Geologic Times*. Tobias Menely and Jesse Oak Taylor, eds. University Park: Penn State University Press, 2017: 239–58.

Søren Frank. *A Poetic History of the Oceans: Literature and Maritime Modernity*. London: Brill, 2022.

Hanna Freed-Thall, ed. "Beaches and Ports." *Comparative Literature* 73, 2 (June 2021): 131–49.

Mary Fuller. *Voyages in Print: English Narratives of Travel to America, 1576–1624*. Cambridge: Cambridge University Press, 1995.

María Antonia Garcés. *Cervantes in Algiers: A Captive's Tale*. Nashville: Vanderbilt University Press, 2005.

Amitav Ghosh. *The Slave of MS H.6*. CSSSC Occasional Papers No. 125. Calcutta, 1990.

Amitav Ghosh. *In an Antique Land*. New York: Vintage, 1994.

Amitav Ghosh. *The Great Derangement: Climate Change and the Unthinkable*. Chicago: University of Chicago Press, 2016.

Amitav Ghosh. *Gun Island*. New York: Farrar, Straus, and Giroux, 2019.

Amitav Ghosh. *The Nutmeg's Curse: Parables for a Planet in Crisis*. Chicago: University of Chicago Press, 2021.

John Gillis. *Islands of the Mind: How the Human Imagination Created the Atlantic World*. London: Palgrave Macmillan, 2004.

John Gillis. *The Human Shore: Seacoasts in History*. Chicago: University of Chicago Press, 2012.

John Gillis. *The Shores around Us*. Seattle: CreateSpace, 2015.

John Gillis. "The Blue Humanities." *Humanities: The Journal of the National Endowment for the Humanities*. www.neh.gov/humanities/2013/mayjune/feature/the-blue-humanities. Accessed 12 May 2022.

Paul Gilroy. *The Black Atlantic: Modernity and Double Consciousness*. Cambridge: Harvard University Press, 1993.

Paul Gilroy. "Never Again: Refusing Race and Salvaging the Human." 2019. Holberg Prize Lecture. www.youtube.com/watch?v=Ta6UkmlXtVo. Accessed 20 September 2022.

Édouard Glissant. *Poetics of Relation*. Betsy Wing, trans. Ann Arbor: University of Michigan Press, 1997.

Matthew Boyd Goldie and Sebastian Sobecki, eds. "Our Sea of Islands: New Approaches to British Insularity in the Late Middle Ages." Special Issue of *Postmedieval* 7 (2016).

David Graeber. *Pirate Enlightenment, or the Real Libertalia*. New York: Farrar, Straus and Giroux, 2023.

David Graeber and David Wengrow. *The Dawn of Everything: A New History of Humanity*. New York: Farrar, Straus and Giroux, 2021.

Jack Greene and Philip Morgan, eds. *Atlantic History: A Critical Appraisal*. Oxford: Oxford University Press, 2008.

Alexis Pauline Gumbs. *Undrowned: Black Feminist Lessons from Marine Mammals*. Chico: AK Press, 2020.

Richard Hakluyt. *The Original Writings and Correspondence of the Two Richard Hakluyts*. E.G.R. Taylor, ed. 2 vols. London: Hakluyt Society, 1935.

Valerie Hansen. *The Year 1000: When Explorers Connected the World—and Globalization Began*. New York: Scribner, 2020.

Donna Haraway. *Staying with the Trouble: Making Kin in the Chthulucene*. Durham: Duke University Press, 2016.

Saidiya Hartman. *Lose Your Mother: A Journey Along the Atlantic Slave Route*. New York: Farrar, Straus, and Giroux, 2007.

Epeli Hau'ofa. *We Are the Ocean: Selected Works*. Honolulu: University of Hawai'i Press, 2008.

Richard Helgerson. *Forms of Nationhood: The Elizabethan Writing of England*. Chicago: University of Chicago Press, 1994.

Jeffrey Herlihy-Mira. "Did Don Quixote Long for Muslim Spain?" *Public Books*, August 12, 2021. www.publicbooks.org/did-don-quixote-long-for-muslim-spain/. Accessed 2 September 2022.

Stefanie Hessler and Thyssen-Bornemisza Art Contemporary, eds. *Tidalectics: Imagining an Oceanic Worldview through Art and Science*. Cambridge: MIT Press, 2018.

Philip Hoare. *Leviathan, or the Whale*. London: Fourth Estate, 2009.
Philip Hoare. *The Sea Inside*. New York: Melville House, 2014.
Philip Hoare. *Risingtidefallingstar: In Search of the Soul of the Sea*. Chicago: University of Chicago Press, 2018.
Isabel Hofmeyr. *Dockside Reading: Hydrocolonialism and the Custom House*. Durham: Duke University Press, 2022.
Gavin Hollis. *The Absence of America: The London Stage 1576–1642*. Oxford: Oxford University Press, 2015.
Homer. *The Odyssey*. Emily Wilson, trans. New York: W. W. Norton, 2018.
Peregrine Horden and Nicholas Purcell. *The Corrupting Sea: A Study of Mediterranean History*. London: Blackwell, 2000.
Christopher Huer. *Into the White: The Renaissance Arctic and the End of the Image*. New York: Zone Books, 2019.
Graham Huggan. *Colonialism, Culture, Whales: The Cetacean Quartet*. London: Bloomsbury, 2018.
Peter Hulme. *Colonial Encounters: Europe and the Native Caribbean, 1492–1797*. London: Methuen, 1986.
Edwin Hutchins. *Cognition in the Wild*. Cambridge: MIT Press, 1995.
Serenella Iovino and Serpil Opperman, eds. *Environmental Humanities: Voices from the Anthropocene*. London: Rowman & Littlefield, 2016.
C.L.R. James. *Mariners, Renegades, and Castaways: The Story of Herman Melville and the World We Live In*. Donald E. Pease, intro. Hanover: University Press of New England, 2001.
Fredric Jameson. *The Political Unconscious: Narrative as a Socially Symbolic Act*. Ithaca: Cornell University Press, 1982.
Stephen C. Jett. *Ancient Ocean Crossings: Reconsidering the Case for Contacts with the Pre-Columbian Americas*. Tuscaloosa: University of Alabama Press, 2017.
Ryan Tucker Jones. *Red Leviathan: The Secret History of Soviet Whaling*. Chicago: University of Chicago Press, 2022.
Claire Jowitt. *The Culture of Piracy, 1580–1630*. London: Routledge, 2010.
Claire Jowitt, Craig Lambert, and Steve Mentz, eds. *The Routledge Companion to Marine and Maritime Worlds, 1400–1800*. London: Routledge, 2020.
Melody Jue. *Wild Blue Media: Thinking Through Seawater*. Durham: Duke University Press, 2020.
Joan Naviyuk Kane. *Dark Traffic*. Pittsburgh: University of Pittsburgh Press, 2021.
Harry Kelsey. *Sir Francis Drake: The Queen's Pirate*. New Haven: Yale University Press, 1998.
Frank Kermode. "Introduction to William Shakespeare." *The Tempest*. London: Methuen, 1954.
Tiffany Lethabo King. *The Black Shoals: Offshore Formations of Black and Native Studies*. Durham: Duke University Press, 2019.
Bernhard Klein, ed. *Fictions of the Sea: Critical Perspectives on the Ocean in British Literature and Culture*. London: Routledge, 2002.
Bernhard Klein and Gesa Mackenthun, eds. *Sea Changes: Historicizing the Ocean*. London: Routledge, 2003.
Karen Ordahl Kupperman. "The Puzzle of the American Climate in the Early Colonial Period." *The American Historical Review* 87 (1982): 1262–89.
Karen Ordahl Kupperman. "Fear of Hot Climates in the Anglo-American Experience." *The William and Mary Quarterly* 41 (1984): 213–40.

Mark Kurlansky. *Cod: A Biography of the Fish that Changed the World*. London: Walker Books, 1997.

Jonathan Lamb. *Scurvy: The Disease of Discovery*. Princeton: Princeton University Press, 2017.

David Lewis. *We, the Navigators: The Ancient Art of Landfinding in the Pacific*. Sir Derek Oulton, ed. 2nd ed. Honolulu: University of Hawai'i Press, 1994.

Simon Lewis and Mark Maslin. *The Human Planet: How We Created the Anthropocene*. New Haven: Yale University Press, 2018.

Longinus. *On the Sublime*. H.L. Havell, trans. Andew Lang, intro. London and New York: Macmillan and Col., 1890. www.gutenberg.org/files/17957/17957-h/17957-h.htm. Accessed 9 June 2021.

Barry Lopez. *Arctic Dreams: Imagination and Desire in an Arctic Landscape*. New York: Vintage, 2001.

Paul E. Lovejoy. "Autobiography and Memory: Gustavus Vassa, Alias Olaudah Equiano, the African." *Slavery & Abolition* 27 (2006): 317–47.

Alison Maas, ed. "A Bibliography to the Study of Sea Literature." 2021. https://sites.williams.edu/searchablesealit/a-bibliography-to-the-study-of-sea-literature/. Accessed 9 September 20201.

Alison Maas, ed. "Zotero Blue Humanities Bibliography." 2022. www.zotero.org/groups/4421701/blue_humanities_searchable_sea_literature/library. Accessed 20 November 2022.

Peter Mancall. *Hakluyt's Promise: An Elizabethan's Obsession for an English America*. New Haven: Yale University Press, 2007.

Gabriel García Márquez. *One Hundred Years of Solitude*. Gregory Rabassa, trans. New York: Harper, 1970.

Yann Martel. *Life of Pi*. New York: Harcourt, 2001.

Leo Marx. *The Machine in the Garden: Technology and the Pastoral Ideal in America*. Oxford: Oxford University Press, 1964.

Predrag Matvejevic. *Mediterranean: A Cultural Landscape*. Michael Henry Heim, trans. Claudio Magris, intro. Berkeley: University of California Press, 1999.

Joy McCann. *Wild Sea: A History of the Southern Ocean*. Chicago: University of Chicago Press, 2018.

Herman Melville. *Moby-Dick, or the Whale*. Hershel Parker and Harrison Hayford, eds. 2nd ed. London: W. W. Norton, 2002.

Maria Rosa Menocal. *The Ornament of the World: How Muslims, Jews, and Christians Created a Culture of Tolerance in Medieval Spain*. New York: Little, Brown, and Company, 2002.

Steve Mentz. *At the Bottom of Shakespeare's Ocean*. London: Bloomsbury, 2009a.

Steve Mentz. "Toward a Blue Cultural Studies: The Sea, Maritime Culture, and Early Modern English Literature." *Literature Compass* 6, 5 (2009b): 997–1013.

Steve Mentz. "Strange Weather in *King Lear*." *Shakespeare* 6, 2 (2010): 139–52.

Steve Mentz. "After Sustainability." *PMLA* 127, 3 (2012a): 586–92.

Steve Mentz. "Hakluyt's Oceans: Maritime Rhetoric in *The Principal Navigations*." *Richard Hakluyt and Travel Writing in Early Modern Europe*. Daniel Carey and Claire Jowitt, eds. London: Routeldge, 2012b: 283–93.

Steve Mentz. *Shipwreck Modernity: Ecologies of Globalization, 1550–1719*. Minneapolis: University of Minnesota Press, 2015.

Steve Mentz. "Hurricanes, Tempests, and the Meteorological Globe." *The Palgrave Handbook of Early Modern Literature and Science*. Howard Marchitello and Evelyn Tribble, eds. London: Palgrave Macmillan, 2017: 257–76.

Steve Mentz. *Break Up the Anthropocene*. Minneapolis: University of Minnesota Press, 2019.

Steve Mentz. *Ocean*. London: Bloomsbury, 2020a.

Steve Mentz. "Swimming in the Anthropocene." *Public Books*, December 2020b. www.publicbooks.org/swimming-in-the-anthropocene/. Accessed 9 June 2021.

Steve Mentz. "Wet Globalization: The Early Modern Ocean as World-System." *A Cultural History of the Sea in the Early Modern Age*. Steve Mentz, ed. London: Bloomsbury, 2021a: 1–23.

Steve Mentz. "Ice/Water/Vapor." *The Cambridge Companion to Environmental Humanities*. Jeffrey Jerome Cohen and Stephanie Foote, eds. Cambridge: Cambridge University Press, 2021b: 185–98.

Steve Mentz. "A Poetics of Planetary Water: The Blue Humanities after John Gillis." *Coastal Studies and Society* (2022a). https://journals.sagepub.com/doi/10.1177/26349817221133199. Accessed 20 November 2022.

Steve Mentz. *Swim Poems*. Massapequa: Ghostbird Press, 2022b.

Steve Mentz. "Swimming a Long Way Together." *Belfield Literary Review* 2 (Spring 2022c): 198.

Steve Mentz. "Blue Humanities." *Posthuman Glossary*. Rosi Braidotti and Maria Hlavajova, eds. London: Bloomsbury, 2018: 129–32.

Steve Mentz and James Smith. "Learning an Inclusive Blue Humanities: Oceania and Academia through the Lens of Cinema." *Humanities* 9, 67 (2020). www.mdpi.com/2076-0787/9/3/67. Accessed 12 May 2022.

Jason W. Moore. *Capitalism in the Web of Life: Ecology and the Accumulation of Capital*. London: Verso, 2015.

Timothy Morton. *Hyperobjects: Philosophy and Ecology after the End of the World*. Minneapolis: University of Minnesota Press, 2013.

John Muir. *John Muir: Nature Writings*. William Cronon, ed. New York: Library of America, 1997.

Astrida Neimanis. *Bodies of Water: Posthuman Feminist Phenomenology*. London: Bloomsbury, 2017.

Astrida Neimanis. "The Weather Underwater: Blackness, White Feminism, and the Breathless Sea." *Australian Feminist Studies* 34, 102 (2019): 490–508.

Adam Nicolson. *The Seabird's Cry: The Lives and Loves of the Planet's Great Ocean Voyagers*. New York: Henry Holt, 2018.

Adam Nicolson. *The Sea Is Not Made of Water: Life Between the Tides*. London: William Collins, 2021.

Diana Nyad. *Other Shores*. New York: Random House, 1978.

Charles Olson. *Call Me Ishmael*. New York: Grove Press, 1947.

Charles Olson. *The Maximus Poems*. George F. Butterick, ed. Berkeley: University of California Press, 1985.

Nicholas Orme. *Early British Swimming: 55 BC–AD 1719*. Exeter: University of Exeter Press, 1993.

Lincoln Paine. *The Sea & Civilization: A Maritime History of the World*. New York: Vintage Books, 2013.

Stephen Parmenius. *De navigatione Humphredi Gilberti*. London, 1582.

J.H. Parry. *The Discovery of the Sea*. New York: Dial Press, 1974.

Giacomo Parrinello, ed. "Coastal Studies." *Private Shared Zotero Bibliography*. 2021. www.zotero.org/groups/2503094/coastal_studies. Accessed 9 September 2021.

Kimberly Patton. *The Sea Can Wash Away All Evils: Modern Marine Pollution and the Ancient Cathartic Ocean*. New York: Columbia University Press, 2006.

Michael Pearson. *The Indian Ocean*. London: Routledge, 2003.

John Peck. *Maritime Fiction: Sailors and the Sea in British and American Novels, 1719–1917*. London: Palgrave Macmillan, 2001.

Craig Santos Perez. *From Unincorporated Territory: [guma']*. Oakland: Omnidawn Publishing, 2014.

Craig Santos Perez. "Praise Song for Oceania." *Habitat Threshold*. Oakland: Omnidawn Publishing, 2020.

John Durham Peters. *The Marvelous Clouds: Toward a Philosophy of Elemental Media*. Chicago: University of Chicago Press, 2016.

Nathaniel Philbrick. *In the Heart of the Sea: The Tragedy of the Whaleship Essex*. New York: Penguin, 2001.

T.J. Piccirillo. *Blue Humanities Logo*. Branford (CT). Image file used by permission of artist. 2021.

Elspeth Probyn, Kate Johnston, and Nancy Lee, eds. *Sustaining Seas: Oceanic Space and the Politics of Care*. London: Rowman & Littlefield, 2020.

Jonathan Pugh and David Chandler. *Anthropocene Islands, Entangled Worlds*. London: Westminster University Press, 2021.

Nicholas Purcell and Peregrine Horden. *The Corrupting Sea: A Study of Mediterranean History*. London: Wiley-Blackwell, 2000.

David B. Quinn. *The Hakluyt Handbook*. 2 vols. London: Hakluyt Society, 1974.

David B. Quinn and Neil M. Cheshire, eds. *The New Found Land of Stephen Parmenius: The Life and Writings of a Hungarian Poet, Drowned on a Voyage from Newfoundland, 1583*. Toronto: Hakluyt Society, 1972.

David Quint. *Cervantes's Novel of Modern Times: A New Reading of Don Quijote*. Princeton: Princeton University Press, 2003.

Jennifer Raff. *Origin: A Genetic History of the Americas*. New York: Twelve, 2022.

Kritish Rajbhandari. "Postcolonial Fiction, Oceans, and Seas." *Oxford Research Encyclopedias, Literature*, July 2022. https://doi.org/10.1093/acrefore/9780190201098.013.1376. Accessed 14 September 2022.

Marcus Rediker. *Villains of All Nations: Atlantic Pirates in the Golden Age*. Boston: Beacon Press, 2004.

Sara Rich. *Shipwreck Hauntography: Underwater Ruins and the Uncanny*. Amsterdam: Amsterdam University Press, 2021.

Brian Russell Roberts. *Borderwaters: Amid the Archipelagic States of America*. Durham: Duke University Press, 2021.

Callum Roberts. *The Unnatural History of the Sea*. London: Shearwater, 2007.

Neil Roberts. *Freedom as Marronage*. Chicago: University of Chicago Press, 2015.

Kim Stanley Robinson. *Antarctica*. New York: Bantam, 2010.

Kim Stanley Robinson. *New York 2140*. New York: Orbit, 2017.

Monique Roffey. *The Mermaid of Black Conch*. New York: Alfred A. Knopf, 2022.

Helen Rozwadowski. *Vast Expanses: A History of the Oceans*. London: Reaktion, 2018.

Helen Rozwadowski. "'Bringing Humanity Full Circle Back into the Sea': *Homo aquaticus*, Evolution, and the Ocean." *Environmental Humanities* 14 (2022): 1–28.

Salman Rushdie. *Haroun and the Sea of Stories*. New York: Granta, 1991.

Stuart B. Schwartz. *Sea of Storms: A History of Hurricanes in the Greater Caribbean from Columbus to Katrina*. Princeton: Princeton University Press, 2015.

James C. Scott. *Against the Grain: A Deep History of the Earliest States*. New Haven: Yale University Press, 2017.

William Shakespeare. *Hamlet*. Ann Thompson and Neil Taylor, eds. London: Arden Shakespeare, 2006.

William Shakespeare. *The Tempest*. Virginia Mason Vaughan and Alden T. Vaughan, eds. London: Bloomsbury, 2011.

Leanne Shapton. *Swimming Studies*. New York: Blue Rider Press, 2012.

Christina Sharpe. *In the Wake: On Blackness and Being*. Durham: Duke University Press, 2016.

Teresa Shewry. *Hope at Sea: Possible Ecologies in Oceanic Literature*. Minneapolis: University of Minnesota Press, 2015.

Peter Sloterdijk. *In the World Interior of Capitalism: For a Philosophical Theory of Globalization*. Wieland Hoban, trans. Boston: MIT Press, 2013.

Peter Sloterdijk. *You Must Change Your Life: On Anthropotechnics*. Wieland Hoban, trans. New York: Polity, 2014.

Stephanie Smallwood. *Saltwater Slavery: A Middle Passage from African to American Diaspora*. Cambridge: Harvard University Press, 2007.

Rivers Solomon. *The Deep*. With Daveed Diggs, William Hutson, and Jonathan Snipes. New York: Saga Press, 2019.

Edmund Spenser. "One Day I Wrote Her Name . . ." *Amoretti 75*. *The New Oxford Book of Sixteenth-Century Verse*. Emrys Jones, ed. Oxford: Oxford University Press, 1991: 282.

Athelstan Spilhaus. *Atlas of the World with Geophysical Boundaries*. Philadelphia: American Philosophical Society, 1991.

Philip E. Steinberg. *The Social Construction of the Ocean*. Cambridge: Cambridge University Press, 2001.

Philip E. Steinberg and Kimberly Peters. https://www.thelittleowlnyc.com/#menus "Volume and Vision: Toward a Wet Ontology." *Harvard Design Magazine* 39 (2014): 124–29.

Philip E. Steinberg and Kimberly Peters. "A Wet World: Rethinking Place, Territory, and Time." *Society and Space* (2015a). www.societyandspace.org/articles/a-wet-world-rethinking-place-territory-and-time. Accessed 27 September 2022.

Philip E. Steinberg and Kimberly Peters. "Wet Ontologies, Fluid Spaces: Giving Depth to Volume through Oceanic Thinking." *Environment and Planning D: Society and Space* 33, 2 (2015b): 247–64.

Philip E. Steinberg and Kimberly Peters. "The Ocean in Excess: Toward a More-Than-Wet Ontology." *Dialogues in Human Geography* 9, 3 (2019): 293–307.

Bill Streever. *Cold: Adventures in the World's Frozen Places*. New York: Little, Brown, 2009.

Christina Thompson. *Sea People: The Puzzle of Polynesia*. New York: Harper, 2019.

Vergil. *The Aeneid*. H. Rushton Fairclough, trans. G.P. Goold, rev. Cambridge: Loeb, 1999.

Vergil. *The Aeneid*. Shadi Bartsch, trans. New York: Random House, 2021.

Dan Vitkus. *Piracy, Slavery, and Redemption: Barbary Captivity Narratives from Early Modern England*. New York: Columbia University Press, 2001.

Derek Walcott. *Omeros*. New York: Farrar, Straus, & Giroux, 1990.

Derek Walcott. "The Sea Is History." *Selected Poems*. Edward Baugh, ed. New York: Farrar, Straux and Giroux, 2007: 137–39.

Sheila Watt-Cloutier. *The Right to Be Cold: One Woman's Fight to Protect the Arctic and Save the Planet from Climate Change*. Minneapolis: University of Minnesota Press, 2018.

John B. West. "Torricelli and the Ocean of Air: The First Measurements of Barometric Pressure." 2013. https://journals.physiology.org/doi/full/10.1152/physiol.00053.2012?rfr_dat=cr_pub++0pubmed&url_ver=Z39.88-2003&rfr_id=ori%3Arid%3Acrossref.org. Accessed 12 May 2022.

Walt Whitman. *The Sea Is a Continual Miracle Sea Poems and Other Writings by Walt Whitman.* Jeffrey Yang, ed. Hanover: University Press of New England, 2017.

Madi Williams. *Polynesia, 900–1600.* York: ARC Humanities Press, 2021.

Robert Sean Wilson. *Be Always Converting, Be Always Converted: An American Poetics.* Cambridge: Harvard University Press, 2009.

Laura Winkiel, ed. "Hydro-Criticism." Special Issue of *ELN* 57, 1 (2019).

Tim Winton. *Breath.* New York: Farrar, Straus, and Giroux, 2008.

Sylvia Wynter. *Sylvia Wynter: On Being Human as Praxis.* Katherine McKittrik, ed. Durham: Duke University Press, 2014.

Patricia Yaeger, ed. "Oceanic Studies." Special Issue of *PMLA* 125, 3 (2010).

Jeffrey Yang. "Introduction: Apologia for the Sea." *The Sea Is a Continual Miracle: Sea Poems and Other Writings by Walt Whitman.* Hanover: University Press of New England, 2017.

Marina Zurkow. *More & More (the Invisible Oceans).* Brooklyn: Punctum, 2016.

Essential Reading in the Blue Humanities

This short bibliography provides readers with points of entry. These thirty-six titles should not displace the full Works Cited for this volume, the collaboratively produced Zotero Bibliographies for "Coastal Studies," or Alison Maas's more focused "Blue Humanities" bibliography, first produced for Richard King's "Searchable Sea Literature" website and now also on Zotero. Nonetheless, I hope this fairly short list of three dozen books will be useful. Note that I have selected only one title per author, though most of these writers have produced substantial bodies of work. I have also included neither essay collections nor special issues of journals; an incomplete list of those can be found in chapter 2, "Blue Humanities Thinking."

Hester Blum. *The News at the End of the Earth: The Print Culture of Polar Exploration*. Durham: Duke University Press, 2019.

W. Jeffrey Bolster. *The Mortal Sea: Fishing the Atlantic in the Age of Sail*. Cambridge: Harvard University Press, 2012.

Dionne Brand. *A Map to the Door of No Return: Notes to Belonging*. New York: Penguin Random House, 2002.

Dan Brayton. *Shakespeare's Ocean: An Ecocritical Voyage*. Charlottesville: University of Virginia Press, 2012.

Karen Eva Carr. *Shifting Currents: A World History of Swimming*. London: Reaktion, 2022.

Rachel Carson. *The Sea around Us*. Katherine L. Howe, drawings. New York: Oxford University Press, 1951.

Margaret Cohen. *The Novel and the Sea*. Princeton: Princeton University Press, 2010.

Kevin Dawson. *Undercurrents of Power: Aquatic Culture in the African Diaspora*. Philadelphia: University of Pennsylvania Press, 2018.

Elizabeth DeLoughrey. *Allegories of the Anthropocene*. Durham: Duke University Press, 2019.

Sidney Dobrin. *Blue Ecocriticism and the Oceanic Imperative*. London: Routledge, 2021.

Lowell Duckert. *For All Waters: Finding Ourselves in Early Modern Wetscapes*. Minneapolis: University of Minnesota Press, 2017.
David Gange. *The Frayed Atlantic Edge: A Historian's Journey from Shetland to the Channel*. New York: Williams Collins, 2020.
John Gillis. *The Human Shore: Seacoasts in History*. Chicago: University of Chicago Press, 2012.
Éduoard Glissant. *Poetics of Relation*. Betsy Wing, trans. Ann Arbor: University of Michigan Press, 1997.
Alexis Pauline Gumbs. *Undrowned: Black Feminist Lessons from Marine Mammals*. Chico: AK Press, 2020.
Stefan Helmreich. *Alien Ocean: Anthropological Voyages in Microbial Seas*. Berkeley: University of California Press, 2009.
Philip Hoare. *Risingtidefallingstar*. London: Fourth Estate, 2017.
Isabel Hofmeyr. *Dockside Reading: Hydrocolonialism and the Custom House*. Durham: Duke University Press, 2022.
Karin Animoto Ingersoll. *Waves of Knowing: A Seascape Epistemology*. Durham: Duke University Press, 2016.
Melody Jue. *Wild Blue Media: Thinking Through Seawater*. Durham: Duke University Press, 2020.
Richard King. *Ahab's Rolling Sea*. Chicago: University of Chicago Press, 2019.
Steve Mentz. *Ocean*. London: Bloomsbury, 2020.
Tiffany Lethobo King. *The Black Shoals: Offshore Formations of Black and Native Studies*. Durham: Duke University Press, 2019.
Andrew Lipman. *The Saltwater Frontier: Indians and the Contest for the American Coast*. New Haven: Yale University Press, 2015.
Astrida Neimanis. *Bodies of Water: Posthuman Feminist Philosophy*. London: Bloomsbury, 2017.
Craig Santos Perez. *Navigating Chamoru Poetry: Indigeneity, Aesthetics, and Decolonization*. Tucson: University of Arizona Press, 2021.
Elspeth Probyn. *Eating the Ocean*. Durham: Duke University Press, 2016.
Jonathan Pugh and David Chandler. *Anthropocene Islands, Entangled Worlds*. London: University of Westminster Press, 2021.
Helen Rozwadowski. *Vast Expanses: A History of the Oceans*. London: Reaktion, 2018.
Christina Sharpe. *In the Wake: On Blackness and Being*. Durham: Duke University Press, 2016.
Teresa Shewry. *Hope at Sea: Possible Ecologies in Oceanic Literature*. Minneapolis: University of Minnesota Press, 2015.
Stephanie Smallwood. *Saltwater Slavery: A Middle Passage from African to American Diaspora*. Cambridge: Harvard University Press, 2008.
Alice Te Punga Somerville. *Once Were Pacific: Māori Connections to Oceania*. Minneapolis: University of Minnesota Press, 2012.

Nicole Starosielski. *The Undersea Network*. Durham: Duke University Press, 2015.

Philip Steinberg. *The Social Construction of the Ocean*. Cambridge: Cambridge University Press, 2001.

Jace Weaver. *Red Atlantic: American Indigenes and the Making of the Modern World, 1000–1927*. Chapel Hill: University of North Carolina Press, 2017.

Index

Abulafia, David 65, 78n5, 80; *The Boundless Sea* 80
Adamastor 69, 72; *see also* Camões, Luis vaz de
Alaimo, Stacy xiv, xixn5, 19, 20, 21, 30, 139; *Bodily Natures* xixn5; *Exposed* 35n13, 36n54; "Science Studies and the Blue Humanities" (*Configurations*) 20, 35n22
Allen, Nicholas, Nick Groom, and Jos Smith 20; *Coastal Works* 20, 35n27
Allewaert, Monique 95, 105n9; *Ariel's Ecology* 95
Al-Ramli, Muhsin 88–90
Anderson, Hans Christian 128
Anderson, Jon 45, 52n22
Annales School 28
Anson, George 54
Anthropocene 8, 11, 12, 22, 133
Anthropos, Old Man 12
Aquaman xvii
Aquatic Ape, hypothesis 132
Ariel's song 27, 32
Ariosto, Ludovico 71
Arista, Noelani 44–2, 52n16; *The Kingdom and the Republic* 41–2
Aristotle 2–3, 14, 15n6; *see also Poetics*
Atlantic History 19
Auden, W. H. 30, 37n56, 46; *The Enchaféd Flood* 30, 37, 56
Austen, Jane 18

Bailyn, Bernard 34n1, 35n11, 130n9
Baker, Samuel 55, 63n5
Bambara, Toni Cade 129
Banks, Sir Joseph 40
Barents Sea 110
Barents, Willem 5
Barthes, Roland 121
Battuta, Ibn 67
Baucom, Ian 27, 36n43
Beaches 121
Beaulieu, Marie-Claire 21; *A Cultural History of the Sea (Antiquity)* 21; *see also* Cohen, Margaret, *Cultural History of the Sea*
Beowulf 132
Bergvall, Caroline 111, 115n10; *Drift* 111, 115n10
Bering Straight 112
Bermuda 25, 28; *see also Sea-Venture*
"Beyond the Atlantic" 27
Black Atlantic 19, 31; *see also* Gilroy, Paul
Blackmore, Josiah 73, 79n17
Blakemore, Richard 105n18
"blue counterchallenge" (to green thinking) 24
Blue Cultural Studies 19
Blue Ecocriticism 29; *see also* Dobrin, Sidney
Blue humanities, "inclusive" 5; *see also* Mentz, Steve; Smith, James
Blue Humanities Logo 23–4, 36n36; *see also* Piccirillo, T.J.
"Blue Marble" (photography 24
Blum, Hester 15n3, 15n8, 15n15, 19, 21, 34n1, 35n16, 54; "Archipelagos/ Oceans/American Visuality" 35n20; *The News at the End of the Earth* 15n3, 15n15, 20, 35n24, 37n57, 54; *The View from the Masthead* 19, 35n10; "Oceanic Studies" 35n16
Boccaletti, Giulio 66, 78n8; *Water* 66
Bodek, Richard and Joseph Kelly 105n11
Bolster, W. Jeffrey 64n15, 113, 115n13, 130n20; *Black Jacks* 130n20; *The Mortal Sea* 113, 115n13
Bona Esperanza (ship) 108, 110

Botkin, Daniel 13, 16n41; *Discordant Harmonies* 16n41
Bould, Marc 92n7
Bradford, William 113
Brady, Emily 57, 63n10; "environmental sublime" 57–8
Brand, Dionne 31, 37n62, 93, 100, 105n2
Brathwaite, Kamau 9, 21, 29; *see also Tidalectics*
Braudel, Fernand 28, 36n45; *The Mediterranean and the Mediterranean World in the Age of Philip II* 28, 36n45, 80
Brayton, Daniel 19, 21, 34n2, 35n12, 36n37; *Shakespeare's Ocean* 34n2, 35n12, 37n57
Brilvitich, Charles 130n20
Brooke, Rupert 134
Brown, Vincent 129n4
Burke, Edmund 47, 48, 53n32; *see also* sublime
Byron 27

Cabot, John 59
Camões, Luis vaz de 66, 68, 69–73, 77, 79; *The Lusiads* 66, 69–73
Campbell, Alexandra, and Michael Paye 20; "Blue Humanities" special issue of *Humanities* 20, 34n5, 35n23
"capacity" (as feature of ocean) 25, 26–7; *see also* Perez, Craig Santos, "Praise Song for Oceania"
Caribbean Studies 19
Carr, Karen Eva 90, 92n16, 141n2; *Shifting Currents* 90, 141n2
Carretta, Vincent 122–5, 130n18
Carroll, Siobhan 19n22, 77
Carson, Rachel 7, 9, 23, 50, 118, 120–2, 125, 130n12; *The Edge of the Sea* 120, 130n12; *The Sea Around Us* 23, 27, 36n42
Cervantes, Miguel de 87–90, 92n9; "The Captive's Tale" 87–90
Cesairé, Aimé 28, 36n50, 94, 100, 105n3; *Un Tempête* 28, 94
Champlain, Samuel de 140–1, 142n20, 142n22
Chancellor, Richard 110
Chaplin, Joyce 52n8; *Round About the Earth* 52n8; *see also* circumnavigation
Chen, Cecilia, Janine MacLeod, and Astrida Neimanis 20; *Thinking with Water* 20, 35n27
Circumnavigation 39; *see also* Chaplin, Joyce
Clark, Andy 30, 36n55
Clewis, Robert 53n27; *The Sublime Reader* 53n27
clipping (hip-hop trio) 125; *see also* Diggs, Daveed
Clouds 3
"coastal history" 15n4; *see also* Land, Isaac
Coastal Studies (Zotero Bibliography) 18
Cod (fish) 112–13
Cohen, Jeffrey Jerome 23, 30; *Prismatic Ecology* 23, 36n35; *Stone* 36n54
Cohen, Margaret 6, 15n3, 21, 83, 92n4, 121, 130n14, 142n21; *The Aesthetics of the Undersea* 21, 36n30 (*see also* Quigley, Killian); "Chronotypes of the Sea" 15n3; *The Cultural History of the Sea* (vol 5 Age of Empire) 21; *Cultural History of the Sea* (6 vols) 21, 36n31; *The Novel and the Sea* 16n23, 19n5, 35n10
Coleridge, Samuel Taylor 45, 55, 63n6; *Rime of the Ancient Mariner* 45, 55, 57–61, 62
Collectivities xvi
Colombian Exchange, the 65, 78n1
Columbus, Christopher 65
Connecticut 1, 11; *see also* Short Beach
"connectivity" 80–2
Connery, Christopher 105n19
Conrad, Joseph 83
Cook, Captain James 39, 40, 52n13, 54
Corbain, Alain 135, 141n12
Cox, Lynne 132, 137, 141n15; *Grayson* 137, 141n15
Craciun, Adraina 21
Critical Ocean studies 1
Crosby, Alfred 78n1; *see also* Colombian Exchange
Cruikshank, Julie 108, 115n3; *Do Glaciers Listen?* 108
Cryosphere 3, 5, 12
Cuffe, Paul 122
Cugoano, Ottobah 122
Currents, ocean 56, 62–3

Da Gama, Vasco 54
Dana, Richard Henry 6
Daston, Lorraine 4–5, 15n13
Davis, John 5, 15n14, 59
Daws, Vanessa xv, 22, 133, 138–9, 141n18; "Pluralize the Anthropocene!" (painting) 22–4, 36n32, 138;

Psychoswimography 138–9, 141n18; "Swimming a Long Way Together" (project) xv, xvii, 138
Deakin, Roger 133
"Deep, The" (song) 125; *see also* clipping (hip-hop trio); Diggs, Daveed
Defoe, Daniel 6, 99; *King of the Pirates* 99; *Robinson Crusoe* 96, 133
DeLoughrey, Elizabeth 19, 21, 29, 44; *Allegories of the Anthropocene* 20, 35n13, 35n24; *Routes and Roots* 19, 29, 35n10, 52n14
Demuth, Bathsheba 64n14, 108, 115n5; *Floating Coast* 108, 115n5
Dening, Greg 121, 130n17
Derrida, Jacques 47
Devienne, Elsa 121, 130n14
Dias, Bartholomew 54
Dickinson, Emily xv, xviii, 1, 7–9, 13, 14, 16n24; "An Everywhere of Silver" 7–9, 32; "difference" (as feature of water) 25
Digby, Everard 132, 134–5, 141n3; *De arte natandii* 132, 134–5; *see also* Middleton, Christopher
Diggs, Daveed 125; *see also* clipping (hip-hop trio)
DiLeo, Jeffrey 20, 35n21; *symploke* Blue Humanities special issue 20, 35n21
Diouf, Syviane 96, 105n10
Disorientation xvi
Dobrin, Sidney 19, 31, 35n12, 36n37, 37nn59–60
Donald, Gerald 125; *see also* Drexiya
Drake, Francis 54, 90, 96, 98
Drexiya 77, 125–8, 125–7, 131n33; *Bubble Metropolis* 125; *The Quest* 127, 131n33; *see also* Stinson, James; Donald, Gerald
"dry narratives" xiv, 63n4; *see also* "wet narratives"
Duckert, Lowell 5, 15n16, 115n4; *For All Waters* 15n16, 115n4
Durrell, Lawrence 9
"dynamic ecology" 13; *see also* Botkin, Daniel

Ecstein, Lars, and Anja Schwarz 40, 52n10
Elden, Stuart 45
Eperjesi, John 125, 131n29
Ephemerality 21
Equiano, Olaudah 122–5, 130n18; *The Interesting Narrative* 122–5, 130n18
Essex (whaleship) 118, 130n10
Experimental writing 21

Faulkner, William 96
"feel for the water" 133
Foucault, Michel 98, 106n20, 123, 130n21; "heterotopia" 98, 123
Francois, Anne-Lise 8, 13; "Ungiving Time" 8
Frank, Søren xv, xix n6; *A Poetic History of the Oceans* xv, xixn6
Freed-Thall, Hannah 120, 130n13

Garcés, María Antonia 87–90, 92n10
Garcia Márquez, Gabriel 85
Gauguin, Paul 45
"Geometrical projection of two thirds of the sphere" 38, 52n1
Ghosh, Amitav 67–9, 78n10, 79n12, 85–6; *In an Antique Land* 67–9; *Gun Island* 85–6, 92n8; *The Nutmeg's Curse* 69
Gilbert, Humphrey 59, 107, 115n2
Gillies, John 6–12, 14, 121, 130n14, 130n15; "The Blue Humanities" 6, 16n21; *The Human Shore* 6, 9, 10n28; *Islands of the Mind* 6, 9n27
Gilroy, Paul 35n11, 116, 122, 129n2, 130n22; *The Black Atlantic* 116, 129n2
Gleitze, Mercedes xv
Glissant, Édouard xv, 9, 34n2, 35n11, 90, 100, 105n1, 116, 129n1; *Poetics of Relation* 90, 129n1
Goldie, Matthew Boyd, and Sebastian Sobecki 20, 35n18; "Our Sea of Islands" (*postmedieval*) 20, 35n18
Gore, Al 50
Graeber, David, and Davd Wengrow 66, 78, 105n7, 105n16; *The Dawn of Everything* 66
Great Gott Island 9; *see also* Gillies, John
Greene, Jack, and Philip D. Morgan 35n11, 130n9
Gumbs, Alexis Pauline 31, 37n62, 128–9, 131n34; *Undrowned* 128–9, 131n34

Hakluyt, Richard 109, 115n8
Hamilton-Patterson, James 133, 136–7, 141n14; *Playing with Water* 141n14; *Seven-Tenths* 136–7, 141n14
Hansen, Valerie 78n2
Haraway, Donna 30, 37n55
Harman, Graham 47–8, 53n29; "unsublime ecology" 47

Hartman, Saidiya 31, 37n62, 117–18, 130n7
Hau'ofa, Epeli 39, 52n6
Helgerson, Richard 115n9
Hendrix, Jimi 125
Heraclitus 12–13, 14
Herlihy-Mera, Jeffrey 88–90, 92n12
Heroes, ecological 49–50; "no ecological heroes!" 49
Hessler, Stefanie and the Thyssen-Bornemisza Art Collective 20–1, 105n4; *Tidalectics* 21; *see also* Brathwaite, Kamau
Heuer, Christopher 5, 15n16; *Into the White* 5, 15n16
Hoare, Philip 133, 138–29, 141n16; *Leviathan* 138, 141n16; *Risingtidefallingstar* 138, 141n16; *The Sea Inside* 138, 141n16
Hofmeyr, Isabel and Kerry Bystrom 19n21, 20, 21, 35n17, 76–8; *Dockside Reading* 76–8; hydro-colonialism 76–8; "Oceanic Routes" (*Comparative Literature*) 20
Hollis, Gavin 36n48
Homer 18, 19, 92, 133; *The Odyssey* 19; *see also* Odysseus
Horden, Peregrine, and Nicholas Purcell 28, 34n2, 36n46, 81–2, 92n2; *The Corrupting Sea* 28, 34n2, 36n46, 92n2; *see also* "connectivity"
Huggan, Graham 131n31
Hulme, Keri 42
Hulme, Peter 94, 105n7
human bodies (of water) xii
humidity 94, 124–5
hurricanes 94, 102
Hutchins, Edwin 30, 36n55
"hydro-criticism" 1, 19

immersion, in water xvi, 139
Indigenous Thinking 17, 101–3, 104–5, 111–12, 113–14
Iovino, Serenella 30, 36n54; *see also* Opperman, Serpil
"isolomania" 9; *see also* Gillies, John; *Islands of the Mind*
Ivan the Terrible 110

James, C.L.R. 118, 130n11
Jameson, Fredric 140, 142n23
Jamestown 113
Jett, Stephen C. 65, 78n3
Jonah 46
Jones, Ryan Tucker 64n14
Journal of Transnational American Studies 20; "Archipelagoes/Oceans/American Visuality" special issue 20
Jowitt, Claire, Craig Lambert, and Steve Mentz 21, 97, 105n14; *The Routledge Companion to Marine and Maritime Worlds, 1400–1800* 21, 35n29
Jue, Melody 10, 14n31; *Wild Blue Media* 10, 16n31

Kane, Joan Naviyk 113–14, 115n14, 115n16; "Dark Traffic" 113–14, 115n16
Kant, Immanuel 47
Keats, John 21
Kelsey, Harry 106n21
Kermode, Frank 28, 36n49
King, Tiffany Lethabo 37n61
Klein, Bernhard 19, 21, 34n1; *Fictions of the Sea* 19, 34n1, 35n10, 37n57; *Sea Changes* 19, 34n1, 35n10
Kupperman, Karen Ordahl 131n27
Kurlansky, Mark 112–13, 115n11; *Cod* 112–13, 115n11

Lamb, Jonathan 19n19, 21; *Cultural History of the Sea (Age of Enlightenment)* 21; *see also* Cohen, Margaret, *Cultural History of the Sea*; *Scurvy* 79n19
Lambourn, Elizabeth 21; *Cultural History of the Sea (Medieval)* 21; *see also* Cohen, Margaret, *Cultural History of the Sea*
Land, Isaac 15n4; *see also* "coastal history"
Lewis, David 40, 41n10
Lewis, Simon, and Mark Maslin 117, 129n5
Life Between the Tides 16n40
Linnaeus 4
Longinus 47, 53n28; *On the Sublime* 47
Long Island Sound xi
Lopez, Barry 15n14
Lorde, Audre 129
Lovejoy, Paul 130n19
Lyotard, Jean-Francois 47

Maas, Alison 18, 34n8, 35n9; *see also* Searchable Sea Literature
Mackentheun, Gesa 35n10; *see* Klein, Bernhard
Magellan, Ferdinand 39, 54
Magris, Claudio 82
Marley, Bob 101
Maroons/marronage 95

Martel, Yann 44; *Life of Pi* 44, 52n19
Marx, Leo 28, 36n49
Matvejevic, Predrag 81, 92n3
McCann, Joy 63n1; *Wild Sea* 63n1
McKittrick, Katherine 35n11; *see also* Wynter, Sylvia
Melville, Herman xv, 15n5, 18, 32; *Moby-Dick* xixn10, xvii–xviii, 2, 15n5
Menocal, María Rosa 88, 92n11
Mentz, Steve xv, xixn4, 21; "After Sustainability" 16n35, 141n4; *At the Bottom of Shakespeare's Ocean* 17, 19, 25, 31n3, 35n10, 36n37, 36n40, 37n58; "Blue Humanities" 36n33; *Break Up the Anthropocene* 36n34; *Cultural History of the Sea (Early Modern)* 21, 29 (*see also* Cohen, Margaret, *Cultural History of the Sea*); "Experience is Better Than Knowledge" 141n19; "Hakluyt's Ocean" 115n2; "Hurricanes, Tempests, and the Meteorological Globe" 16n34, 105n7; "Ice/Water/Vapor" 15n3, 15n10, 34n1, 105n13; "Is Compassion an Oceanic Feeling?" 141n1; *Ocean* 20, 34n6, 35n24, 53n34, 79n16, 92n6; "A Poetics of Planetary Water" 14n1; "Plural Anthropocenes in Lausanne" 36n41; "The Restlessness of the Tides" 16n39; "Seep" xixn5; *Shipwreck Modernity* xiv, xixn4, 20, 29, 35n24, 36n40, 130n23; "Strange Weather in *King Lear*" 13, 16n42; "Swimming a Long Way Together" (poem) xv–xvi, xix n7; "Swimming in the Anthropocene" 53n34; "Swimming Lessons" 141n4; *Swim Poems* xixn7; "Toward a Blue Cultural Studies" 16n22, 17, 34n3, 35n14
Mentz, Steve and James Smith 15, 52n19; "Learning an Inclusive Blue Humanities" 15n19, 52n12
Mentz, Steve, and Martha Elena Rojas 20; The Sea and Nineteenth-Century Anglophone Literary Culture 20, 35n25
Mercator Projection 55
Middle Passage 116
Middleton, Christopher 135, 141n9; *see also* Digby, Everard
Milton, John 47, 71; *Paradise Lost* 47, 71
"mimesis" 3; *see also* Aristotle
Moby-Dick xii, xv, 2; "Brit" 2, 112; "Epilogue" 139–40; "The Grand Armada" 67, 73–5; "Loomings" 82–3; "Nantucket" 111–12; "The Pacific" 45–6; "The Quadrant" 33–4; "Queequeg in His Coffin" 103–4; "Wheelbarrow" xvii–xviii; "The Whiteness of the Whale" 118–20; "Will the Whale Diminish?" 61–2; *see also* Melville, Herman
Monsoon 66
Moore, Jason 39, 52n4, 117, 129n5; *see also* "world ecology"
Morton, Timothy 30, 36n54
Muir, John 5, 15n14
"multilingualism" 93

Narcissus 82–3
Neimanis, Astrida 10, 14, 16n32, 16n33, 21, 30, 134, 141n7; *Bodies of Water* 10, 16n33, 20, 36n54, 141n7; "The Weather Underwater" 16n32
Nicolson, Adam 12–13, 14, 16n40, 58; *The Sea is Not Made of Water* 12–13, 16n40; *see also Life Between the Tides*
Noah/Noah's Ark 62, 112
Northwest/Northeast Passages 107, 109
Novaya Zembla 5, 108
Nyad, Diana 133, 141n6

O'Brian, Patrick 83
Ocean as archive 29
"ocean deficit" 19, 31; *see also* Brayton, Dan; Dobrin, Sidney
ocean history 1
Oceania 18, 25, 26–7, 39–42, 43
"oceanic feeling" 132
"Oceanic Routes" (*Comparative Literature*) 20; *see also* Hofmeyr, Isabel; Kerry Bystrom
"Oceanic Studies" (*PMLA* cluster) 20; *see also* Yaeger, Patricia
"ocean intimacy" 41
Odysseus/*The Odyssey* 46, 69, 83–4, 86–7, 90–2, 123, 132, 133
"offshore trajectory" 17, 26, 29
Olson, Charles xii, xiv, xviiin3, 46; *Call Me Ishmael* 46, 53n24; *The Maximus Poems* xii
Opperman, Serpil 30, 36n54; *see also* Iovino, Serenella
Orme, Nicholas 134, 141n10
Oswald, Alice 27
Ovid 4, 27, 71

Paine, Bob 13
Paris Plages 121

Parkhurst, Anthony 113
Parrinello, Giacomo 34n7
Parry, J.H. 52n3; *The Discovery of the Sea* 52n3
Patton, Kimberly 46, 121, 130n16; *The Sea Can Wash Away All Evil* 46, 53n23, 130n16
Pearson, Michael 65, 78n4
Peck, John 19; *Maritime Fiction* 19, 34n5, 35n10
Perez, Craig Santos xv, xviii, 18, 24, 29, 42–4, 114; "Chanting the Waters" 32; *[guma']* 42–4, 52n17; *Habitat Threshold* 25; "Praise Song for Oceania" 25–33, 34n4, 36n39
Peters, John Durham 4–5, 15n12; *The Marvelous Clouds* 4–5, 15n12
Philbrick, Nathaniel 130n10
Physical properties of water xii
Piccirillo, T.J. 23–4, 36n36; *see also* Blue Humanities Logo
Pirates 97–100
Plymouth 113
Poe, Edgar Allen 57
"poetics" 2
Poetics 2–3, 15n6; *see also* Aristotle
"poetics of planetary water" 1–16
"polar ecomedia" 54; *see also* Blum, Hester
Polarity, of water 117
Polynesian triangle 40
Posthuman, blue humanities as 34, 97, 100
"post-sustainability" 50
Pound, Ezra 115n7
Powell, Manushag 97, 99, 105n14
Poys, John Cowper 134
Psalm 107 ("They that go down to the sea. . .") 46
Pugh, Jonathan and David Chandler 9–10, 16n29, 94, 105n6; *Anthropocene Islands* 9, 16n29

Quebec 113
Queequeg xvii–xviii; *see also* Melville, Herman
Quigley, Killian 21; *Aesthetics of the Undersea* 21, 36n30; *see also* Cohen, Margaret
Quint, David 88–9, 92n13

Racehorse, HMS 124
Rachel Carson Center (Munich) xviiin2
Raff, Jennifer 107, 115n1; *Origins* 107, 115n1
Rajbhandari, Kritish 78n9
Rediker, Marcus 97, 100, 105n14, 130n6; *The Slave Ship* 100, 130n6
Rich, Adrienne 10; "Diving into the Wreck" 10
Rich, Sara 9–10, 14, 16n30; *Shipwreck Hauntography* 10, 16n30
River civilizations 66–7
Roberts, Brian Russell 92n1
Roberts, Callum 112–13, 115n12
Roberts, Neil 105n12
Robinson, Kim Stanly 30, 56–7, 63n9
Roffey, Monique xv, 100–3, 106n24, 128; *The Mermaid of Black Conch* 100–3, 127
Romanticism 6, 24, 133, 136–7
Rosier, James 113
Rozwadowski, Helen 1, 15n2, 131n33; *Vast Expanses* 1, 15n2
Rushdie, Salman 3, 15n9, 75–6, 85; *Haroun and the Sea of Stories* 15n9, 19n20, 67, 75–6; *Midnight's Children* 76; *Quichotte* 76
Russia 110

Samuelson, Meg 21
Sancho, Ignatius 122
Sandy, Hurricane 11, 12
Scales, shifting xiv
Schwartz, Stuart B. 95, 105n8
Scott, James C. 78n6
"Seafarer, The" (poem) 108–11
Searchable Sea Literature Bibliography 18; *see also* Maas, Alison
Sea-Venture (ship) 28
"seep" xiv, xix n5; *see also* Mentz, Steve
Sekula, Allan 121, 130n14
Sex tourism 72
Shakespeare, William xv, xviii, 24, 123, 133; *Hamlet* 4, 8, 15n11, 59, 63n12; *King Lear* 13, 48; *The Tempest* xviii, 25–33, 36n38, 123, 126, 131n22
Shapton, Leanne 133, 135–6, 141n13; *Swimming Studies* 135–6, 141n13
Sharpe, Christina 10, 31, 37n62, 77, 117, 130n8
Shelly, Percy Bysshe 48; "Mont Blanc" 48, 57
Sherman, William 123
Shewry, Theresa 21, 41, 52n15
Shipwreck Modernity xiv, xix n4; *see also* Mentz, Steve
Short Beach, Connecticut ix, xi, 1; *see also* Connecticut
Sinbad 46
Sloterdijk, Peter 39, 52n2, 97, 105n15

Smallwood, Stephanie 106n23, 116, 129n3; *Saltwater Slavery* 116, 129n3
Smith, James 15n19
Smith, John 83, 113; "technology" 83
Sobecki, Sebastian 21; *see also* Goldie, Matthew Boyd
Solomon, Rivers 125–8, 131n30; *The Deep* 125–8, 131n30
Somerville, Alice Te Punga 40, 52n11; *Once Were Pacific* 40, 52n11
Spenser, Edmund 8, 16n25, 71; "One day I wrote her name upon the strand" 8, 16n25
Spilhaus, Athelstan 55; "The Spilhaus Projection" 55–6
Sprawson, Charles 133, 134, 141n8; *Haunts of the Black Masseur* 134, 141n8
Steinberg, Philip 19, 21, 44, 108, 115n6; *The Social Construction of the Ocean* 19, 35n10, 52n20
Steinberg, Philip and Kimberly Peters 35n13, 444; "more-than-wet ontology" 45, 52n21; "The Ocean in Excess" 52n21; "wet ontology" 44, 52n21
Stinson, James 125; *see also* Drexiya
Streever, Bill 5, 15n19
Sublime, the 46–51
Sullivan, Robert 42
Surf/surfing 12, 46–51
"swimmer poetics" 133
Swimming 8, 132–41
"Swimming a Long Water Together" (poem) xv–xvi, xixn7; *see also* Mentz, Steve
"Swimming a Long Way Together" (art project) xv, xvii; *see also* Daws, Vanessa
Swim poetry 33
Swinburne, Algernon 134
symploke (Blue Humanities special issue) 20

Tasso, Torquato 71
Taussig, Michael 121
"technology" 83
Thompson, Christina 40; *Sea People* 40
Thorpe, Ian 132
Thunberg, Greta 50
Thwaites. Glacier 7
"tidalectics" 21; *see also* Brathwaite, Kamau; Hessler, Stefanie
Torma, Franziska 21; *Cultural History of the Sea (Global Age)* 21; *see also* Cohen, Margaret, *Cultural History of the Sea*
Torricelli, Evangelista 3
"transcorporeality" xiv; *see also* Alaimo, Stacy
"triangular trade" 116
Tuan, Yi-Fu 9
Tupaia 40, 52n13; Tupaia's Map 41

Urbain, Jean-Didier 121

Vapor (gaseous water) 3
Verne, Jules 125
Vikings, transatlantic voyages 107
Virgil 18, 123
Virginia 25
Vitkus, Dan 97, 105n14

Walcott, Derek 28, 94, 100, 105n5; *Omeros* 28, 94; "The Sea is History" 94
Watt-Clouthier, Sheila 5, 15n18, 114, 115n15
Welty, Eudora 96
West, John B. 15n7
"wet globalization" 28, 97
"wet narratives" xiv, 55, 63n4; *see also* "dry narratives"
Whitman, Walt xv, xviii, 1, 11–12, 13, 14, 16n37, 133; "Song of Myself" 11–12, 16n37
Williams, Madi 52n7; *Polynesia* 52n7
Williams, Tennessee 134
Willoughby, Hugh 108–11
Wilson, Robert Sean 40, 52n5
Winkiel, Laura 20, 35n14; "Hydro-Criticism" (*ELN*) 20
Winton, Tim 46–51, 53n31; *Breath* 47–51
Wittfogel, Karl 66
Wordsworth, William 45, 48, 414n5; "Lines Composed a Few Miles Above Tintern Abbey" 141n5; "Sea Shell" 45; *The Prelude* 48, 57
"world ecology" 39; *see also* Moore, Jason
World Ocean xii, 27, 39
Wynter, Sylvia 35n11; *see also* McKittrick, Katherine

Yaeger, Patricia 20, 35n15; *see also* "Oceanic Studies" (*PMLA* cluster)
Yang, Jeffrey 11, 16n36; *The Sea is a Continual Miracle* 11, 16n36

Zurkow, Marina 30, 36n54

Made in the USA
Las Vegas, NV
16 January 2024